THE U.S. NAVY AND THE VIETNAM WAR
Edward J. Marolda and Sandra J. Doyle, *Series Editors*

The Approaching Storm

Conflict in Asia, 1945–1965

Edward J. Marolda

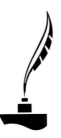

NAVAL HISTORY & HERITAGE COMMAND
DEPARTMENT OF THE NAVY
WASHINGTON, DC
2009

Secretary of the Navy's Advisory Subcommittee on Naval History

Dr. John B. Hattendorf (Chair)
Dr. Charles C. Chadbourn III
Lieutenant General George Ronald Christmas, USMC (Ret.)
Rear Admiral William J. Holland, USN (Ret.)
Ms. Christine G. Hughes
Captain William Spencer Johnson IV, USN (Ret.)
Dr. J. P. London
The Honorable Robin B. Pirie Jr.
Mr. Fred H. Rainbow
Admiral J. Paul Reason, USN (Ret.)
Dr. James R. Reckner
Dr. Clifford L. Stanley
Dr. William L. Stearman
Captain Channing M. Zucker, USN (Ret.)

Published by
Naval History & Heritage Command
805 Kidder Breese Street SE
Washington Navy Yard, DC 20374-5060
www.history.navy.mil

Book design by Dean Gardei and Gwynn Fuchs

U.S. GOVERNMENT OFFICIAL EDITION NOTICE

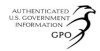

Use of ISBN

This is the Official U.S. Government edition of this publication and is herein identified to certify its authenticity. Use of 978-0-945274-58-2 is for U.S. Government Printing Office Editions only. The Superintendent of Documents of the U.S. Government Printing Office requests that any reprinted edition clearly be labeled as a copy of the authentic work with a new ISBN.

Library of Congress Cataloging-in-Publication Data

Marolda, Edward J.
   The approaching storm : conflict in Asia, 1945–1965 / Edward J. Marolda.
      p. cm. – (The U.S. Navy and the Vietnam War)
   Includes bibliographical references.
   ISBN 978-0-945274-57-5 (alk. paper)
1. Vietnam War, 1961–1975—Naval operations, American. 2. United States. Navy—History—Vietnam War, 1961–1975. 3. United States. Navy—History—20th century. 4. Southeast Asia—History—1945– 5. East Asia—History—1945– I. Title.
DS558.7.M35 2008
959.704'3450973—dc22   2008004081

∞ The paper used in this publication meets the requirements for permanence established by the American National Standard for Information Sciences "Permanence of Paper for Printed Library Materials" (ANSI Z39.48-1984).

For sale by the Superintendent of Documents, U.S. Government Printing Office
Internet: Bookstore.gpo.gov; Phone: toll free 866-512-1800; DC area 202-512-1800; Fax: 202-512-2104
Mail: Stop IDDC, Washington, DC 20402-0001

CONTENTS

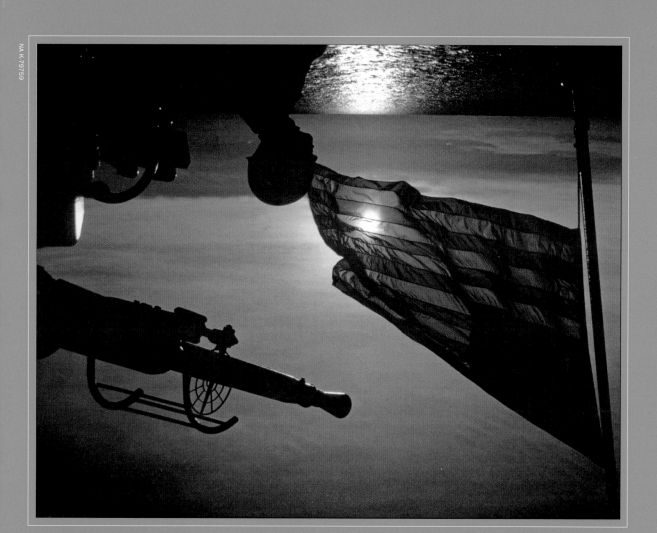

PREFACE

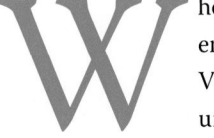hen the U.S. Seventh Fleet embarked the last of 50,000 Vietnamese evacuees, got underway from Vietnam's southern coast, and set a course for the Philippines on the evening of 2 May 1975, it marked the end of America's longest war. For more than 25 years, the United States and its allies had fought to preserve the independence of free governments in South Vietnam, Laos, and Cambodia, but that effort had failed. Vietnamese, Laotian, and Cambodian Communist movements and military forces now held sway over the entire Indochinese peninsula.

The struggle for Southeast Asia, however, was only one episode in the even longer Cold War that began in 1946 and ended with the collapse of global communism in the late 1980s. The 58,000 Americans who sacrificed their lives in Vietnam marched in the same proud ranks as the tens of thousands of their compatriots who fought and died to achieve ultimate victory in the Cold War.

The U.S. Navy was in the forefront of the fight. More than 2.6 million Sailors and Marines served in the combat theater at one time or another. It is the objective of this series, The U.S. Navy and the Vietnam War, to honor the faithful service to their country of those men and women who, in John Paul Jones' immortal words, went "in harm's way" to fight for freedom.

Between 2008 and 2015, the 50th anniversary of the onset of major combat operations in 1965, the Naval History and Heritage Command and the Naval Historical Foundation will collaborate in publishing well-illustrated, engagingly written, and authoritative booklets that detail the Navy's major involvement in the conflict. We have enlisted to the cause distinguished authors and charged them with producing interpretative essays based on research in primary sources and the best secondary works. First in the series, *The Approaching Storm* covers the global, regional, and ideological stimulants of the conflict, setting the stage for subsequent booklets on the fight for the rivers and canals of Vietnam, naval special warfare, the POW experience, the Rolling Thunder bombing campaign, Navy medicine at war, coastal operations, the Linebacker bombing campaign, Navy leaders, naval advisors and the Vietnam Navy, sealift and naval logistics, Seabees and construction, naval intelligence, and the seaborne evacuations from Indochina.

It is important for this and future generations of Americans to understand that in the war for Southeast Asia our Sailors fought with skill, courage, and perseverance in often trying circumstances. They were sorely tested but never failed to do their duty.

Edward J. Marolda
Sandra J. Doyle
Series Editors

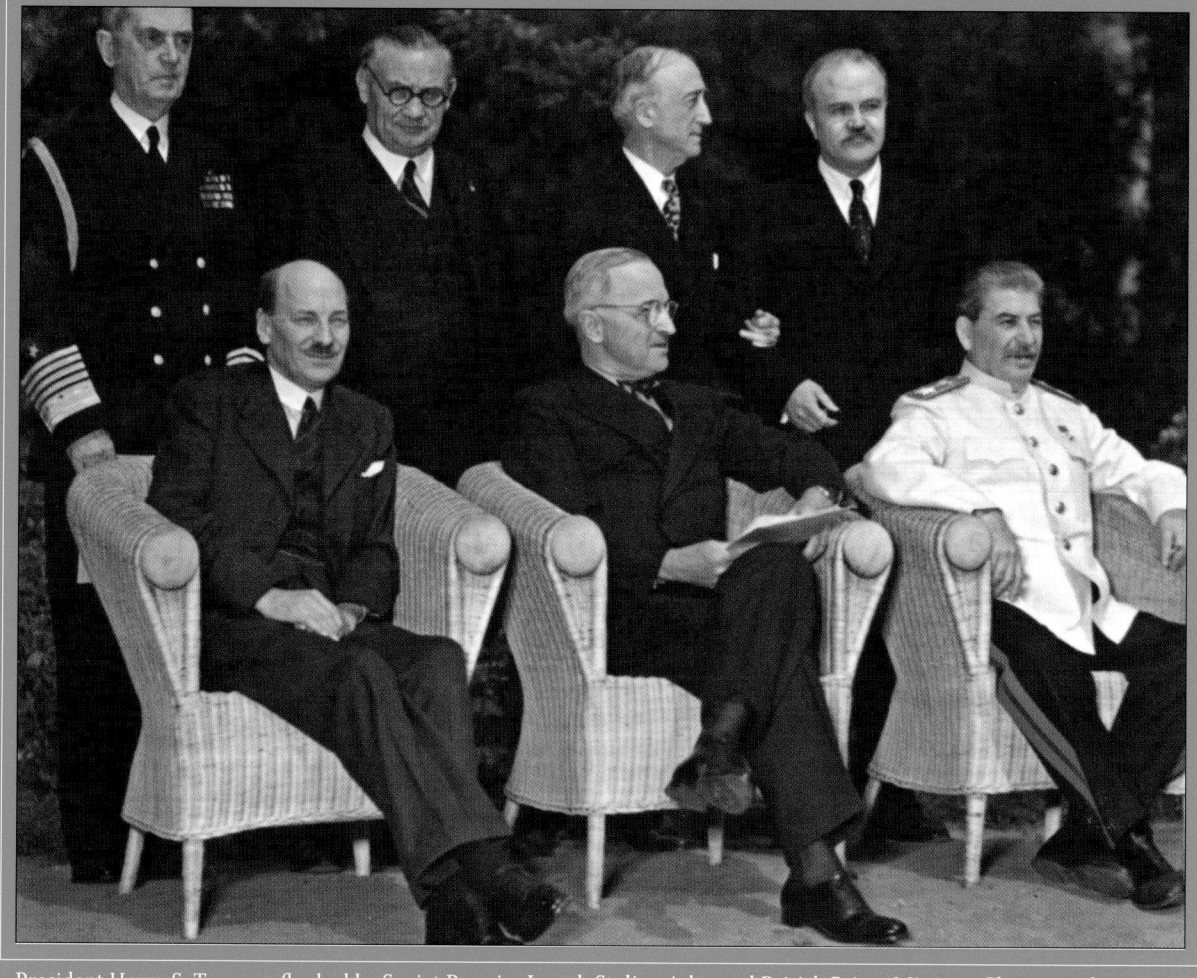

President Harry S. Truman, flanked by Soviet Premier Joseph Stalin, right, and British Prime Minister Clement Atlee, pose for a group photo at the Potsdam Conference in the summer of 1945. Within a year, animosities among the Western allies and the Soviet Union would ignite a "cold war" that lasted more than 45 years.

America's participation in the Vietnam conflict dates to the waning days of World War II, when certain victory over Japan prompted the Allies and Asian peoples of many ideological persuasions to change the political landscape. France, Great Britain, the Netherlands, and other European countries planned to reestablish control over their colonies in China, India, and Southeast Asia. The Soviet Union intended to extend its influence in Northeast Asia in general and northern China in particular. Anticolonial resistance movements, in many cases led by Communists, prepared for military and political action to seize control of Korea, China, and Indochina.

The United States emerged from World War II as a military, political, and economic colossus. American leaders were determined never to allow a return to the destructive isolationist foreign policy of the prewar years or the rise of any nation that could launch another surprise attack on the United States—there would be no more Pearl Harbors. Accordingly, the United States government prepared to exert strong influence over the course of events in postwar Asia.

Before his death in April 1945, President Franklin D. Roosevelt had adamantly opposed the efforts of European colonial powers to reconstitute their Asian empires. His successor, Harry S. Truman, however, was much less passionate on that issue. He was less concerned about Great Britain and France returning to Hong Kong and Indochina than he was about Joseph Stalin's Soviet Union establishing political and military domination over Europe.

Backed up by the massive and powerful Red Army that occupied much of Eastern Europe at the end of World War II, Soviet authorities established absolute control over the governments and economies of Poland, Romania, Bulgaria, eastern Germany, and Czechoslovakia. Stalin applied strong diplomatic and military pressure on the governments of Greece, Turkey, and Iran for territorial and other concessions. His aggressive behavior led Truman to champion a foreign policy approach that opposed Soviet or Communist global inroads, stimulated the economies of Western Europe with the Marshall Plan, and in 1949 prompted a military alliance, the North Atlantic Treaty Organization (NATO).

Along with these developments, the Truman administration deployed ground and air forces to Western Europe and directed the preparation of contingency plans for war (nuclear and conventional) with the Soviet Union. The U.S. Navy strengthened its naval units in the Mediterranean, formally establishing in 1949 the U.S. Sixth Fleet to operate there. ⌁

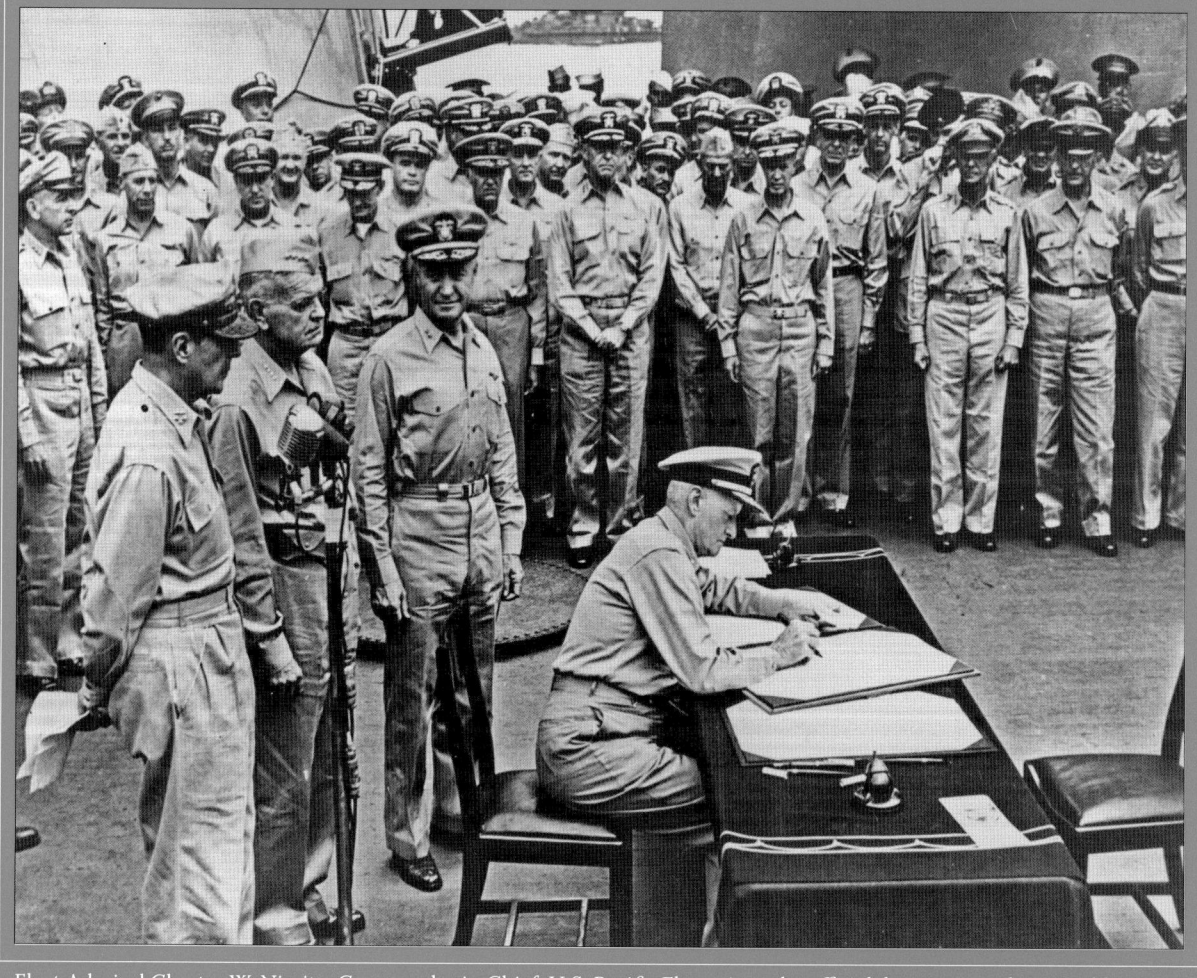

Fleet Admiral Chester W. Nimitz, Commander in Chief, U.S. Pacific Fleet, signs the official document ending World War II on 2 September 1945. Many of the U.S. Army and Navy officers around him on board battleship *Missouri* (BB 32) were determined to preserve America's new hard-won preeminence in East Asia and the Pacific Ocean.

For the Navy, however, especially after the Pacific campaign of World War II, the Pacific Ocean continued to be the big picture. At the end of the war, the American navy was the globe's preeminent naval power, operating 98 aircraft carriers, 24 battleships, 96 cruisers, 445 destroyers, 259 submarines, and thousands of amphibious and logistic ships; 24,000 aircraft; 6 Marine divisions; and 4 million Sailors and Marines under arms. Nowhere was American strength at sea more evident than in the vast reaches of the Pacific. When General Douglas MacArthur accepted the surrender of the Empire of Japan on board battleship *Missouri* (BB 63) on 2 September 1945, there was no conceivable rival to the mighty American armada. Moreover, U.S. political and economic power reigned supreme throughout the Pacific and East Asia.

Navy leaders, and many Army leaders, meant to keep it that way. They were determined to sustain the monumental victory over Japan, purchased at an enormous cost in American lives and national treasure, by preventing the postwar rise of hostile Asian nations or navies.

Influential naval leaders feared that the Marxist-Leninist ideology championed by Stalin's Soviet Union, Mao Tse-tung's (Mao Zedong) Chinese Communist movement, and Kim Il Sung's Korean Communists threatened to destroy all that the

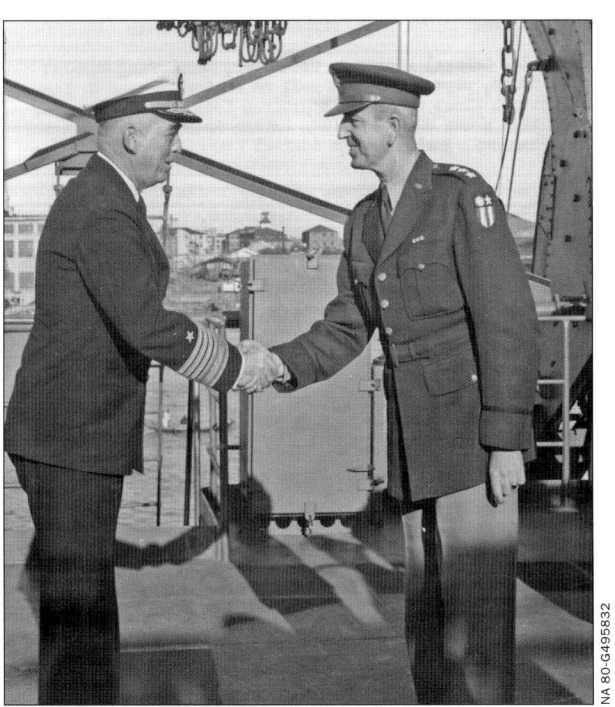

Admiral Thomas C. Kinkaid, Commander U.S. Seventh Fleet, left, greets Army Lieutenant General Albert C. Wedemeyer, in charge of all American forces in China, on board flagship *Estes* (AGC 12) in November 1945. Wedemeyer and key naval leaders feared that the Soviet Union had designs on Northeast Asia.

United States had accomplished in the region. Only a few weeks after the Soviet Union entered the war in the Far East on 9 August 1945, Stalin's armies had advanced far into northern Korea and Manchuria. The Soviets crushed the 1.6-million-man Japanese Kwantung Army in Manchuria and occupied the old Russian naval base at Port Arthur (Lushun).

Under pressure from the Soviets, the Chinese Nationalist government of Chiang Kai-shek (Jiang Jieshi) agreed to Soviet control of major railroads and commercial ports in Manchuria and to the basing of Soviet naval vessels at Port Arthur. Washington leaders understood that this heavy-handed Soviet presence would continue, even after the Red Army had secured the surrender of the Kwantung Army and withdrawn to the USSR, as called for in wartime Allied agreements.

General Albert C. Wedemeyer, commander of the China Theater, and other American military leaders were also concerned that before the Soviets withdrew their forces from Manchuria and Korea, they would enable the Chinese and Korean Communists to move in behind them and establish political and military control over the region. Indeed, the day after Soviet entry into World War II, Mao secretly directed his forces to move into the cities and other population centers of northern China and begin taking the surrender of Japanese troops there.

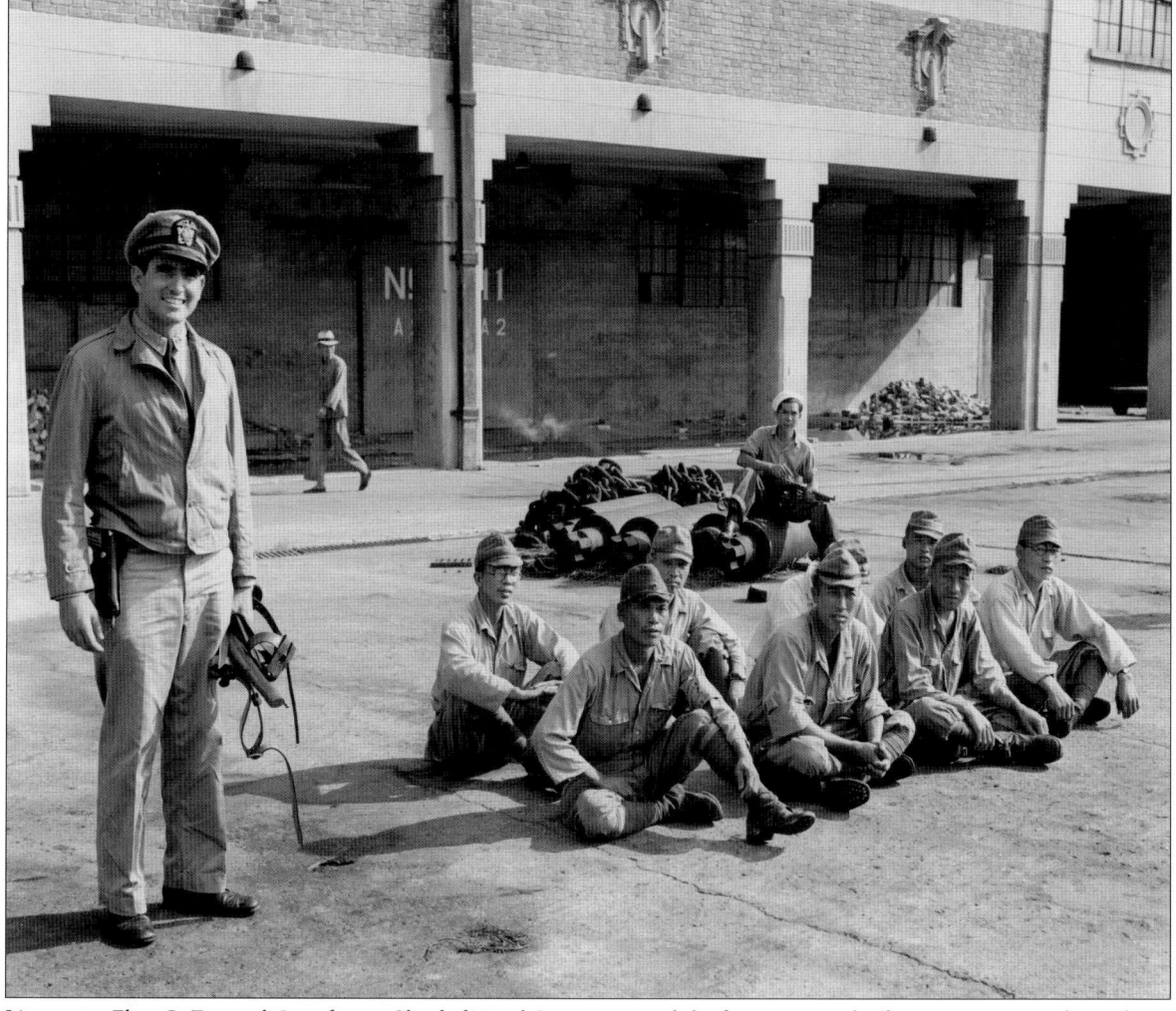

Lieutenant Elmo R. Zumwalt Jr., a future Chief of Naval Operations and the first U.S. naval officer to conn a naval vessel into the port of Shanghai at the end of World War II, stands watch over captured Japanese sailors. His presence symbolized the U.S. Navy's strong postwar interest in China.

As a counterweight to this growing Soviet and indigenous Communist presence in Northeast Asia, the Truman administration wasted little time deploying Army and Marine troops to southern Korea and northern China. U.S. commands moved to establish a military presence in those ports and communications centers not yet under Soviet control. In General Order No.1, promulgated by President Truman on 15 August 1945, military commands were informed that only Chiang Kai-shek's government, and not the Chinese Communists, could accept the surrender of Japanese forces in China (except Manchuria), northern Indochina, and on the island of Taiwan (Formosa).

In late September and early October, the U.S. Seventh Fleet cleared mines from the approaches to Chinese ports and transported to north China almost 50,000 Marines of the 1st Marine Division, 6th Marine Division, and 1st Marine Aircraft Wing. The troops established a presence in Tsingtao (Qingdao), Tientsin (Tianjin), Bejing, and other population centers and along area rail lines. During late 1945 and 1946, Chinese Communist troops attacked or sniped at Marines guarding bridges and railway lines. During this period, Mao's troops killed seven U.S. Marines and wounded another score.

The Truman administration also directed the Seventh Fleet to transport three Chinese Nationalist

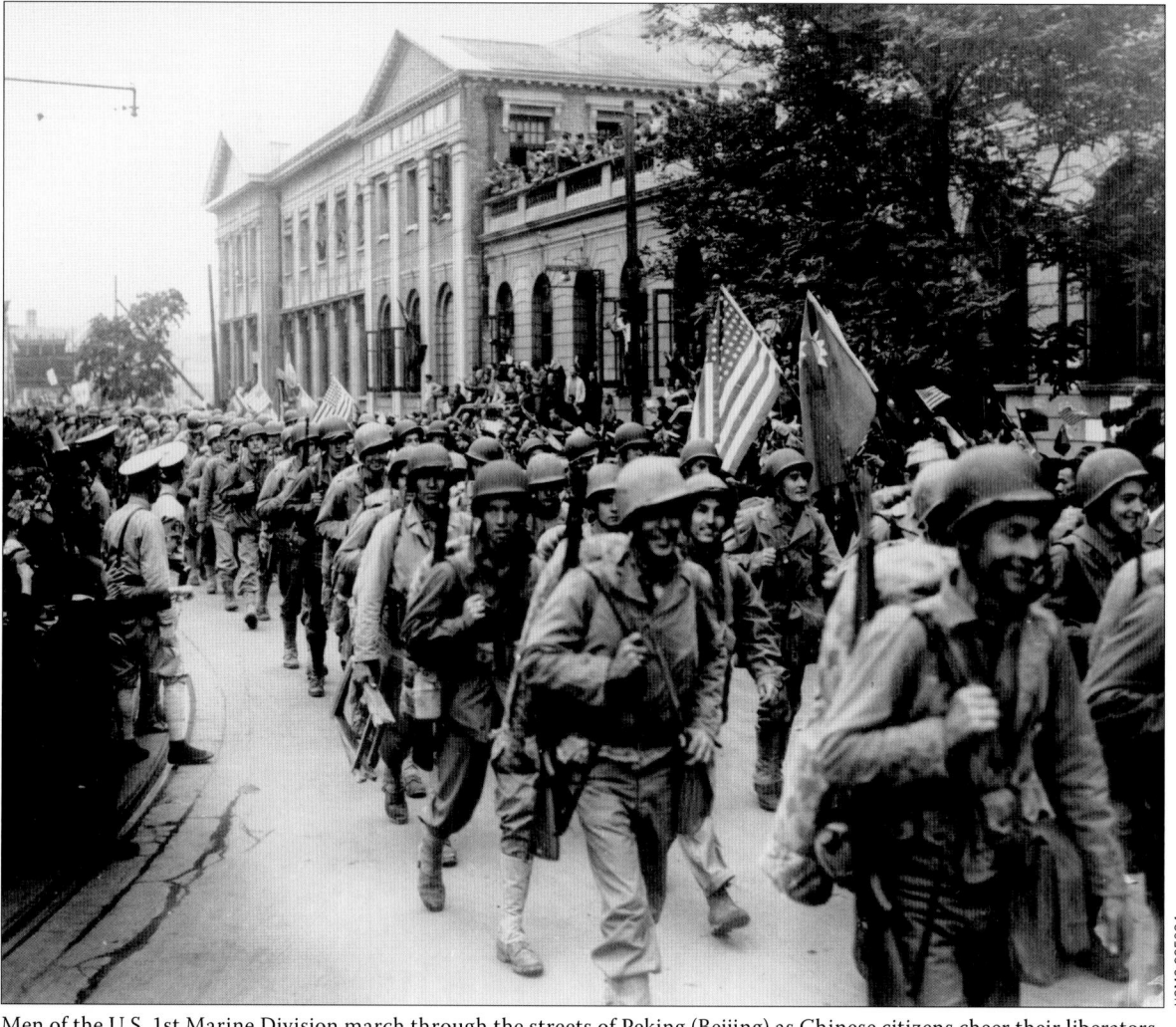

Men of the U.S. 1st Marine Division march through the streets of Peking (Beijing) as Chinese citizens cheer their liberators from the Japanese. Smiles would fade from the faces of these Marines as they found themselves caught up in the bloody Chinese civil war.

armies to northern China and Manchuria during the fall of 1945. Soviet authorities worked to delay and complicate these American and Chinese Nationalist deployments while enabling Mao's Communists to take control of ports and cities in the region. Nationalist troops carried by U.S. naval vessels were prevented from landing in several Manchurian ports. When the Soviets disarmed the Kwantung Army in the north, they turned over many Japanese weapons and stocks of ammunition to the Communists.

This collusion between Stalin's government and the local Communists reinforced the inclination of many Navy leaders to press for an increase in U.S. support for Chiang's government. During World War

II, Admiral Ernest J. King, Commander in Chief, U.S. Fleet and Chief of Naval Operations, saw China as the logical springboard for the invasion of Japan. To pave the way for an American amphibious landing in China, he posted to the capital at Chungking (Chongqing) Commodore Milton "Mary" Miles, who headed Naval Group China. The dynamic, unorthodox officer created an effective and wide-ranging guerrilla and intelligence-gathering operation in close cooperation with Chiang and his top military officers. The Joint Chiefs of Staff vetoed King's wartime plan for a landing in China, but the Navy continued to value its connection to Chiang and saw him as the best hope against Communist aspirations in Northeast Asia.

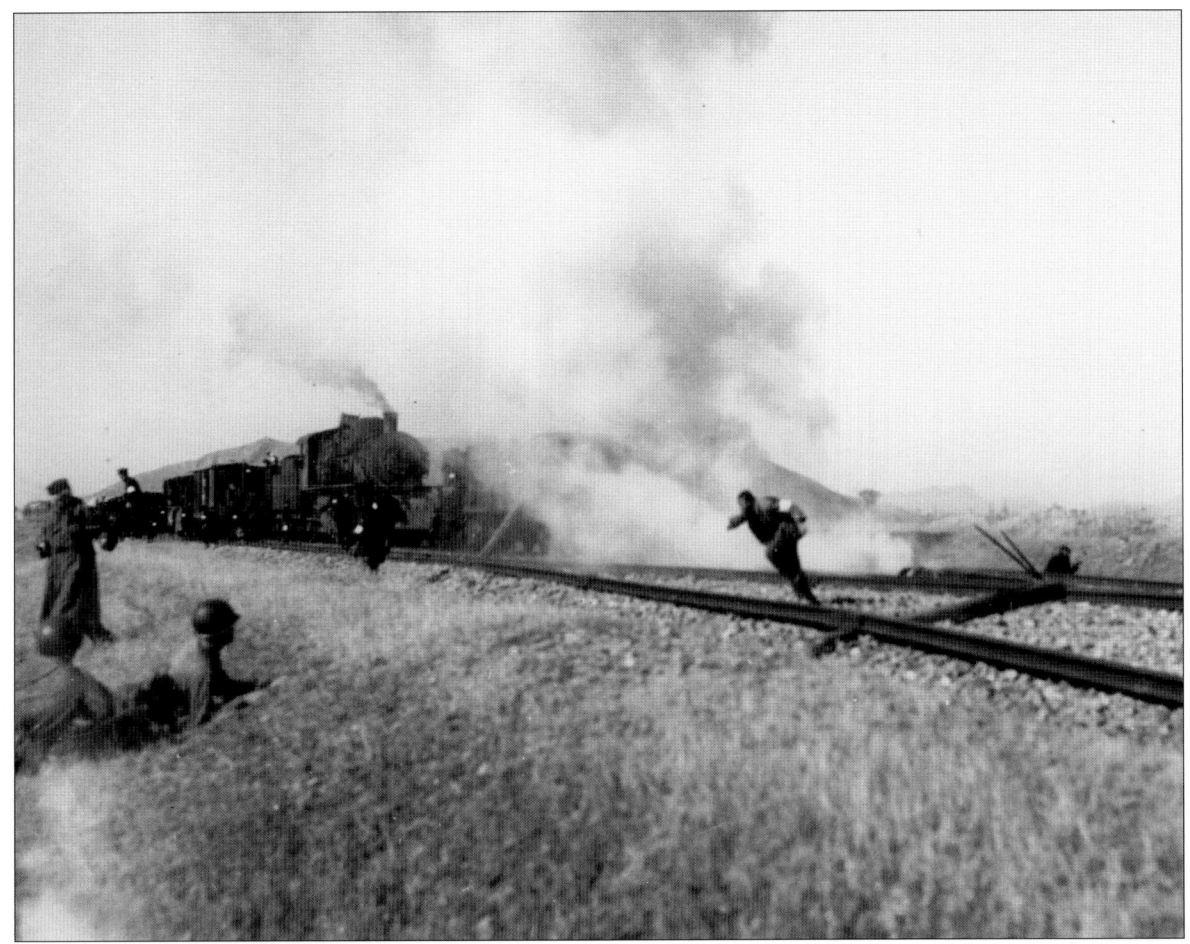

A mine planted along railroad tracks explodes as Chinese workmen and American Marines seek cover. Convinced that the United States favored their Chinese foes, Mao Tse-tung's troops increasingly targeted U.S. forces in northern China.

This appreciation of Chiang and his government was hardly universal among Americans. Army General Joseph "Vinegar Joe" Stillwell had been outspoken in his condemnation of Chiang for wartime timidity and military ineptitude. Others focused on Chiang's failure to rid his government of corrupt and venal officials and military officers. At the same time, some U.S. Army officers who had been part of the so-called Dixie Mission (meant to establish contact with the Communists and gather intelligence) to Mao's headquarters at Yenan (Yanan) in 1944 were less critical than others of the Communists. Mao's troops were after all America's wartime allies against the Japanese.

While hardly wanting a Communist takeover of China, Truman and his chief advisors were not prepared to deploy American troops to China to fight the Communists. They appreciated that after four years of a bloody world war, most Americans wanted only peace and a return to normalcy. Moreover, Truman and his State Department were determined to focus America's military resources—stretched especially thin after World War II—on the Soviet threat in Europe.

The President, therefore, dispatched to China on a special mission General George C. Marshall, wartime Chief of Staff of the U.S. Army and a man of enormous national and international stature. Truman sent Marshall on a mission impossible—convince the Nationalists and the Communists to join in a government of national unity. Marshall sincerely believed the effort could and would succeed; he arranged a nationwide cease-fire between the Nationalists and Communists that held for several months.

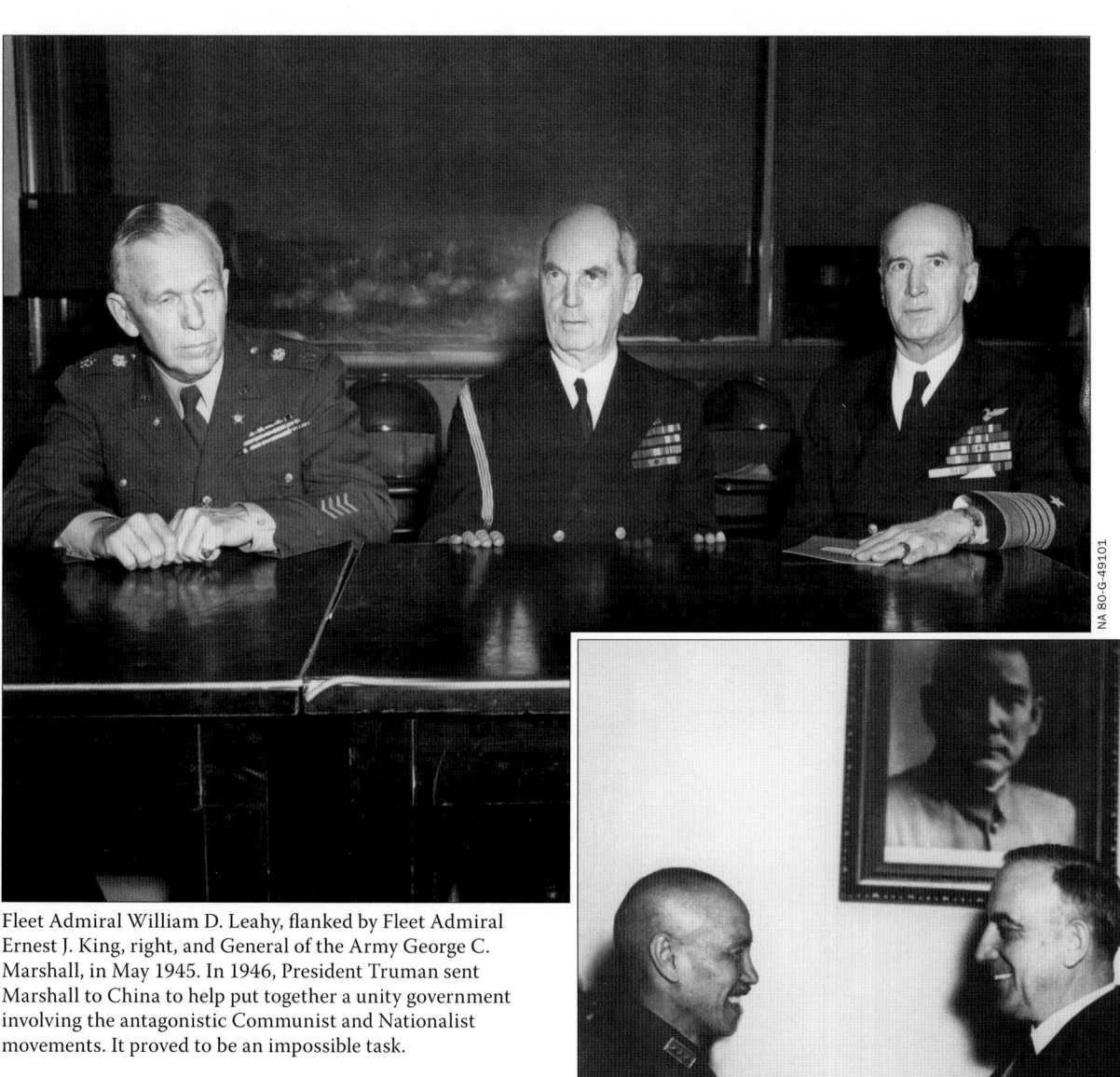

Fleet Admiral William D. Leahy, flanked by Fleet Admiral Ernest J. King, right, and General of the Army George C. Marshall, in May 1945. In 1946, President Truman sent Marshall to China to help put together a unity government involving the antagonistic Communist and Nationalist movements. It proved to be an impossible task.

The mission, however, was doomed even before it began. The contending Chinese parties had fought a bloody, no-holds-barred civil war since 1927. Their bitter feud had only been postponed in the face of the Japanese threat. But Chiang—and some American leaders—understood that the Communists would be satisfied with nothing less than the fulfillment of their dream: a revolutionary change to China's social, political, and economic makeup and its place in the world. Both sides used the cease-fire for tactical advantage—the Communists to solidify their control in northern China and the Nationalists to curry favor with the Americans and build up military strength for the coming countrywide Armageddon. ⚓

Generalissimo Chiang Kai-shek, left, congratulates Vice Admiral Daniel E. Barbey, a successful World War II amphibious commander, after presenting him with an award. The Chinese leader curried favored with American naval officers, many of whom had a higher opinion of Chiang than their Army counterparts.

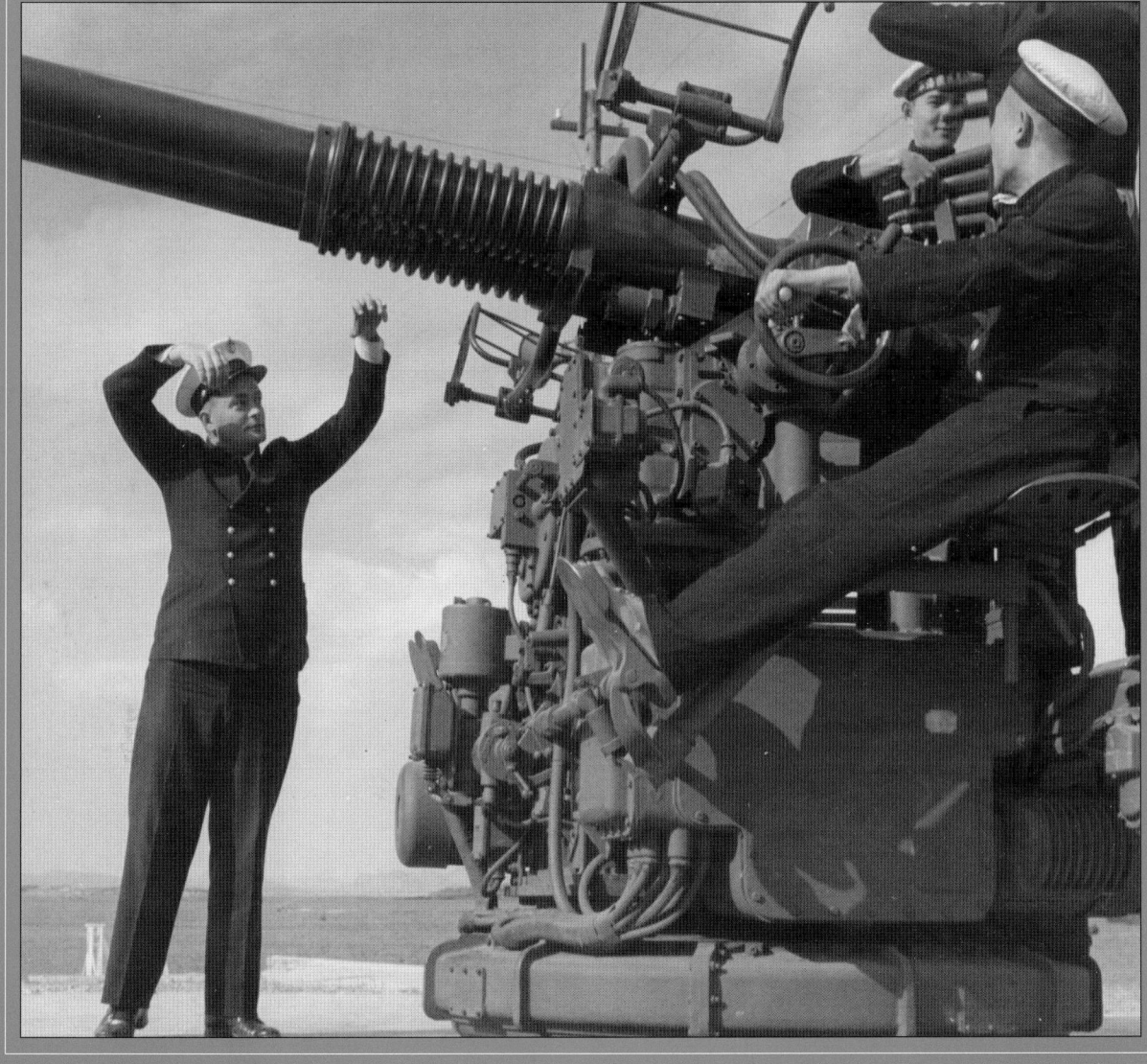

Chief Gunner's Mate J. D. Lyons instructs Chinese Nationalist sailors in the operation of an American-made antiaircraft weapon. The U.S. Navy mounted a substantial advisory effort in China during the late 1940s.

NH 390340

Believing he had a preponderance of military power, Chiang struck first. Nationalist forces stormed into Manchuria and retook a number of cities held by the Communists. By the end of 1948, however, the tide had turned. Mao's troops, well led and fired up with Marxist-Leninist and antiforeign zeal, beat one Nationalist army after the other. By the end of 1948, it was clear that the days for Chiang's armed forces and government were numbered.

As the civil war raged across China, American military advisors and other observers reported that Communists were executing prisoners (the Nationalists were often as brutal), government officials, priests, foreign missionaries, and Chinese "reactionaries" by the tens of thousands. Mao's troops seized or destroyed U.S. and other Western commercial enterprises.

American naval and military leaders concluded that a Communist victory in China would be catastrophic to U.S. security interests in the entire Western Pacific. With Chinese Communists in control of the mainland, it was feared that Mao would permit the Soviets to continue basing their

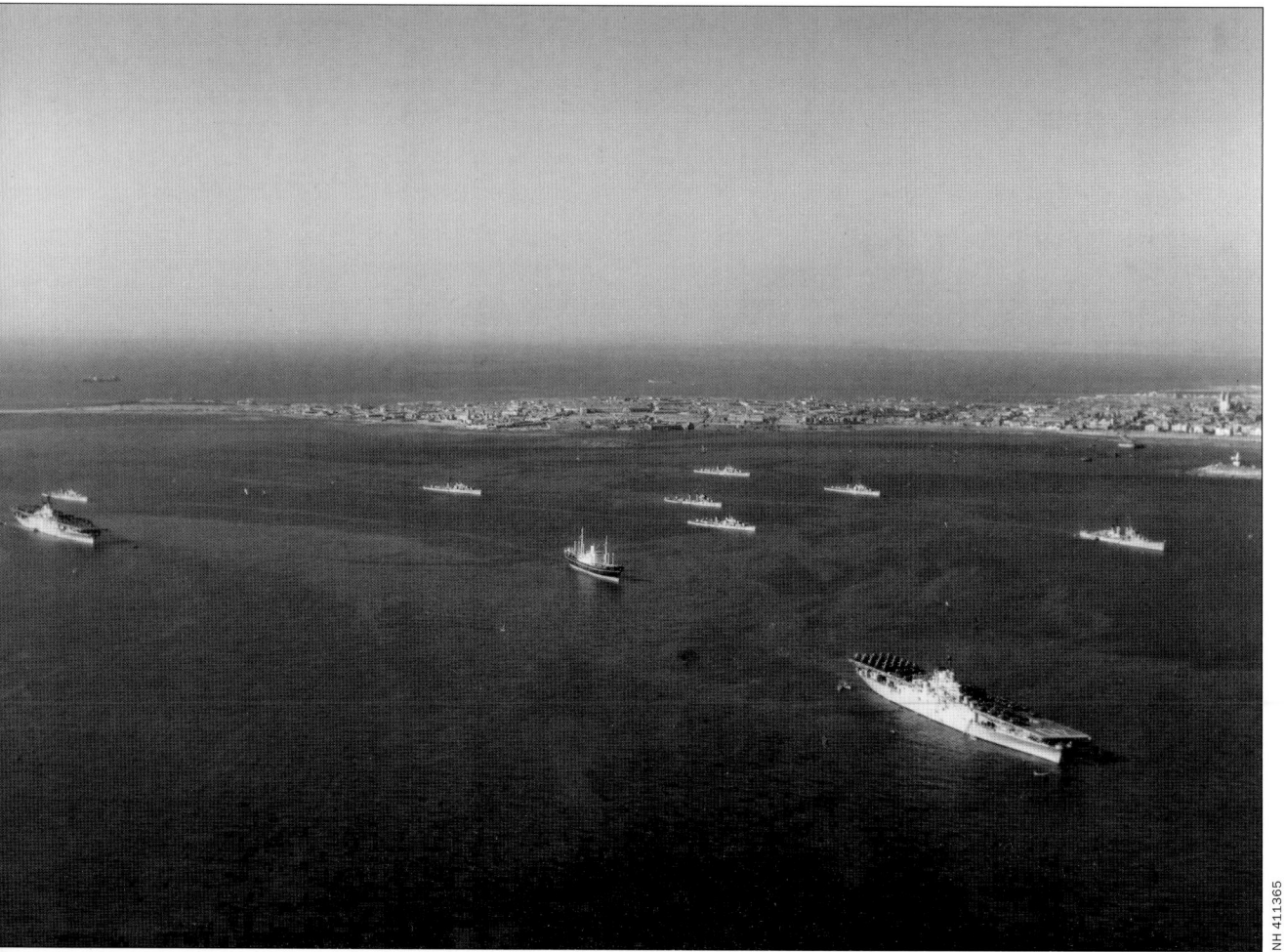

American carriers and other warships lay at anchor in the roadstead of Tsingtao, China, home port of the U.S. Seventh Fleet during the late 1940s.

NH 411365

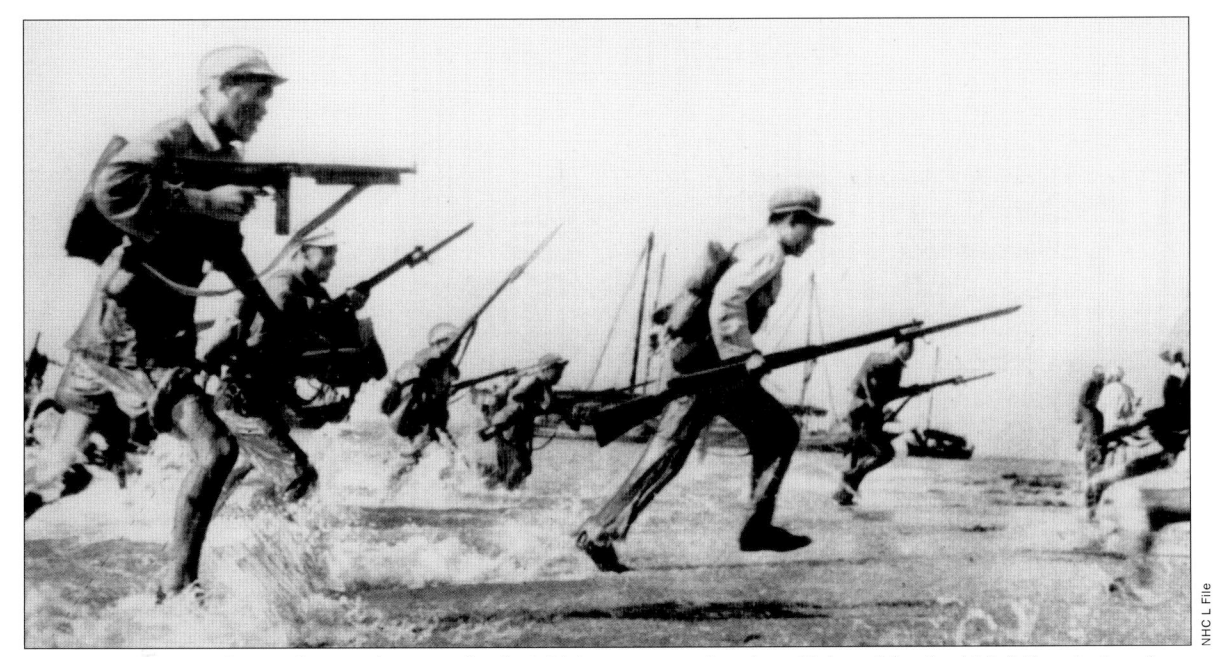

Chinese Communist forces of General Lin Biao's 4th Field Army storm a beach on Hainan Island, which fell to the invaders in April 1950. U.S. Navy observers reasoned that the large island of Taiwan would be Mao Tse-tung's next target.

warships at Port Arthur and indeed all along the coast of China, putting at risk U.S. military forces stationed in Japan and the Philippines.

These military leaders were also concerned that a Communist success in China—the ancient Middle Kingdom—would embolden indigenous movements all around it in Japan, Korea, the Philippines, Malaya, and especially Vietnam to emulate the Chinese model and seek military and political support from Mao's government.

The Truman administration, however, especially after the failure of the Marshall Mission, backed away from a serious commitment to the defense of Chiang's anticommunist government. Truman grew to loath Chiang and, like Stillwell, referred to him derisively as "The Peanut." Marshall, who became Secretary of State in 1948, and his successor, Dean Acheson, pursued a foreign policy that distanced the United States from the conflict in China; they hoped to establish relations with the winner in the civil war. For these reasons, the administration withdrew the Marines from northern China and closed the by-now major U.S. naval base at Tsingtao, home to the U.S. Seventh Fleet. In the spring of 1949, as Communist forces advanced through southern China, the fleet evacuated Tsingtao and withdrew to Subic Bay in the Philippines.

Chiang's government and surviving armed forces fled the mainland ahead of advancing Communist troops and occupied Taiwan and many other offshore islands. The Nationalists handily defeated an ill-planned Communist amphibious assault on the island of Quemoy (Jinmen) in 1949 but failed to prevent the loss of the much larger island of Hainan in the South China Sea during the spring of 1950. Most observers took seriously Mao's often-stated pledge to seize Taiwan and finally eliminate Chiang's Nationalist government. An increasing number of American leaders, concerned about aggressive Soviet and Chinese Communist actions in Europe and Asia, urged Truman to "draw a line in the sand" against Communist inroads.

However, lacking adequate military strength, especially in Asia, the Truman administration resisted actions that might embroil the United States in war with the Communist powers. In fact, early in 1950 Secretary of State Dean Acheson publicly implied in a speech that neither Taiwan nor South Korea fell within America's Western Pacific defensive perimeter.

The Korean War, which erupted on 25 June 1950 when the North Korean People's Army invaded the pro-American Republic of Korea, dramatically altered the administration's appraisal of U.S. strategic interests in the Far East. Truman now was convinced that North Korean leader Kim Il Sung acted in concert with Joseph Stalin and Mao Tse-tung to establish Communist domination over all Asia. On 27 June, the American president ordered U.S. forces into action against the North Korean Communists, and other United Nations forces soon joined the Americans. Truman's perception that Kim and Mao were in league was strengthened when an enormous Chinese Communist army deployed into North Korea late in the fall of 1950 and launched a devastating, all-out offensive against American and other U.N. troops.

We now know that Truman's perception about Communist objectives in Northeast Asia was accurate. Archival materials, memoirs, histories, and other studies available in Moscow, Beijing, and Washington confirm that Stalin and Mao endorsed Kim's plan to attack South Korea. During the ensuing conflict, the Soviets and Chinese assisted Kim with not only massive amounts of military equipment and supplies but also fighter pilots and air defense units.

Washington saw little distinction between Communist designs on Korea, China, and French Indochina on the southern rim of Asia. Earlier ambivalence about the goals of the anti-French Vietnamese resistance movement led by Ho Chi Minh evaporated in the wake of Communist actions in Korea. Truman expected the Chinese Communists, if not the Soviets, to provide arms and supplies, diplomatic support, and perhaps military forces to the anti-French struggle of Ho— a lifelong and dedicated Communist.

Nguyen Sinh Cung (who later took the name Ho Chi Minh) was born in Nghe An Province of northern Vietnam in 1890.

His father, a mandarin and a teacher, facilitated Ho's secondary education at a prestigious academy in Hue. In 1911, Ho moved to Paris, and in the next several years he worked as a gardener, dishwasher, and photography assistant, among other menial jobs, in France, London, and New York. During World War I he returned to France. Although he had been intrigued by the Declaration of Independence and the Constitution as guarantors of certain political rights, he readily embraced the Marxist-Leninist ideas that were inspiring political debate in the French capital. He joined the French Socialist Party and then in 1920, the French Communist Party. He was particularly energized by Lenin's advocacy of

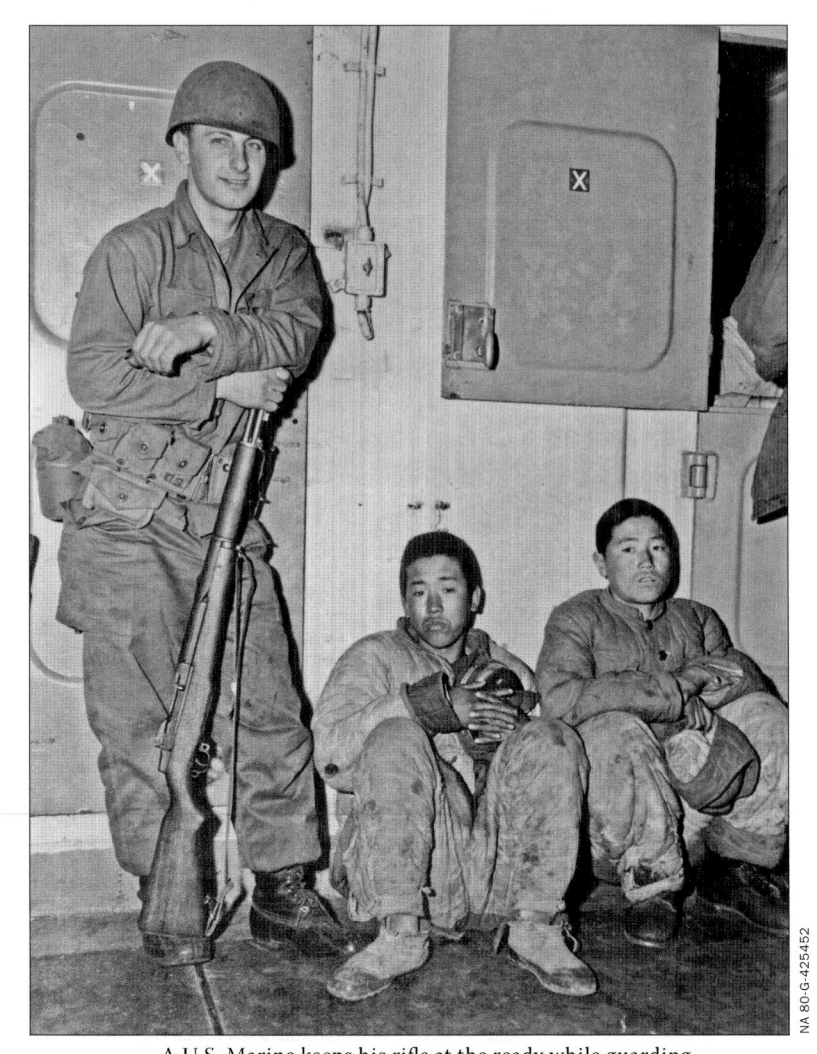

A U.S. Marine keeps his rifle at the ready while guarding Chinese Communist soldiers captured during the brutal fighting for North Korea in late 1950.

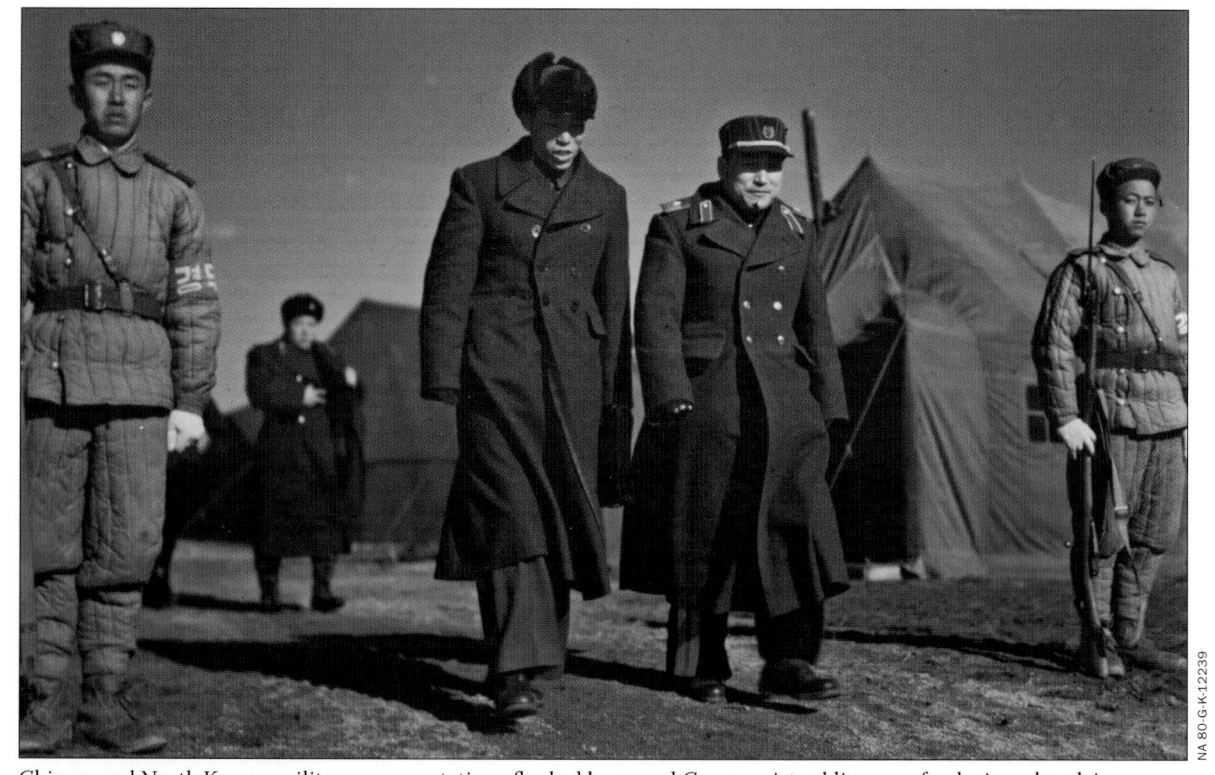

Chinese and North Korean military representatives, flanked by armed Communist soldiers, confer during a break in armistice negotiations at Panmunjom in May 1952. Their superiors, along with Soviet leader Joseph Stalin, colluded in the earlier invasion of the Republic of Korea.

international revolution to free indigenous peoples from their colonial masters.

Three years later he burnished his radical credentials and training at the headquarters of the Communist International (Comintern) in Moscow. Moving on to Canton (Guangzhou) in southern China in 1925, Ho formed the Marxist-Leninist Vietnam Revolutionary Youth League and penned radical tracts. He traveled to Siam, Malaya, and Singapore to help establish Communist parties there. By 1930 Ho was the leading figure in what came to be known as the Indochinese Communist Party. Ho Chi Minh and Mao Tse-tung collaborated frequently during the 1930s on revolutionary, anti-imperialist projects. Ho and the Vietnamese Communists, like all other Marxist-Leninist movements, took up arms against the Axis powers Germany and Japan and made common cause with the United States and the other Allied powers in World War II. The Vietnamese Communists downplayed their ideological underpinnings, joined with noncommunist nationalist groups, and courted American favor and military supplies.

When Ho realized that the United States would not prevent France from reoccupying Indochina after the war, he and his comrades reverted to form. His movement, occupying much of Vietnam in 1946 before French forces reestablished control, began stamping out noncommunist opposition parties and assassinating thousands of village officials, landlords, and key nationalist leaders, including the brother of Ngo Dinh Diem, the future president of South Vietnam. In 1949, Chinese and Vietnamese Communist forces carried out a joint attack against French positions in northern Tonkin.

In January 1950, Ho traveled to China and then on to Moscow. Stalin and Mao recognized the Democratic Republic of Vietnam (DRV), reaffirmed their Marxist-Leninist solidarity with Ho's movement, and promised to provide arms and other military assistance to the anti-imperialist struggle in Indochina. Shortly thereafter, the People's Republic

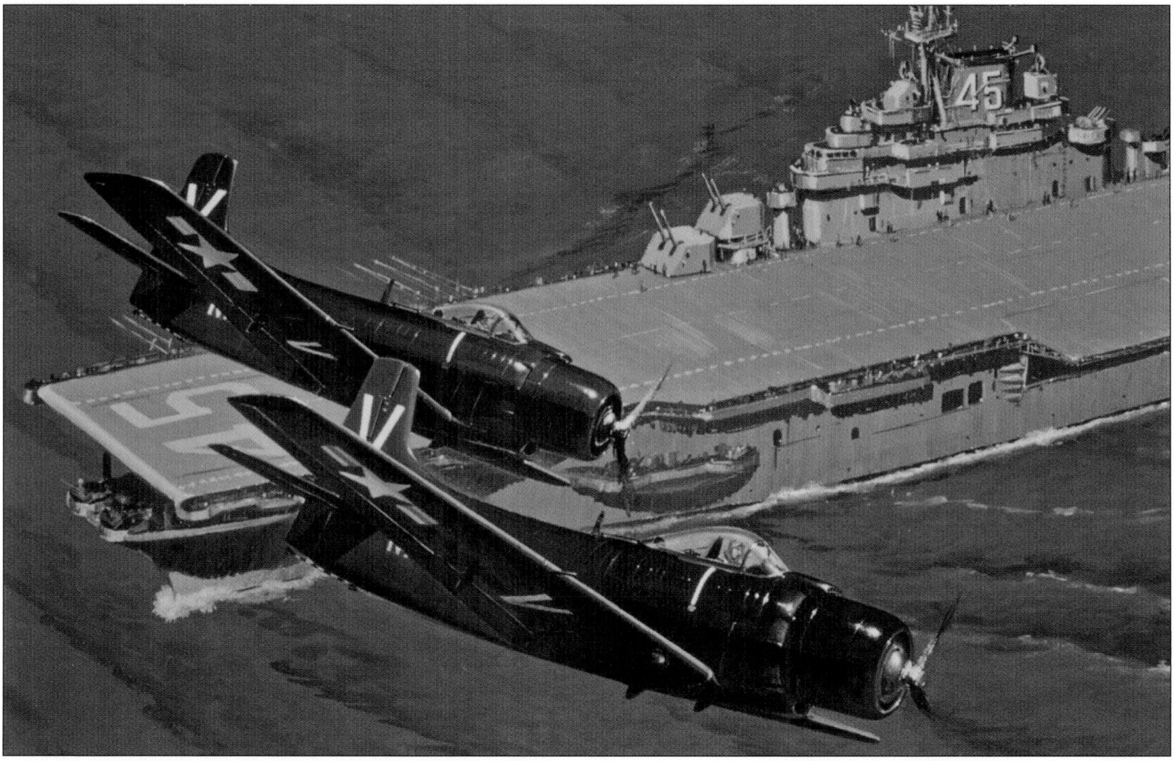

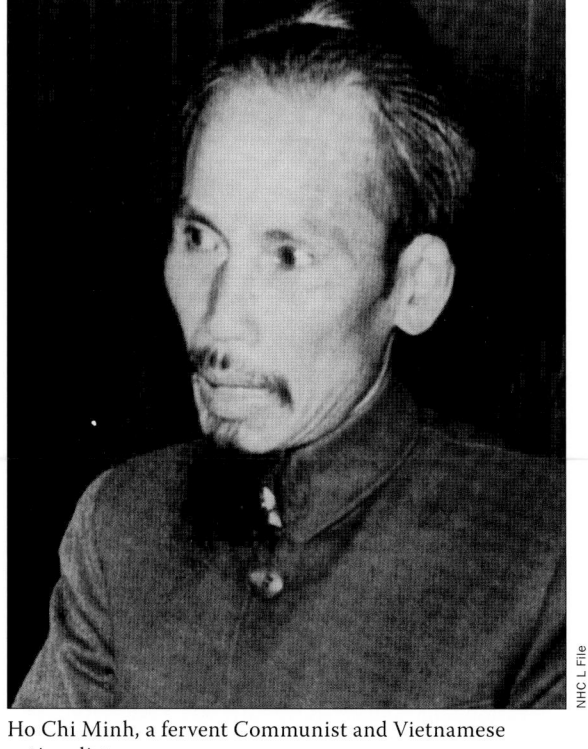

Navy AD Skyraiders fly over carrier *Valley Forge* (CV 45) in this painting by R. G. Smith. The carrier and other warships of the U.S. Seventh Fleet backed up President Truman's pledge to prevent a Communist invasion of Taiwan.

Courtesy Sharlyn Marsh

Ho Chi Minh, a fervent Communist and Vietnamese nationalist.

NHC L File

of China (PRC) began transporting to Tonkin 14,000 rifles, 1,700 machine guns and recoilless rifles, 60 artillery pieces, 300 antitank weapons, and 281 advisors, who included the obese but especially talented Chinese general Chen Geng.

In mid-1950, convinced that Ho and the other Far Eastern Communist leaders were acting in concert to frustrate U.S. policies, the Truman administration moved with unprecedented vigor to reorder the strategic balance in Asia. The President endorsed a huge outlay of funds to strengthen America's military establishment. In addition to authorizing U.S. forces to join the fight against the Communists in Korea, he ordered the Navy to oppose any Chinese Communist invasion of Taiwan. On 29 June 1950, carrier *Valley Forge* (CV 45), with a squadron of the Navy's new F9F Panther jets on board, steamed with the bulk of the Seventh Fleet along the coast of Taiwan in a show of force. The U.S. Navy's presence offshore frustrated Mao's plans to destroy Chiang's Nationalists on the island and thus end the civil war. **13**

Throughout the Korean War, hostilities that involved U.S., Chinese Nationalist, and Chinese Communist forces enflamed the coastal areas of central and southern China. From numerous offshore islands and Taiwan itself, Nationalist guerrillas and regular forces—500,000 men organized in 42 divisions and operating 79 warships and 540 combat aircraft—mined coastal waters, bombed Communist territory, and raided enemy-occupied islands. In October 1952, for instance, a naval assault force stormed an island off Fukien (Fujian) Province, killing or capturing 1,300 Communist troops. The

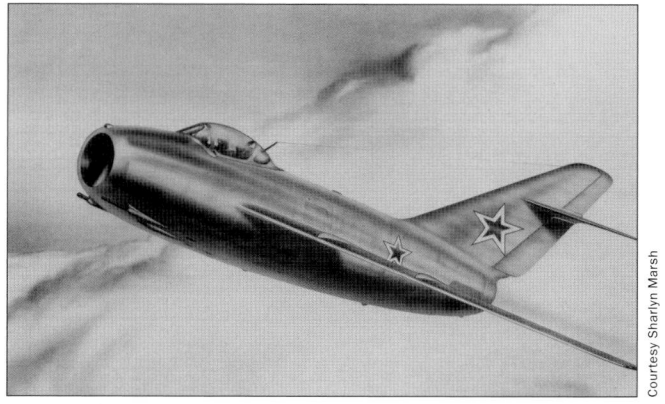

The Soviet-built MiG-15 was the primary fighter interceptor of the People's Republic of China during the early 1950s and posed a great threat to Navy patrol planes operating off the coast of China.

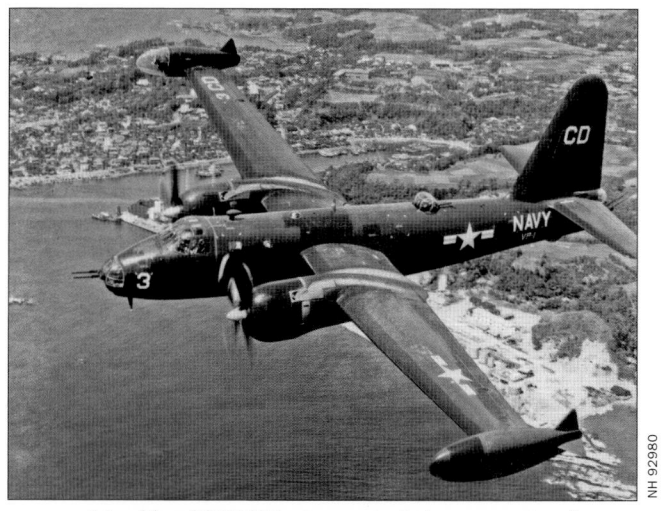

A Lockheed P2V-5 Neptune patrol plane operating from Japan. These aircraft kept watch over the coastal areas of China, especially the 100-mile gap between the mainland and Taiwan, and the waters of the Soviet Far East.

Nationalists also stopped, searched, and seized neutral and other merchant vessels bound for China.

The U.S. Navy established a long-term presence off China. Soon after the outbreak of the Korean War, the Seventh Fleet commander, Vice Admiral Arthur D. Struble, established the Formosa (later Taiwan) Patrol Force. Routinely, three or four American destroyers operated from a base in Taiwan to keep watch on the waters between that island and the Communist mainland. Operating from U.S. naval facilities in Japan and Taiwan, aircraft of the Central Intelligence Agency's Civil Air Transport (CAT) company deployed agents into Communist China.

During the same period, the Seventh Fleet's Fleet Air Wing 1 inaugurated patrols in the Taiwan Strait by seaplanes and land-based patrol aircraft. Pilots were instructed to remain outside of the PRC's 12-mile limit, but in their effort to capture useful photographic intelligence, the aviators sometimes strayed over Chinese territory. Communist interceptor aircraft often climbed into the sky to attack the intruders. In September 1952 off Shanghai, a pair of MiG-15 jets made repeated firing passes on a Navy patrol plane but failed to shoot it down. The Communists were more successful in January 1953 when an antiaircraft unit shot up a P2V Neptune patrol plane flying over the coast, forcing the pilot to ditch just offshore. A U.S. Coast Guard seaplane arrived on the scene and rescued survivors of the P2V, but crashed when it tried to lift off. Under fire from Communist coastal and antiaircraft guns, U.S. and British warships and aircraft came to the assistance of the downed air crewmen and brought ten men to safety.

Twice during the Korean War, the operation of carrier task forces off the coast of China resulted in hostilities. In the spring of 1951, aircraft carriers *Philippine Sea* (CV 47) and *Boxer* (CV 21) and their escorting warships steamed south past the ports of Amoy (Xiamen), Swatow (Shantou), and Foochow (Fuzhou). Carrier aircraft made low-level reconnaissance runs over these cities, prompting Communist antiaircraft units to open up and MiG jets to scramble in opposition. At the end of this operation, characterized by Admiral Arthur W. Radford, commander of the Pacific Fleet, as a "show

of force," he observed that it had been a "powerful deterrent to further expansion of Communism" in Southeast Asia.

The following year, in July, aircraft carriers *Essex* (CV 9) and *Philippine Sea* and eight destroyers, under Rear Admiral A. Soucek, deployed as far south as China's Hainan Island. As many as 53 carrier planes flew over the tropical island and the nearby mainland coast, photographing Communist airfields, naval bases, ports, and military facilities. As the year before, Mao's antiaircraft gunners and jet pilots attacked the American units but failed to knock down any of them. Following the operation, Admiral Radford's spokesman in Hawaii observed to the international press that the object of the mission was to "show that the Navy could bomb the coastal cities of Amoy, Foochow, and Swatow anytime without draining its forces in Korea." Hence, armed conflict involving U.S. and Communist forces occurred not only in Korea from 1950 to 1953 but all along the littoral of Asia. ⚓

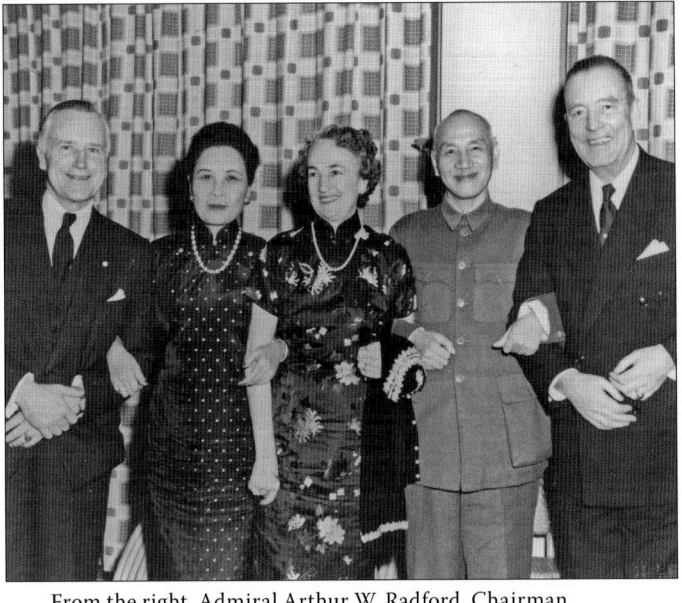

From the right, Admiral Arthur W. Radford, Chairman of the Joint Chiefs of Staff; President Chiang Kai-shek; Mrs. Radford; Madam Chiang Kai-shek; and Walter S. Robertson, Assistant Secretary of State for Far Eastern Affairs, appear arm-in-arm at a social function. Radford advocated a strong U.S. naval presence in waters off Communist China.

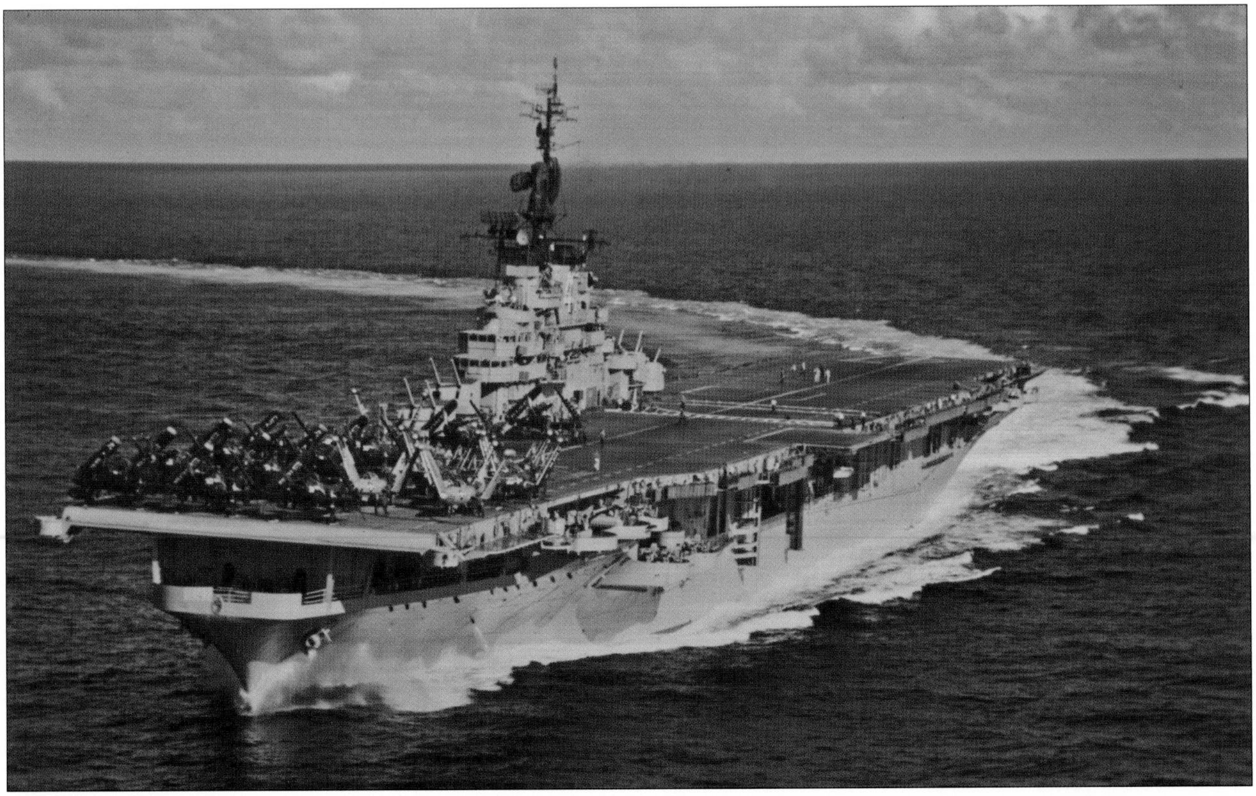

Aircraft carrier *Philippine Sea* (CV 47) steams in the Western Pacific. The Pacific Command deployed carrier task forces along the coast of China throughout the 1950s and early 1960s.

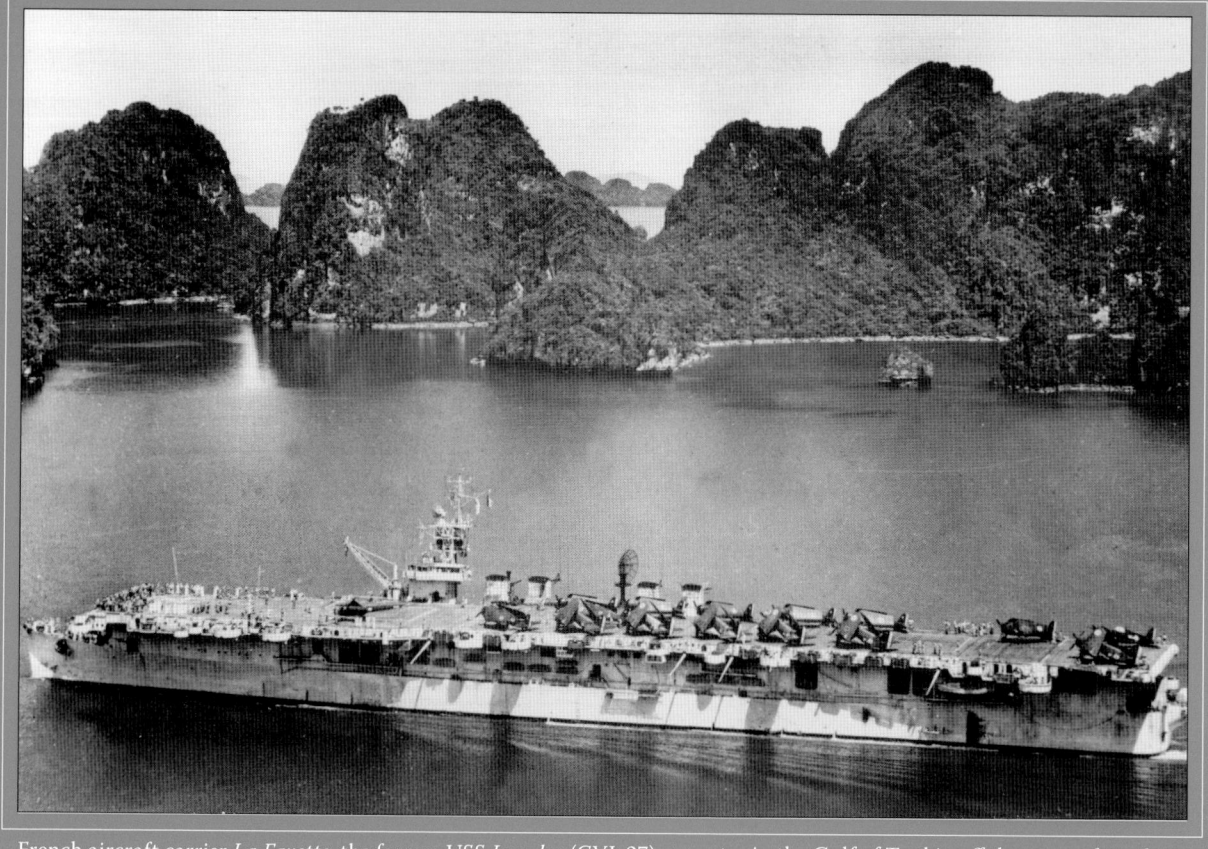

French aircraft carrier *La Fayette*, the former USS *Langley* (CVL 27), operates in the Gulf of Tonkin off the coast of northern Vietnam. The U.S. Navy oversaw a program that provided substantial military assistance to French forces in Indochina.

Truman understood that the Communist threat extended far beyond the Korean peninsula. His National Security Council concluded that the loss of Indochina (Vietnam, Laos, and Cambodia) to the Communists would imperil the rest of Southeast Asia. Consequently, the President directed the provision of military assistance to French and noncommunist Vietnamese forces fighting Ho Chi Minh's Viet Minh guerrillas. In September 1950, Washington established Military Assistance Advisory Group (MAAG), Indochina to administer the aid. The Truman administration wanted to establish independent Vietnamese armed forces, but almost until the end of France's struggle to retain its Asian colonies, Paris insisted that Vietnamese soldiers and sailors be led by French officers and noncommissioned officers.

In the fall of 1950, American naval advisors set up shop in Saigon and began overseeing the transfer to the French of aircraft carriers, aircraft, and amphibious vessels. During the next several years, Washington dispatched one observer group after another to find ways to bolster the French war effort. Even with this American support, however, the French failed to stem the rising tide of support for Ho among the Vietnamese. Many of his countrymen saw "Uncle Ho" as a nationalist first and a Communist second. Indeed, the Viet Minh movement included noncommunist elements.

With the end of the Korean War in July 1953, the Chinese Communists delivered increasing amounts of arms and equipment to the Viet Minh, who forced the French from much of the countryside and then surrounded major population centers. The French attempted to improve their military situation by deploying a huge force of Foreign Legionnaires, paratroopers, and other elite units into the Communist rear at the remote village of Dien Bien Phu, site of a small airstrip. The French object was to prevent a Viet

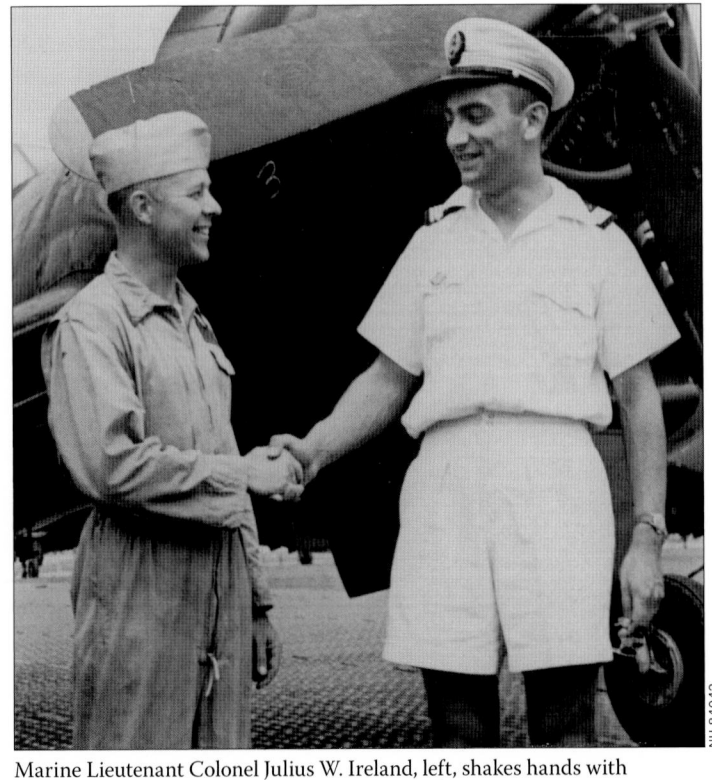

Marine Lieutenant Colonel Julius W. Ireland, left, shakes hands with his French Navy counterpart as the American completes the delivery of F4U Corsair aircraft to the airfield at Tourane (later Danang).

Minh offensive into Laos and at the same time draw enemy forces to the area to be decimated by what was thought to be superior French ground and air power. The French readily deployed these combat forces to Dien Bien Phu in November 1953 and established a number of fortified redoubts around the airstrip.

Sensing an opportunity to destroy the flower of the French military establishment in Indochina, Ho Chi Minh and his gifted military commander, General Vo Nguyen Giap, moved the bulk of their best forces to Dien Bien Phu. Supplied liberally with guns and ammunition by the Chinese Communists, the Viet Minh ringed the French outpost with battle-hardened infantry and positioned hundreds of artillery pieces on surrounding hills. Beginning in March 1954, Ho's troops rained artillery fire on the outgunned French garrison and stormed one strong-

17

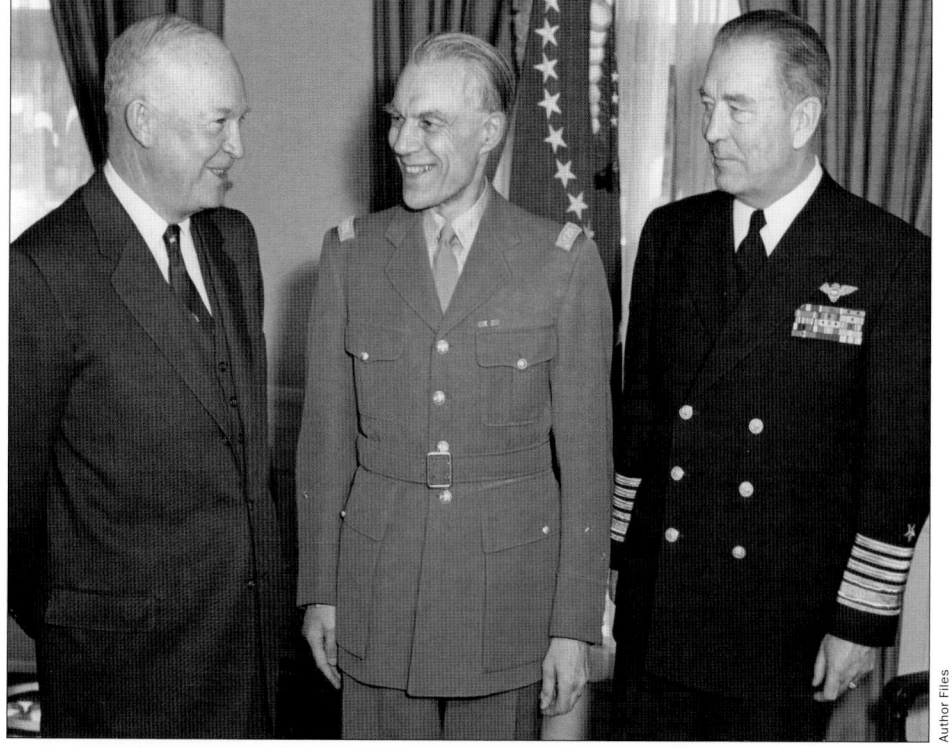

American civilian and military leaders, Radford in particular, advocated attacks by U.S. carrier aircraft on the Communist positions ringing Dien Bien Phu. The President and other top civilian and military leaders, however, doubted that the French could be saved, with or without nuclear weapons.

Before he would consider taking any action, President Eisenhower wanted assurance from Paris that France would accede to eventual Vietnamese independence, accept greater international action to resolve the crisis, retain a strong troop presence in Indochina, and enable the

Author Files

President Dwight D. Eisenhower, left, meets in Washington with General Paul Ély, Chief of Staff of the French Armed Forces, and Admiral Arthur W. Radford to discuss possible U.S. intervention in the Indochina War. Eisenhower decided against the action, despite Radford's advocacy.

point after another. Increasingly lethal Vietnamese antiaircraft fire negated French air power and compelled the parachute delivery of limited reinforcements and supplies. By April the French had sustained thousands of casualties and, fearing the total loss of their forces trapped at Dien Bien Phu, pleaded with Washington for military assistance.

Dwight D. Eisenhower, elected President in November 1952, understood that a defeat of the French army at Dien Bien Phu would compel Paris to give up the struggle for all of Indochina. By the same token, a Viet Minh victory would embolden Communist movements throughout Southeast Asia.

Eisenhower considered the intervention of American forces to redress the balance of power. With the President's approval, Admiral Radford, Chairman of the Joint Chiefs of Staff, directed the deployment of a Pacific Fleet carrier task force to the South China Sea. A number of aircraft in the task force were equipped to drop nuclear bombs. Some

United States to exercise more influence over strategic decision making and military assistance. The French refused Eisenhower's conditions. Based on French recalcitrance and the outright opposition of the British to any joint military action in Indochina, Eisenhower decided against intervention. On 7 May 1954, Ho's Viet Minh forces stormed the last French-held bastion at Dien Bien Phu and marched more than 8,000 French and allied Indochinese troops off to harsh captivity.

In July of that year, representatives of France, the United States, Great Britain, the Soviet Union, the People's Republic of China, the Democratic Republic of Vietnam, and other countries met in Geneva, Switzerland, to discuss ending the conflict in Indochina. In the final agreement, the signatories agreed to the separation of combatants and an election by Vietnamese of all political persuasions in July 1956 to determine the makeup of a unified government. President Eisenhower and Secretary of State John Foster Dulles considered

the Geneva Agreement a disaster for U.S. foreign policy. Admiral Radford told Vice President Richard Nixon that he believed the Geneva agreement to be a "great mistake" for the United States, and Nixon concurred, saying "it is a black day for us." Neither the United States nor the noncommunist government in South Vietnam signed the agreement, even though Washington announced it would not undercut its provisions regarding the introduction into Indochina of military forces or material.

A separate agreement at Geneva called for the transportation and concentration of Communist forces in the Tonkin region of Vietnam at the same time as noncommunist forces that had supported the French were grouped in the Annam and Cochin China regions of central and southern Vietnam. The United States agreed to support the massive movement of noncommunist forces and, as it transpired, civilian refugees from northern to southern Vietnam. Washington ordered the Seventh Fleet to handle the operation, soon named Passage to Freedom. First, the Navy dispatched medical teams to Haiphong and other embarkation points. Lieutenant Tom Dooley and other Navy personnel constructed shelters, latrines, and other accommodations for the tens of thousands of refugees, many of them Catholics, who streamed into the ports. The refugees were deloused to prevent disease and finally helped to board U.S. naval vessels for the voyage south. Between August 1954 and May 1955, the 74 ships of the naval task force and 39 vessels of the Navy's Military Sea Transportation Service delivered 17,800 Vietnamese troops, 293,000 refugees, and more than 8,000 vehicles to Saigon. The authorities in the South constructed housing for the immigrants, who soon became the core of the noncommunist resistance in Indochina.

While buoyed by Operation Passage to Freedom, especially in terms of its success as a humanitarian and public relations action, American leaders continued to be alarmed by the course of events in Asia. The Chinese Communist victory in China and rough handling of allied forces in Korea, coupled with the Viet Minh defeat of French forces in Indochina, boded ill for U.S. interests in the Western Pacific.

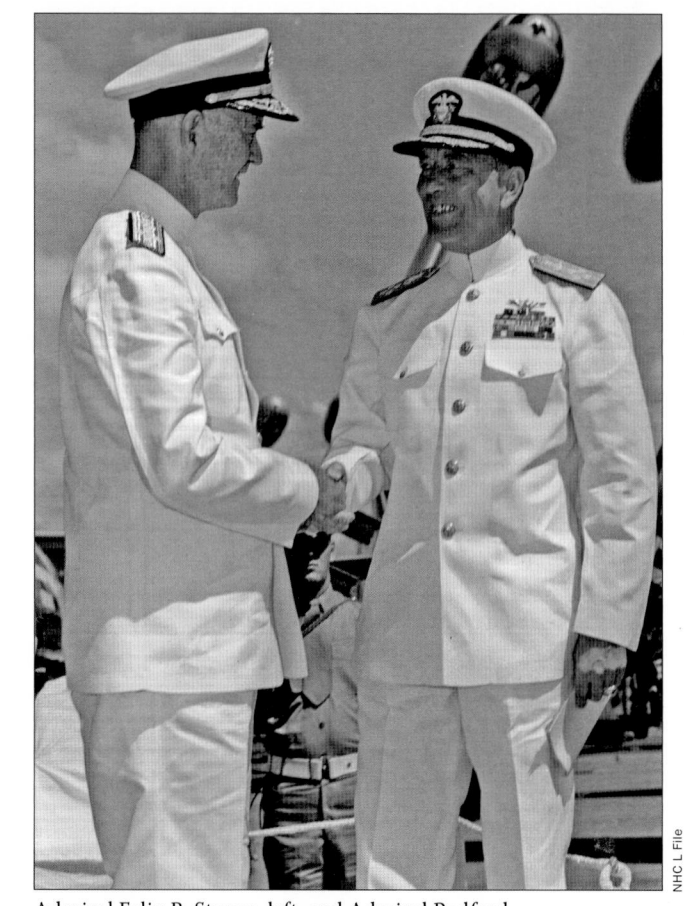

Admiral Felix B. Stump, left, and Admiral Radford exchange pleasantries on board a fleet carrier. U.S. naval leaders were particularly concerned about Communist activities in the Far East during the 1950s.

As a result, the Eisenhower administration, spearheaded by Secretary Dulles, engineered the Manila Pact, signed in September 1954 by the United States, Great Britain, France, Australia, New Zealand, the Philippines, Thailand, and Pakistan. The agreement led to the establishment of the Southeast Asia Treaty Organization (SEATO) whose main purpose was to prevent further Communist inroads in the region. Unlike the NATO alliance, however, SEATO member states would not automatically commit troops to fight aggression in the region; they would first have to confer over a course of action. Even though the Geneva Agreement prohibited South Vietnam, Laos, and Cambodia from joining the alliance, the pact provided the United States and its allies with an international instrument for resisting Communist aggression. ⚓

19

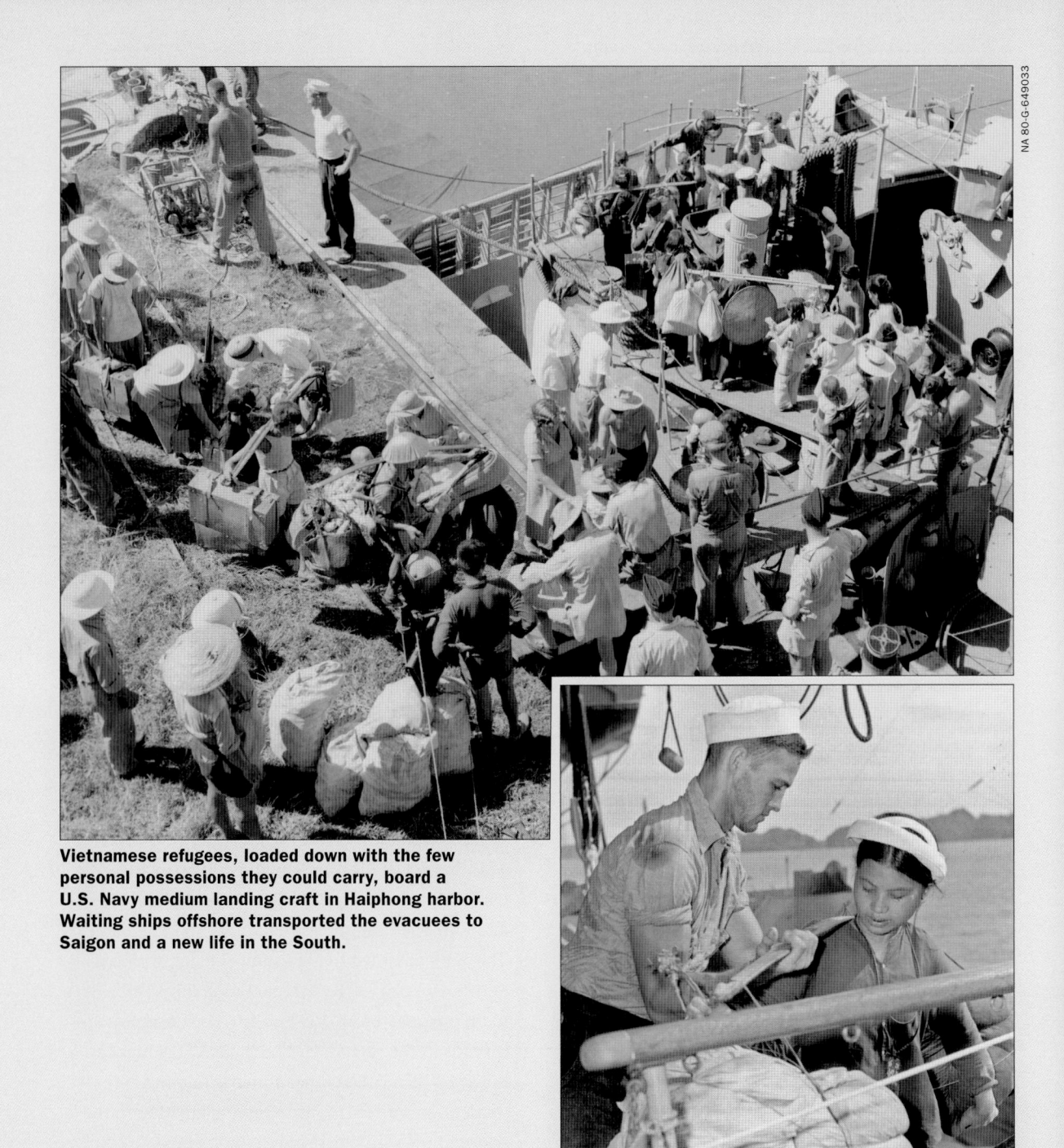

NA 80-G-649033

Vietnamese refugees, loaded down with the few personal possessions they could carry, board a U.S. Navy medium landing craft in Haiphong harbor. Waiting ships offshore transported the evacuees to Saigon and a new life in the South.

A Sailor from attack transport *Bayfield* (APA 33) helps a Vietnamese girl adjust her heavy load so she can board the ship for the voyage south.

NA 80-G-709240

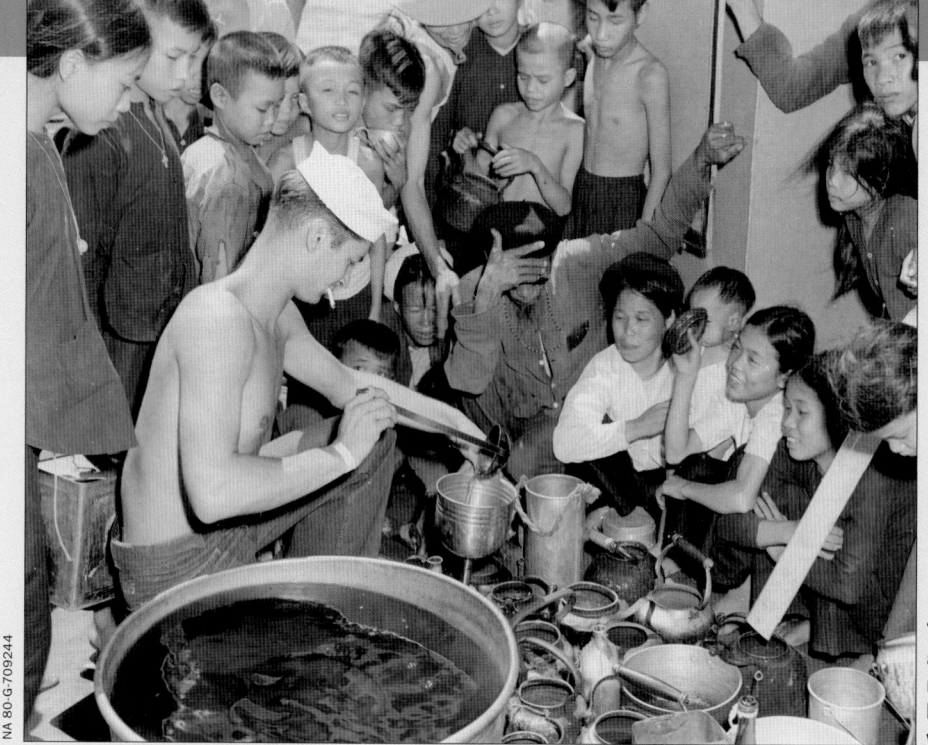

NA 80-G-709244

To the smiles and rapt attention of Vietnamese refugees, another *Bayfield* bluejacket doles out water rations.

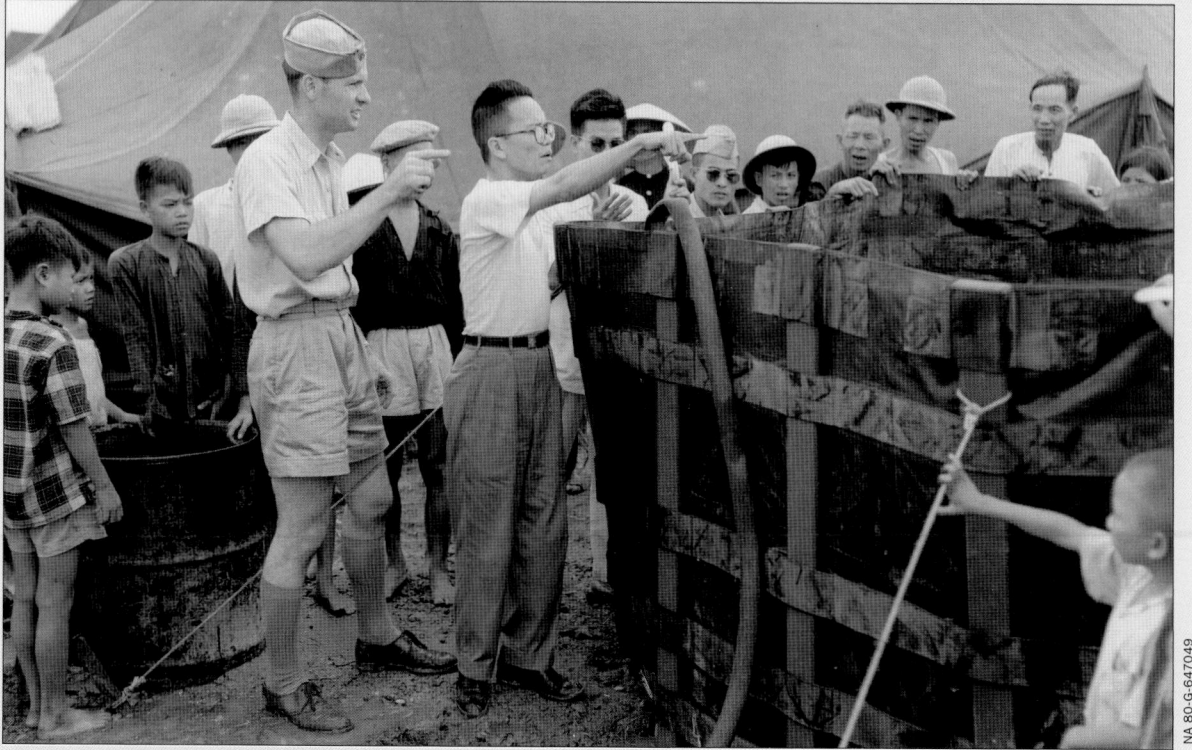

NA 80-G-647049

Lieutenant Tom Dooley, member of a U.S. Navy medical team dispatched to Haiphong in the Tonkin region of French Indochina in August 1954, works with an interpreter to explain to refugees how to keep a water tank free from contamination. Dooley gained international fame and a devoted following later in the 1950s and early 1960s as a doctor ministering to the world's poor.

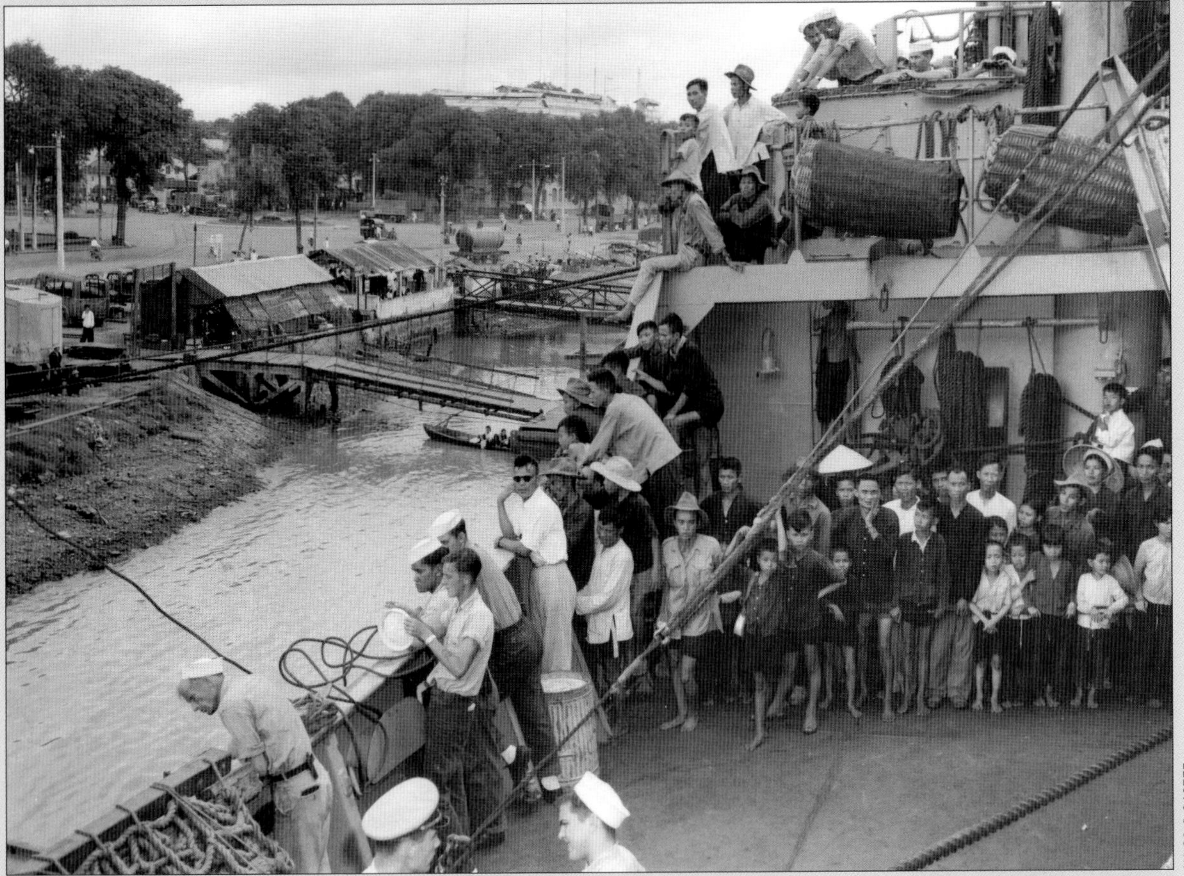

Passage to Freedom

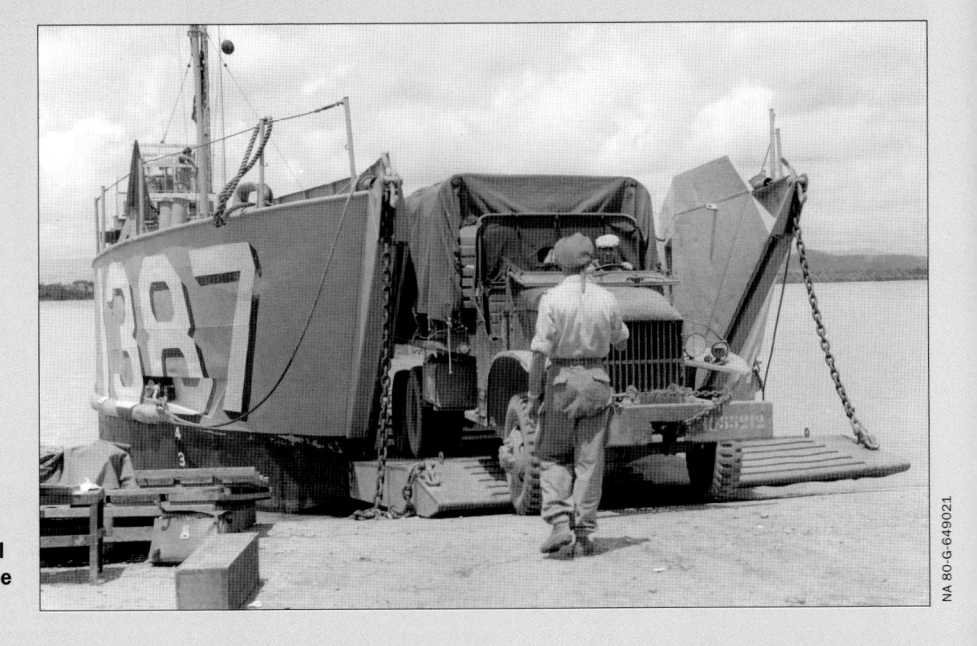

As American Sailors secure their ship to the shore at Saigon, Vietnamese refugees contemplate the land in which they will carve out a new life.

French soldiers load an army vehicle on board U.S. Navy utility landing craft *LCU-1387* in Haiphong for eventual transfer to a military site in southern Indochina.

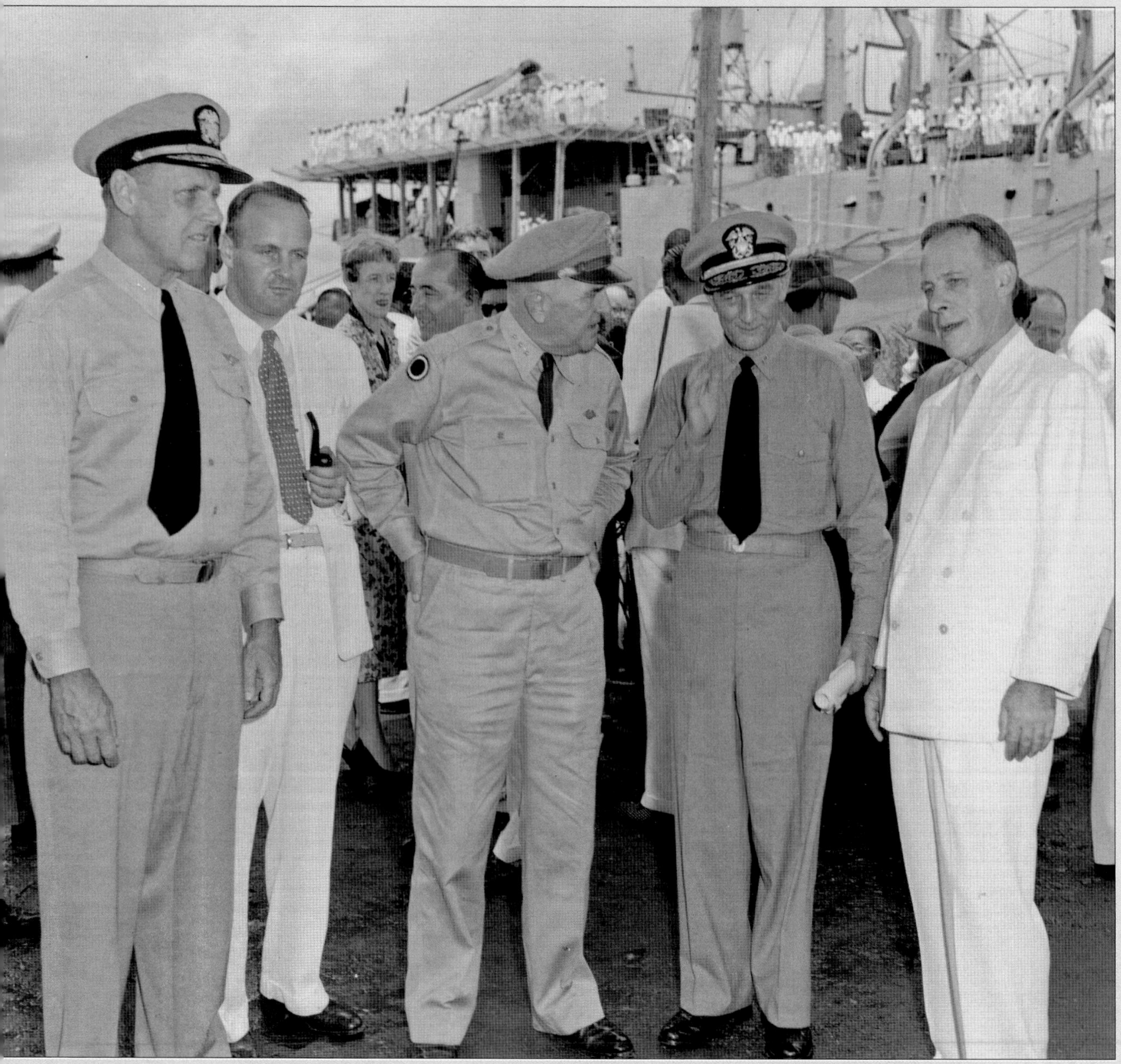

From the left, Rear Admiral Aaron P. Storrs, an unidentified American, Lieutenant General W. O'Daniel, Rear Admiral Lorenzo S. Sabin (commander of the Passage to Freedom operation), and U.S. Ambassador Donald Heath appear at an event to mark the arrival of 100,000 refugees in Saigon.

Southeast Asia.

The United States had already taken steps to solidify opposition to the Communists in Asia. In 1946, the *Hukbalahap*, or Huk guerrillas of the Communist Party of the Philippines, first formed to fight the Japanese, launched a military campaign on the island of Luzon to overthrow the newly independent and pro-American government of the Philippines. Insurgents assassinated landlords and local government officials, preyed on civilians, and organized the population along Marxist-Leninist lines in the areas they controlled. In 1949, guerrillas ambushed and killed Aurora Quezon, head of the Philippine Red Cross and widow of the country's first president, Manuel Quezon. No doubt inspired by Communist successes on the mainland of Asia, the Huks renamed their guerrilla force the People's Liberation Army in 1950.

The Philippine government responded in a manner that considerably reduced the Communist threat by 1954. Ramon Magsaysay, who ultimately became president of the Philippines, improved the Philippine military and local police by getting rid of incompetent officers and promoting effective leaders, won the favor of the civilian population through beneficial economic and political measures, and developed a sophisticated public information campaign that won "hearts and minds" for the government. A key advisor to Magsaysay was Edward Lansdale, a former U.S. Air Force

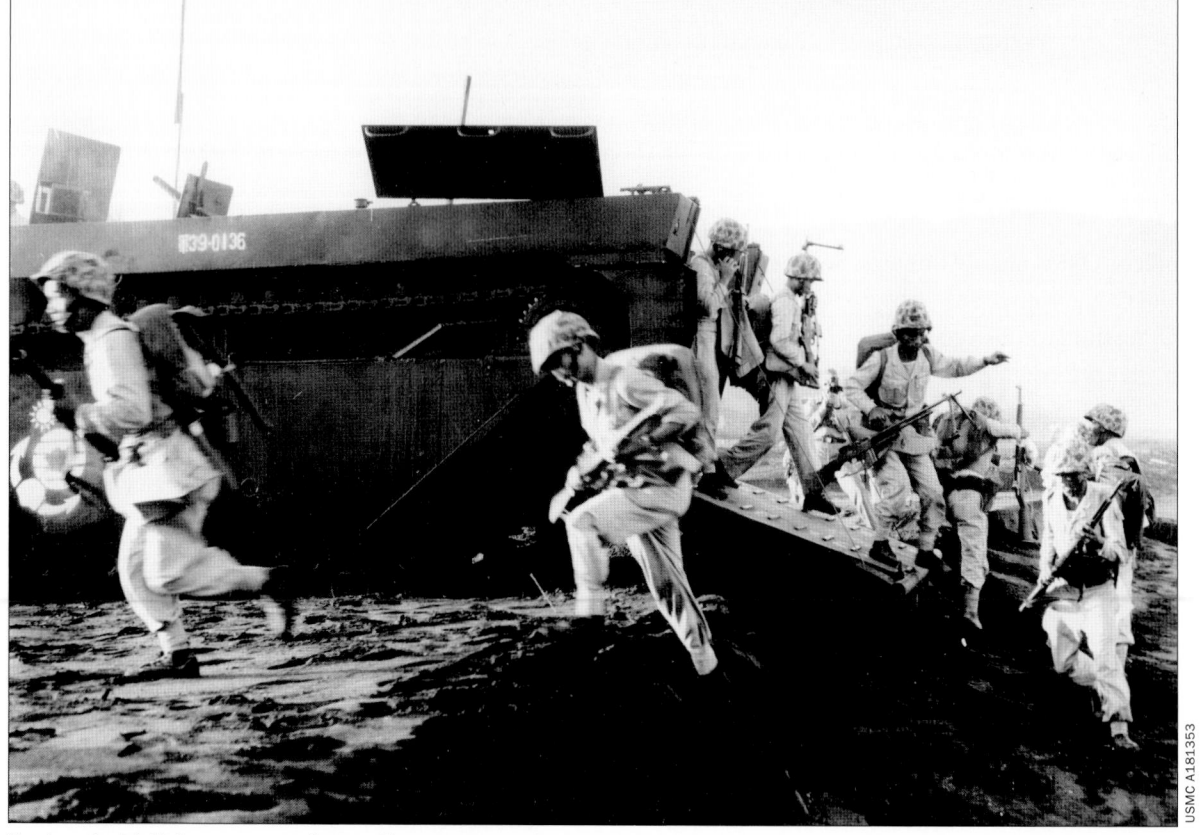

Equipped with U.S. weapons and gear, Chinese Nationalist marines debouch from an American-made tracked landing vehicle during an amphibious exercise. The United States was vital to the survival of Chiang Kai-shek's Republic of China government on Taiwan.

USMC A181353

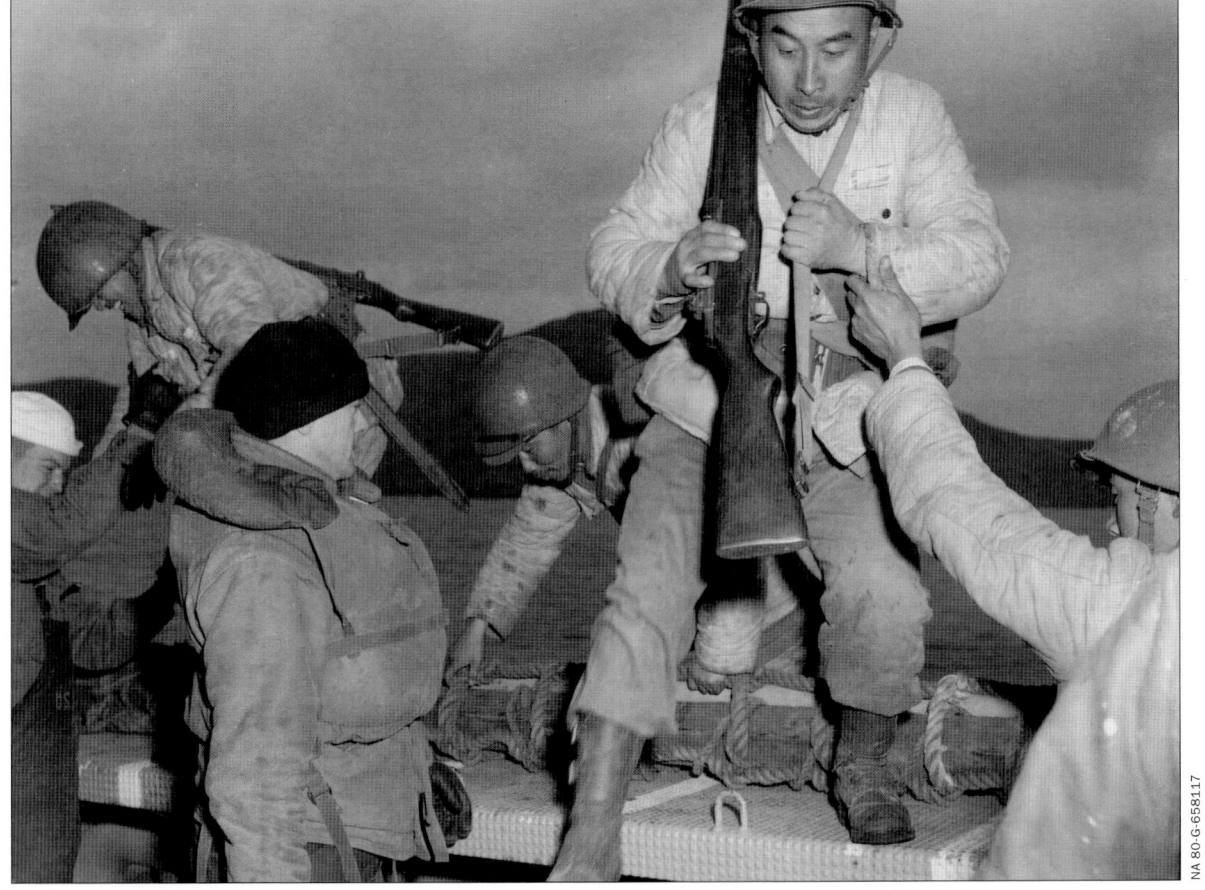

U.S. Navy Sailors of attack transport *Lenawee* (APA 195) help Nationalist soldiers embark on board the ship during the evacuation of the Tachens.

officer, OSS (Office of Strategic Services) operative, and CIA agent.

Washington also gave strong diplomatic backing to efforts by the British Commonwealth to defeat a Communist insurgent movement on the Malay Peninsula, underway since 1948. The so-called Malayan Emergency involved conflict between Chin Peng's Malayan Communist Party (whose members were predominantly ethnic Chinese) and the British colonial government (led by Britons but run for the most part by ethnic Malays). Communist guerrillas sprang ambushes, blew up bridges and government buildings, and worked to disrupt the rubber plantation-based economy. While it took 12 years to do so, about 40,000 British, Malayan, Australian, New Zealand, and other troops successfully countered the Communists by settling much of the Chinese population in fortified villages, thereby separating them from the guerrillas in the jungle who needed that support to survive. Commonwealth naval forces guarded the maritime access to the peninsula, limiting the amount of arms and ammunition Chin Peng's 8,000-man force could bring in from outside sources. Finally, the British adopted an enlightened policy toward the Chinese population that in many ways improved their political, economic, and medical condition. Support for the Communists especially ebbed after 1957 when Great Britain granted Malaya its independence, robbing Chin Peng's movement of its colonial liberation ethos. By 1960, most Communist guerrillas had surrendered, withdrawn in small groups to the remote border area with Thailand, or like Chin Peng fled to Beijing.

Soon after Washington had endured the embarrassment to the West at Geneva, it was faced once again with Chinese Communist moves against the

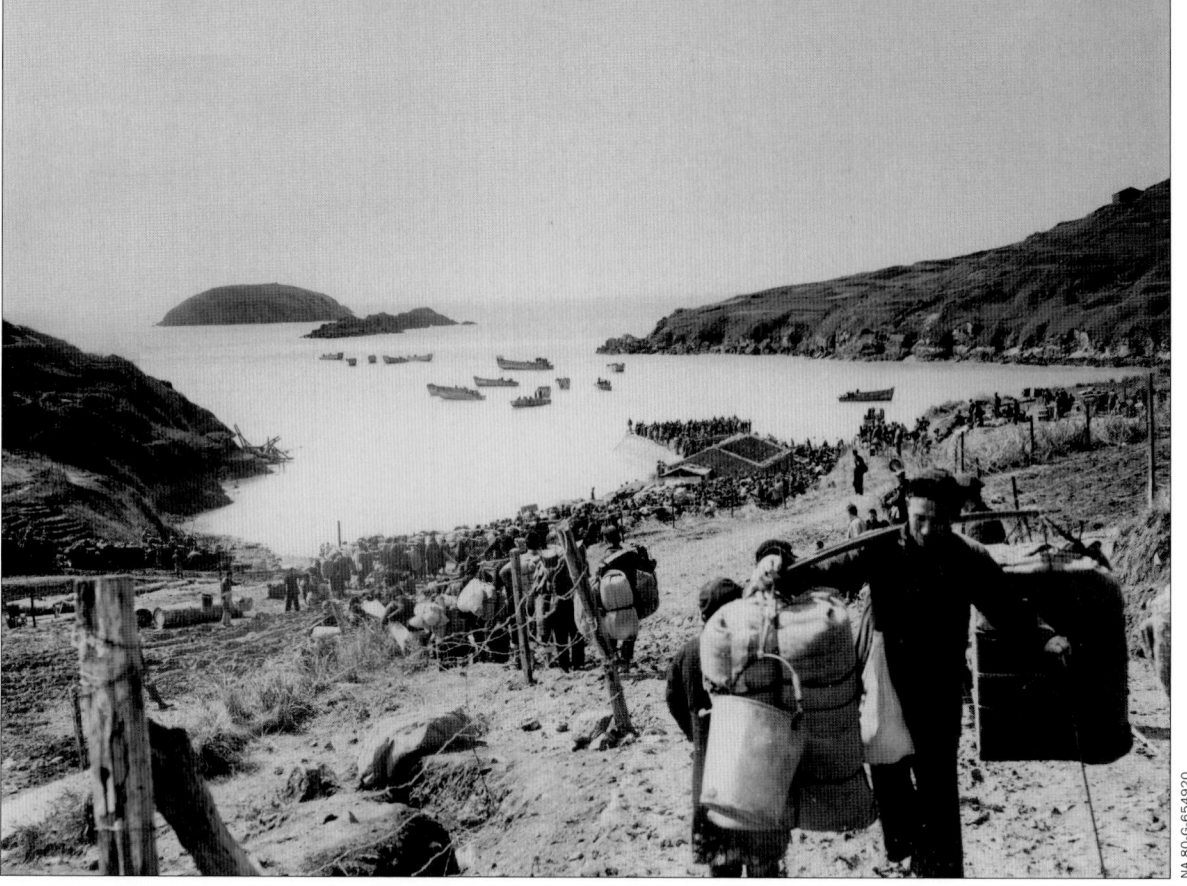

Chinese civilians prepare to board U.S. Navy landing craft during the evacuation of an island in the Tachen group in February 1955. Most of these people would never see their ancestral homes again.

Nationalist forces of Chiang Kai-shek. By then, Washington's pre-Korean War cool attitude toward Chiang had warmed considerably. When Eisenhower entered office, he directed an increasing flow of military advisors and material assistance to the Nationalists. Moreover, the Seventh Fleet continued to patrol the waters between Taiwan and the mainland.

For his part, Mao Tse-tung, emboldened by China's success at having "stood up" to the United States in Korea and the Communist victory at Dien Bien Phu, and needing to bolster support for domestic programs, ordered his forces to capture the Nationalist-held Tachen (Dachen) Island group. In the early afternoon of 18 January 1955, Communist troops stormed ashore from landing craft and by 0200 on the 19th had overwhelmed the 1,086-man Nationalist garrison on the island of Ichiang (Yijiangshan). Other neighboring islands in

the group were clearly at risk.

Consequently, with Seventh Fleet assistance, the Nationalists evacuated 25,000 troops and 18,000 civilians from the remaining Tachens. This was a hollow victory for Mao, however. In a Mutual Defense Treaty, the Eisenhower administration made explicit its intention to defend Taiwan, and hence Chiang's government, against a Communist invasion. All concerned understood that the United States might use nuclear weapons in such a conflict. Whether or not the United States would defend the smaller islands off China was left ambiguous.

By the end of 1954, in response to aggressive post–World War II actions by Communist movements throughout the Far East, the United States had signed security agreements with not only Taiwan but also Japan, the Republic of Korea, the Philippines, Australia, and New Zealand. ↵

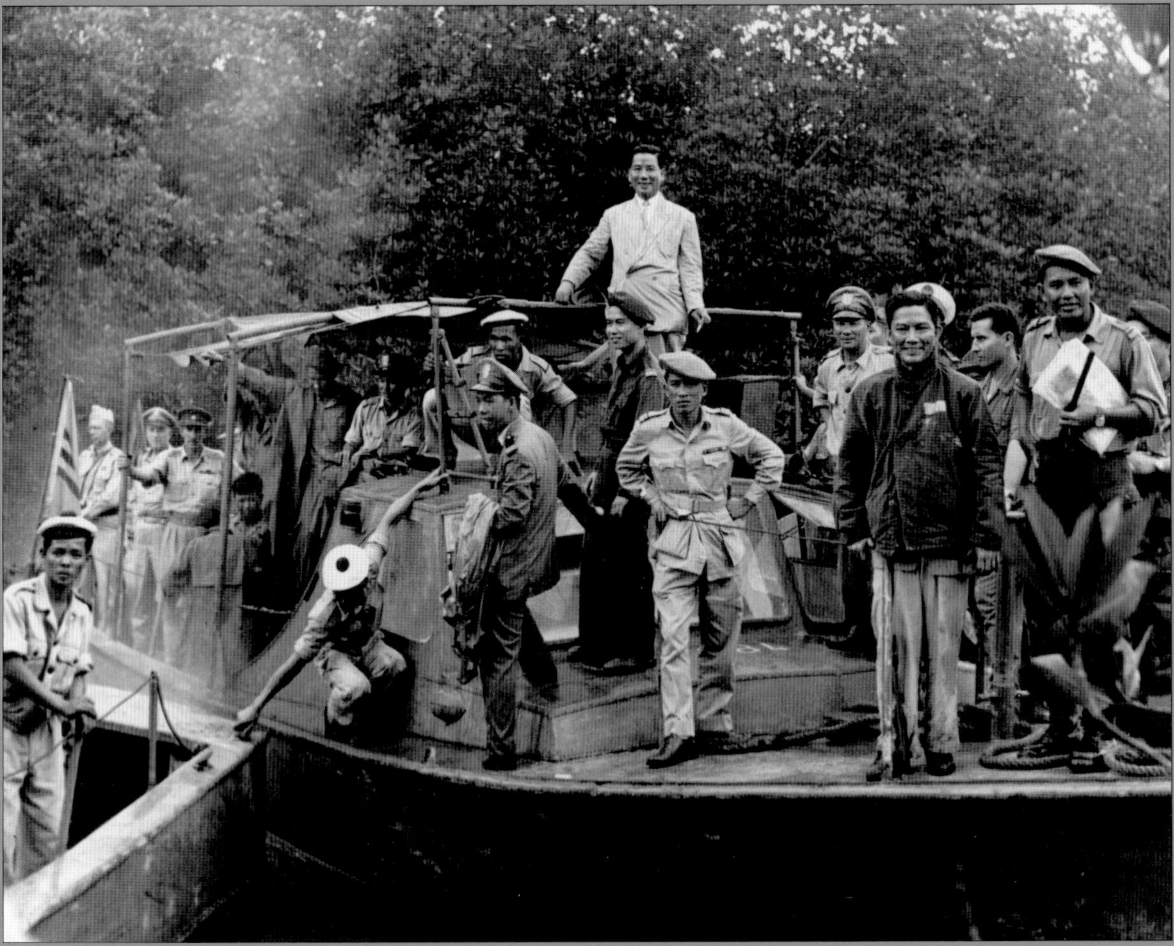

Author File

A smiling South Vietnamese President Ngo Dinh Diem, atop a Vietnam Navy combatant and accompanied by Vietnamese and foreign military personnel, observes an operation near Saigon.

The United States also developed a security relationship with the noncommunist government of South Vietnam. With the end of French control over Indochina, political movements in Tonkin, southern Vietnam, Laos, and Cambodia established separate governments. The temporary dividing line at the 17th parallel between Ho Chi Minh's Communists and the noncommunist Vietnamese to the south began to take on permanence. Ngo Dinh Diem, a fervent anticommunist and reportedly celibate Catholic, took power in Saigon as the head of a new Republic of Vietnam. Diem was born in Quang Binh Province in 1901, the son of a high official in the court of the Vietnamese emperor at Hue. Coming from a well-connected mandarin family, and based on his own intellectual gifts, Diem easily climbed the educational ladder, graduating at the top of his class from the prestigious School of Law and Public Administration in Hanoi. He was appointed a provincial governor at the age of 25. In this capacity, he oversaw the suppression in 1929 of a Communist uprising and thereafter considered himself anticommunist in his political leanings.

He also became fervently anti-French when colonial officials denied him any real authority as Emperor Bao Dai's Minister of the Interior and threatened to arrest him when he resigned in protest in 1933. With the end of World War II, and before the French government returned to Indochina, Diem traveled to Hanoi to dissuade the emperor from cooperating with Ho Chi Minh and the Viet Minh movement. The Communists abducted him on the way, spirited him off to a village near the border with China, and held him for six months, during which time he contracted malaria. Fearing for his life, Diem left Vietnam in 1950 and spent the next four years at seminaries in New Jersey and in Europe. While

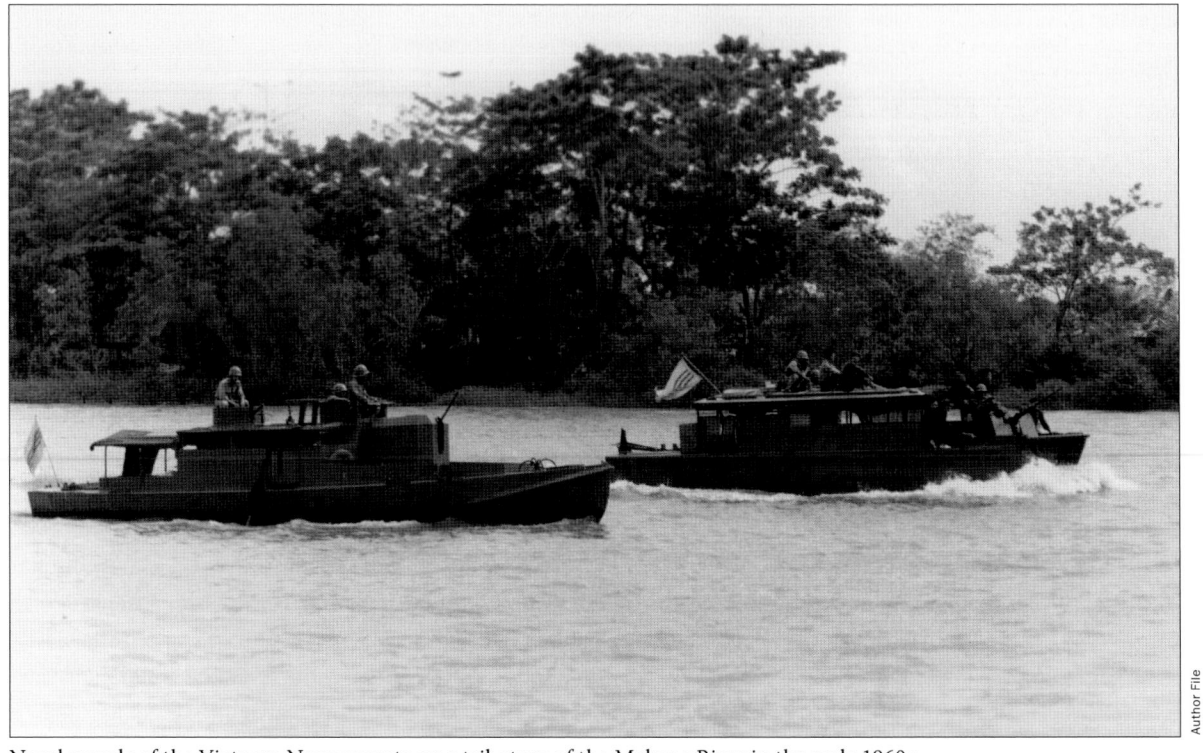

Author File

Naval vessels of the Vietnam Navy operate on a tributary of the Mekong River in the early 1960s.

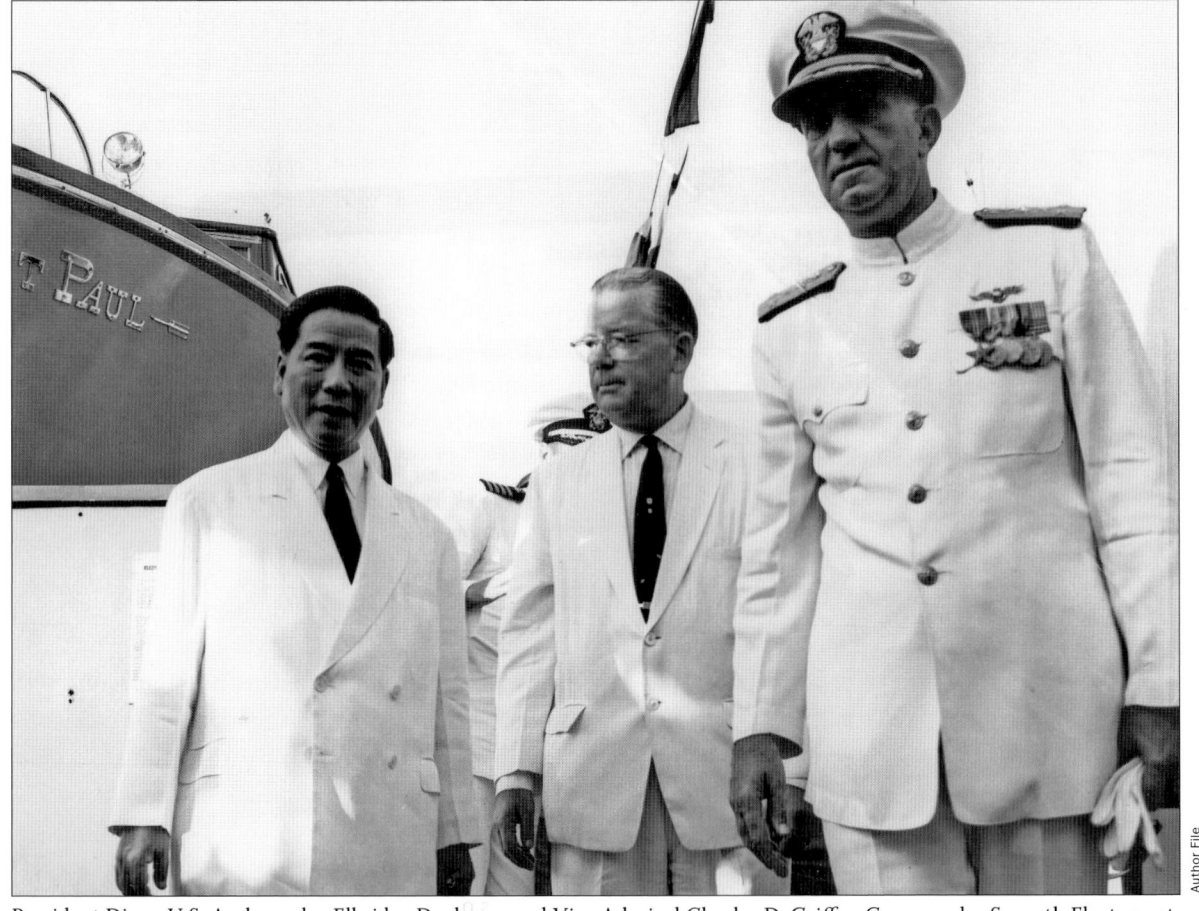

President Diem, U.S. Ambassador Elbridge Durbrow, and Vice Admiral Charles D. Griffin, Commander Seventh Fleet, meet in October 1960 when cruiser *Saint Paul* (CA 73) made a port call to Saigon. Washington used such diplomatic events to show support for Diem.

in the United States, he made contact with Francis Cardinal Spellman, Supreme Court Justice William O. Douglas, junior Senator John F. Kennedy, and other prominent political figures. He reaffirmed his anticommunist and anti-French inclinations. These contacts would soon pay off for him.

In June 1954, Emperor Bao Dai, aware of Diem's gifts as a leader, strong anticommunist credentials, and high-powered American friends, appointed him prime minister. Diem moved quickly and effectively to consolidate his power in the South. Employing Vietnamese ground and naval units, he crushed the Binh Xuyen criminal gang in Saigon and the armed religious groups Cao Dai and Hoa Hao, chased out Viet Minh officials, and engineered a referendum in which he received an inflated 98 percent of the vote. With the support of the Eisenhower administration,

he refused to sponsor national elections, as called for in the Geneva Agreement, because he feared that Ho Chi Minh's Communists would dominate the process and end his political existence.

As Diem in the South and Ho in the North consolidated their political control, American advisors worked to replace French forces (all French troops had departed Vietnam by June 1955) with a modern South Vietnamese military arm. Influenced by the Korean War experience, U.S. Army trainers prepared the new 150,000-man Army of the Republic of Vietnam (ARVN) to repel a conventional Communist invasion across the 17th parallel. Disregarding what the French had learned the hard way about warfare in Indochina, the Americans gave much less attention to preparing their charges for counterguerrilla warfare than did the French.

The Vietnam Navy (VNN), organized and equipped by the French, received the attention of American naval advisors who focused on developing forces for open-ocean, coastal, and river operations. During the late 1950s, the Americans handled the transfer to the VNN of landing ships and craft, trained Vietnamese sailors, and observed their operations. As with many newly formed military organizations, the VNN lacked experienced officers, adequately trained bluejackets, and suitable equipment. The French had provided the VNN with American-made vessels left over from World War II, and after years of hard use, these units were in poor shape.

The recipient of almost two billion dollars in American aid during the last half of the 1950s, Diem instituted measures to strengthen his political base in the South. Almost three quarters of this assistance was devoted to the armed forces and security in general. Diem pushed the development of Vietnamese settlements in the Central Highlands and a road system that he hoped would promote national cohesion. Diem's government successfully managed the influx of over one million mostly Catholic refugees from the North. The government cleared land for the newcomers, built them villages, dams, and irrigation canals, and provided them with farm implements. The countryside bloomed with thousands of new, American-financed schools and a smaller number of hospitals. Diem also pursued land reform in the Mekong Delta that redistributed much of the land to more than half of the tenant farmers, but a sizable minority still paid exorbitant rents to absentee landlords and all had to endure frustrating bureaucratic red tape in the process. South Vietnam's rice production increased from 2.6 million tons in 1954 to 5 million tons in 1959, and rubber production increased by one third.

Like Chiang Kai-shek and Syngman Rhee, Diem was an authoritarian Asian leader who treated opponents harshly and endeavored to manage the political process. He was not a liberal democrat. He asserted firm control of political life in the capital, exposed coup plotters, and between 1955 and 1958 dispatched troops against Communist Party cells in the cities and in the countryside in "denounce the Communists" campaigns. Government forces killed thousands of Communists and imprisoned many more. One study published in Hanoi after the Vietnam War credited Diem's campaigns with reducing Communist Party membership in the South by 90 percent during the period.

On Diem's visits to the United States and during visits to Saigon by Senator Lyndon Johnson and other American political leaders, Diem was lionized as the great hope of the Free World in Southeast Asia. Senator John Kennedy opined that South Vietnam was the "cornerstone of the Free World in Southeast Asia, the keystone to the arch, the finger in the dike."

In 1958, as the peoples of former French Indochina enjoyed a temporary respite from the bloodletting of previous years, Mao again raised the temperature in the Western Pacific. To divert domestic attention from the "Great Leap Forward," an economic and social program that had proven disastrous to the lives of millions of his people, Mao ordered the shelling of Nationalist-held Quemoy and Matsu (Mazu) islands. Thousands of artillery rounds cascaded down on the heads of Chiang's soldiers on Quemoy, located only a few miles from the mainland. Nationalist vessels were unable to resupply the island's defenders. It would be only a matter of time before the Nationalists there would have to surrender.

Determined to prevent the Communists from seizing Quemoy, or worse, invading Taiwan itself, Eisenhower ordered the concentration in Chinese waters of five carriers whose aircraft were equipped to drop nuclear bombs. At that time, American leaders were much more inclined than later to consider the use of such weapons, even in tactical situations.

Washington then ordered U.S. warships to escort Nationalist supply ships to Quemoy. Faced with the prospect of nuclear war with the United States, and absent Soviet support (Soviet Premier Nikita Khrushchev implied to Mao that the Chinese were on their own), Mao forbade his forces from attacking the American ships. Although shelling continued— on odd days—the Communists allowed resupply convoys to reach the island untouched on even days.

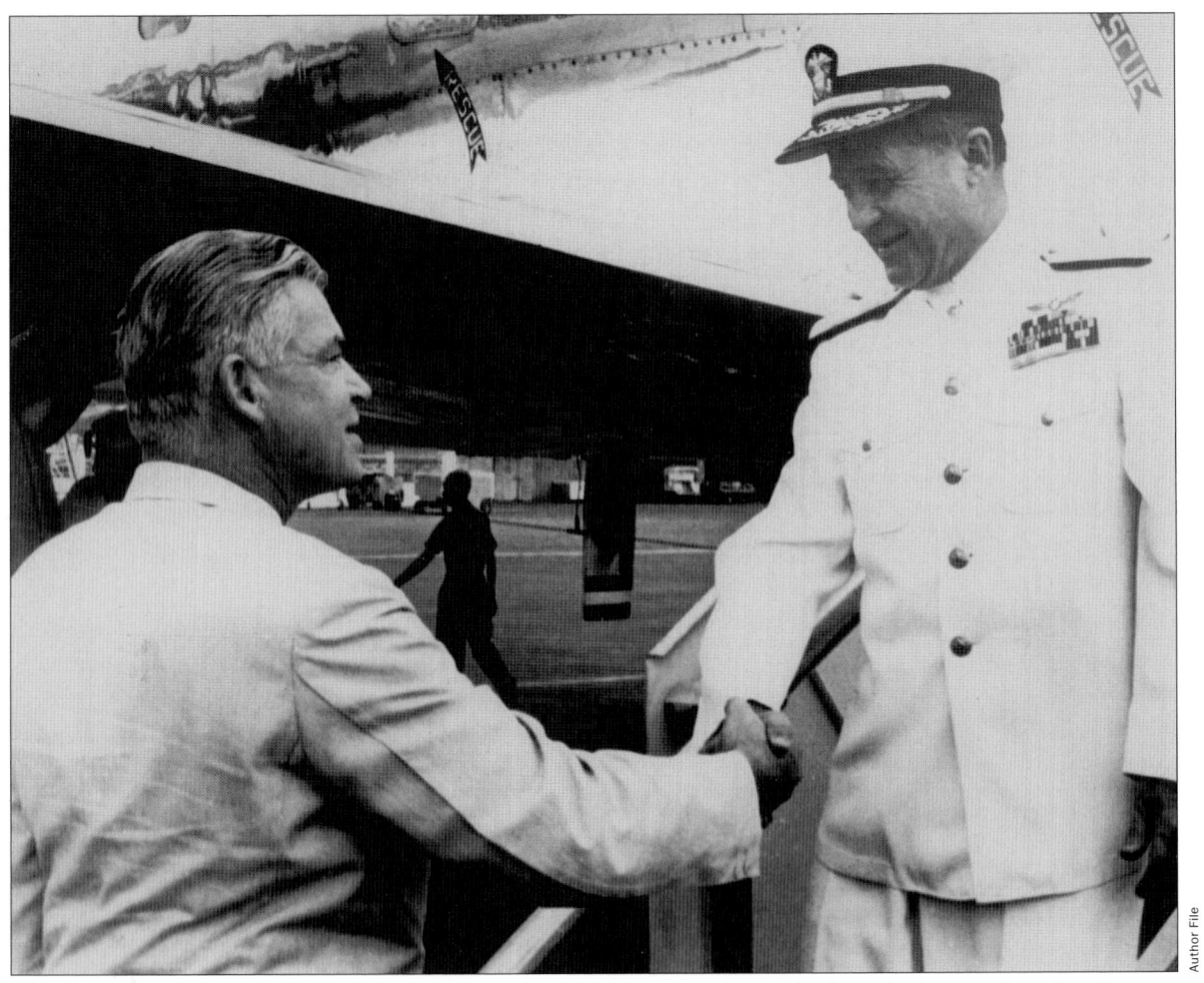

U.S. Ambassador Frederick Nolting greets Admiral Harry D. Felt, Commander in Chief, Pacific Command, as the officer arrives in Saigon.

This was a tacit admission by Mao that his action to embarrass the U.S.-Nationalist allies had failed. The crisis soon ebbed.

American leaders became convinced that Mao and his Communist allies were determined to pursue a new, more belligerent approach toward their neighbors. Typical of the views expressed were those of Admiral Herbert G. Hopwood, Commander in Chief, U.S. Pacific Fleet: "[W]e are entering a new era of intensified cold and limited war in South and South East Asia. . . . The CHICOMS [previously] attempted to win friends and influence the new and violently nationalistic governments in this area. . . . They have now decided to use force and/or threat of [force] as a major instrument of policy."

Washington was determined to counter the Communists by providing governments and parties in the region with political, economic, and military assistance. There were no easy choices with regard to friendly governments or leaders. The United States helped preserve the independence of South Korea, Taiwan, and the Philippines during the Cold War but to do so required doing business with a succession of dictators and other odious figures. The same applied in Indochina. At one point during a long confrontation in Laos, Admiral Harry D. Felt, Commander in Chief, Pacific Command (CINCPAC), expressed his regret that the leader of the government in the capital of Vientiane was "no George Washington." He added, however, that "he is anti-communist which is what counts most in the sad Laos situation." ⚓

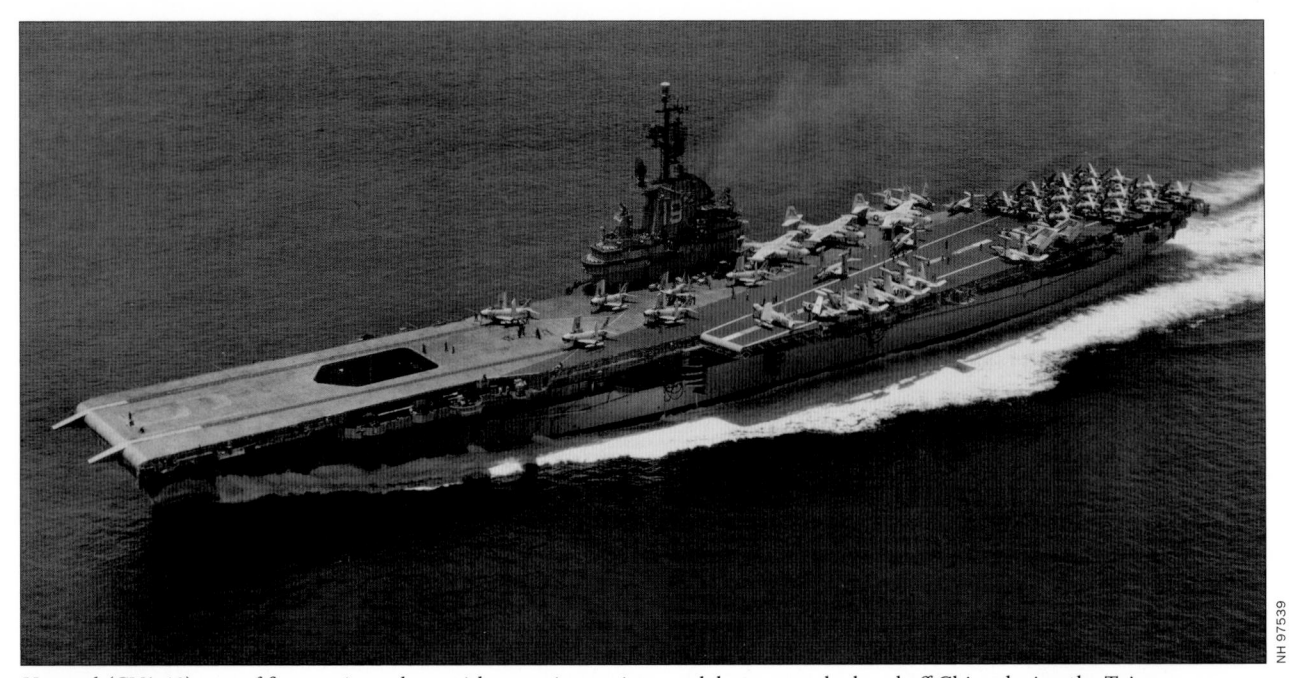

NH 97539

Hancock (CVA 19), one of five carriers, along with escorting cruisers and destroyers, deployed off China during the Taiwan Strait crisis of 1958.

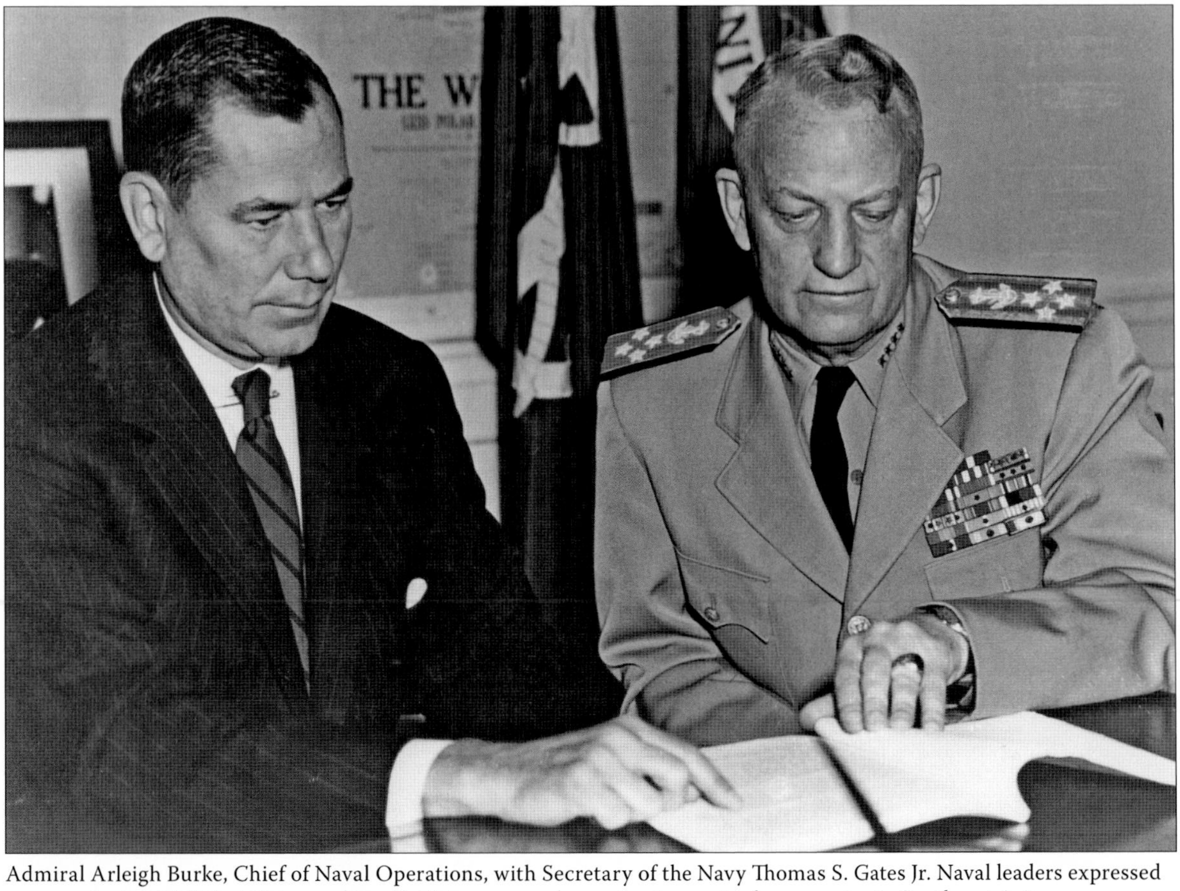

USN 1041065

Admiral Arleigh Burke, Chief of Naval Operations, with Secretary of the Navy Thomas S. Gates Jr. Naval leaders expressed concern during 1959 that China and North Vietnam were becoming increasingly aggressive in Southeast Asia.

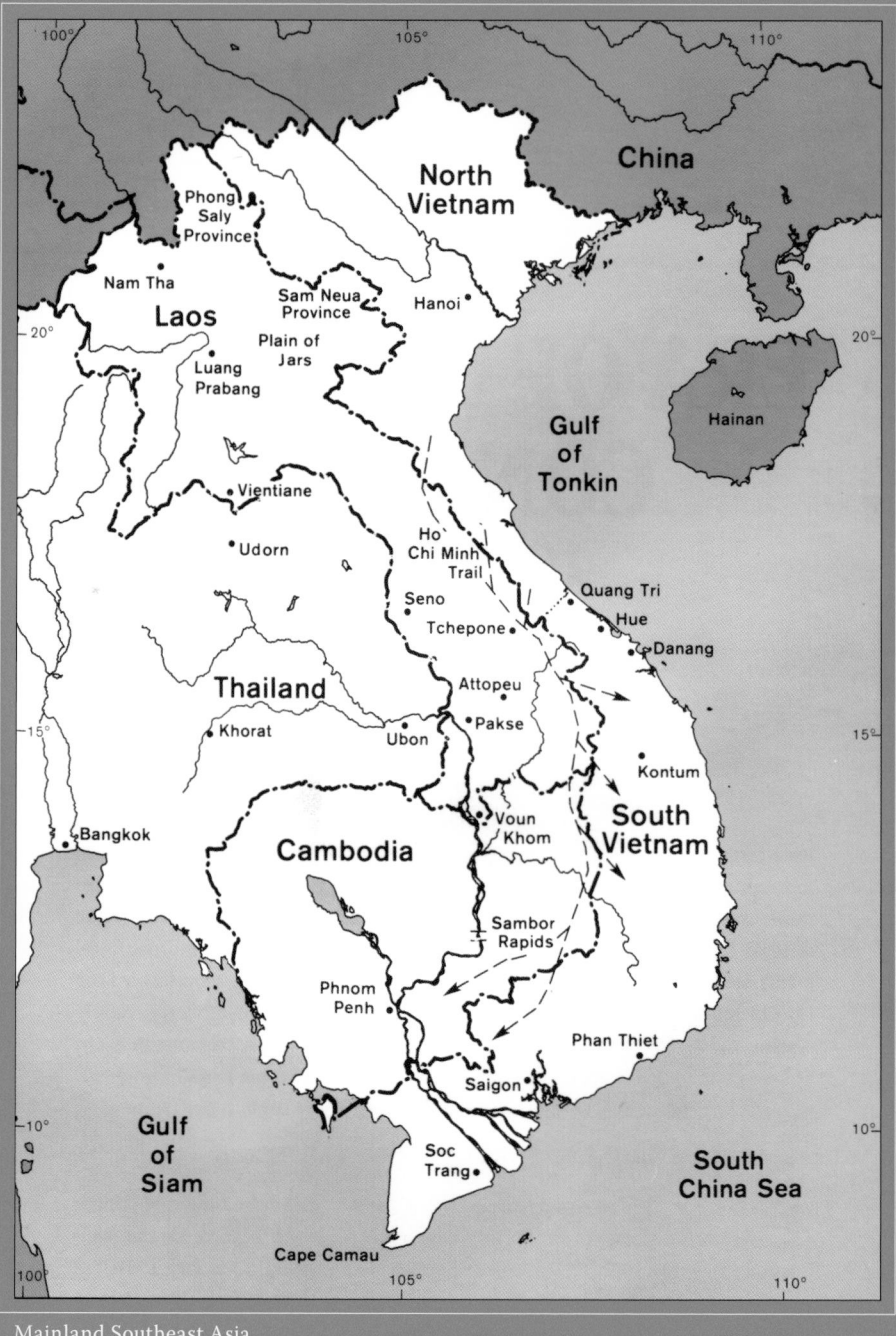

Mainland Southeast Asia.

In May 1959, Ho Chi Minh, with Chinese support, decided on a campaign of armed struggle to unify all Vietnam. The North Vietnamese also intended to dominate the Indochinese peninsula and facilitate the establishment of Marxist-Leninist governments in Laos and Cambodia. The Communists had solidified their control of the North Vietnamese population and feared that if they waited too long, Diem would do the same in the South. Indeed, Diem had already imprisoned or killed thousands of Communists in the Republic of Vietnam, as well as many other noncommunist political opponents.

That month Hanoi began returning to South Vietnam, via southern Laos, Communists who had gone north in 1954. During 1959 and 1960, 4,500 Communist "cadres" made their way south over what came to be known as the Ho Chi Minh Trail. They linked up with their southern brethren and soon formed the National Liberation Front of South Vietnam, the military arm of which was commonly referred to by the South Vietnamese and Americans as the Viet Cong.

To help secure the route through southern Laos, Hanoi provided Laotian Communists—the Pathet Lao—who were already locked in conflict with the

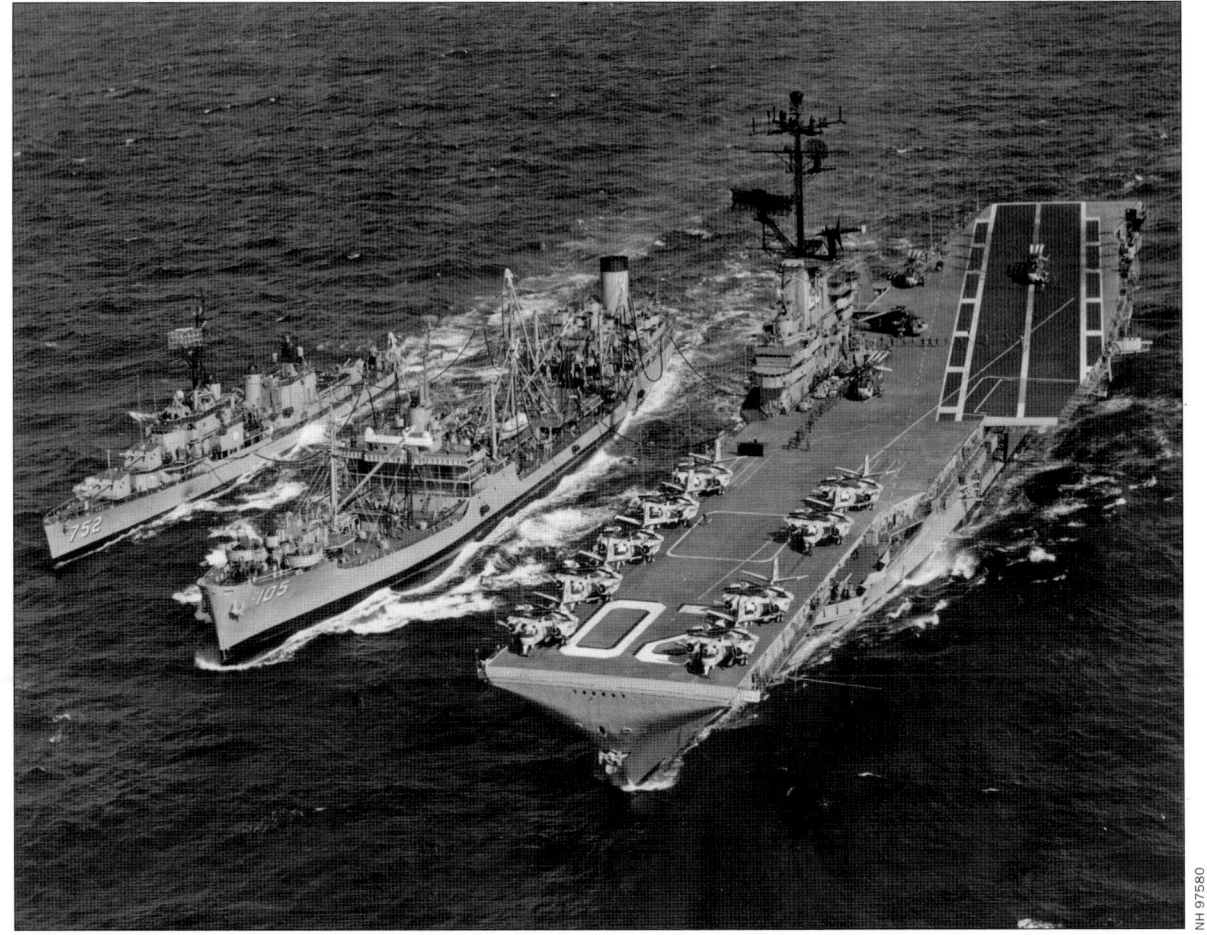

Aircraft carrier *Bennington* (CVS 20) and destroyer *Alfred A. Cunningham* (DD 752) refuel from fleet oiler *Mispillion* (AO 105) while underway.

NH 97580

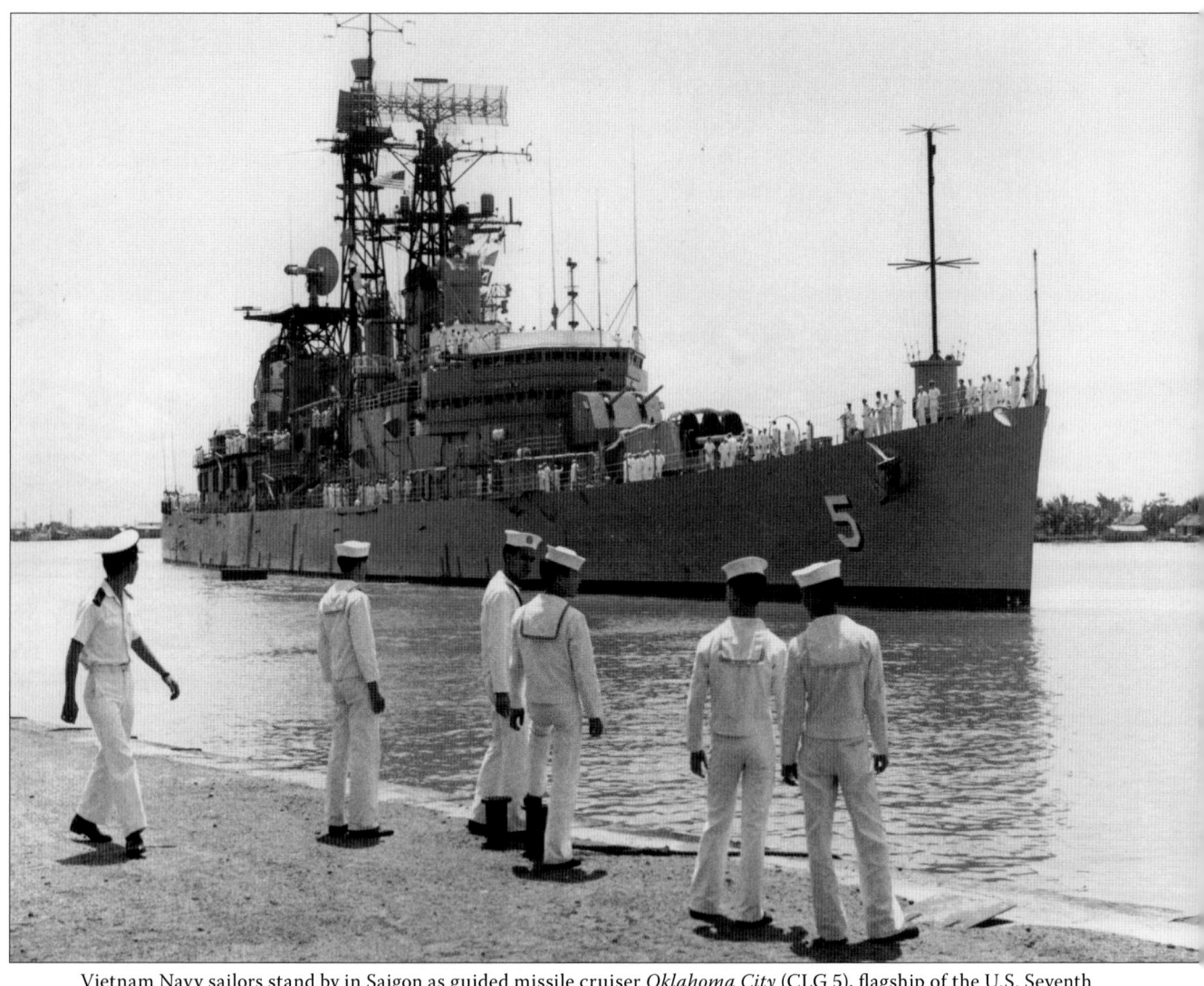

Vietnam Navy sailors stand by in Saigon as guided missile cruiser *Oklahoma City* (CLG 5), flagship of the U.S. Seventh Fleet, pulls into port for a "show-the-flag" visit in July 1964. These diplomatic events increased along with U.S. concern for the security situation in Southeast Asia.

anticommunist government in Vientiane, with military advisors, weapons, and supplies. A Soviet airlift provided the Pathet Lao with arms, ammunition, and equipment.

In 1959 and 1960, the Pathet Lao launched major attacks against government forces. In each instance, Seventh Fleet carrier and amphibious task forces deployed into the South China Sea in a show of force. These visible demonstrations of U.S. resolve helped persuade the Pathet Lao to cease their attacks and agree to cease-fire negotiations with Vientiane.

It took more than that in May of 1962 when the Pathet Lao overran a government-held town and

threatened to topple the pro-American government of Laos. President John F. Kennedy ordered the deployment into Thailand of major U.S. forces and their movement forward to the border with Laos. The 3rd Marine Expeditionary Brigade, which included sizable infantry, air, and Seabee components and a U.S. Army infantry regiment, were prepared to enter Laos and fight the Laotian Communists. Backing up these American ground forces ashore were aircraft carriers *Hancock* (CVA 19) and *Bennington* (CVS 20). Persuaded that the United States would not allow a Communist takeover in Laos, the Pathet Lao and their Soviet,

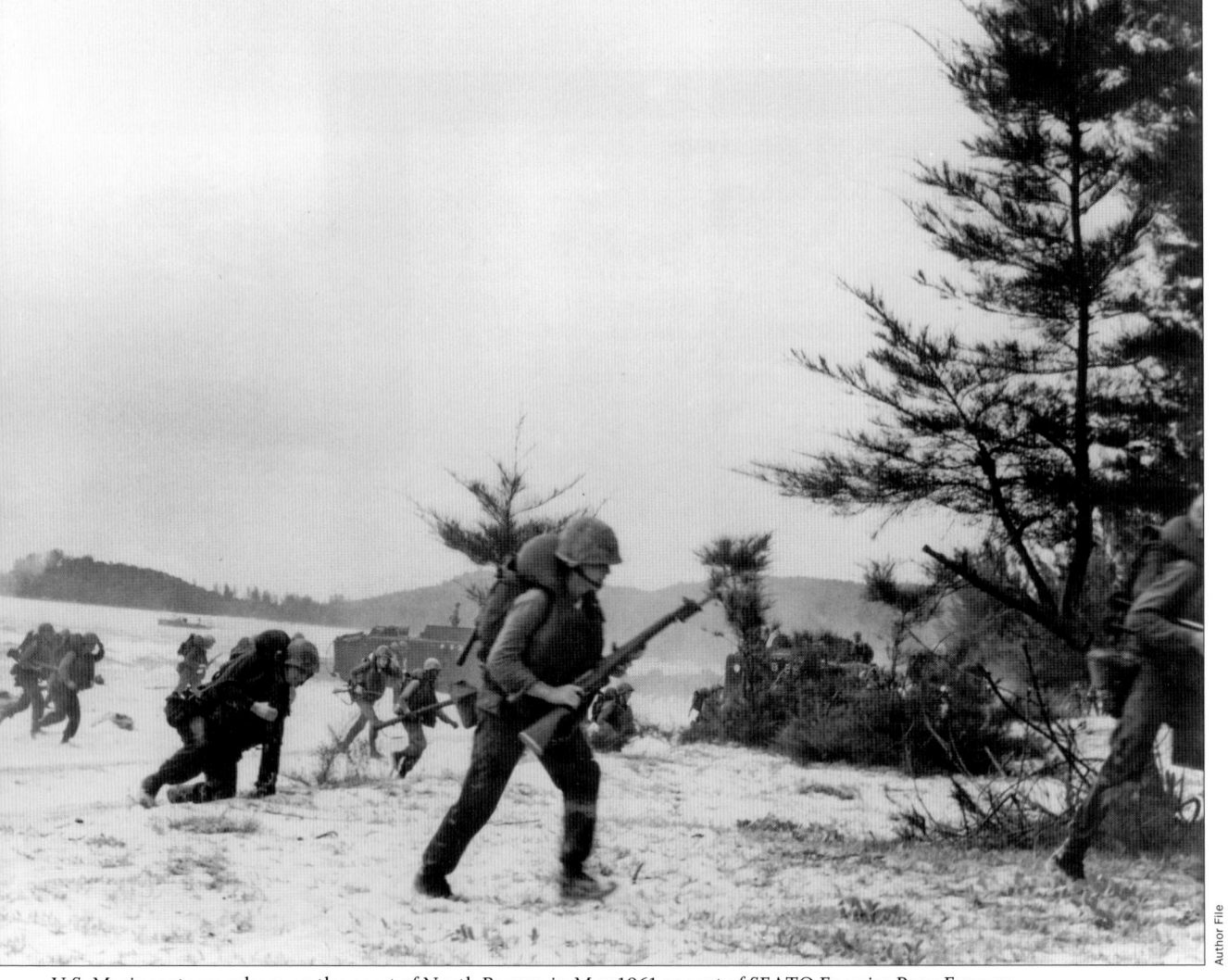

U.S. Marines storm ashore on the coast of North Borneo in May 1961 as part of SEATO Exercise Pony Express.

Chinese, and North Vietnamese supporters agreed to a compromise. In Geneva, Switzerland, on 23 July 1962, the contending Laotian parties agreed to join in a coalition government. The United States and North Vietnam pledged to withdraw their military forces from Laos and respect the country's neutrality—a pledge kept by neither country.

Meanwhile, to bolster friendly governments concerned about the growing militancy of the Communist nations, Washington dramatically increased the U.S. Navy's presence in Southeast Asia. In the early sixties, American warships made port calls in South Vietnam, Thailand, Indonesia, and even Cambodia, whose capital was far up the Mekong River at Phnom Penh. Numerous multinational exercises took place, including "Pony Express" off Borneo that involved 60 ships and 26,000 sailors and marines from SEATO member states. Naval, air, and logistic bases blossomed in the Philippines and on Okinawa.

Many American leaders, including members of the Joint Chiefs of Staff, thought that remote, undeveloped Laos was a poor place to fight the Communists, especially if China intervened there in force. There was much greater support for making a stand in Thailand and South Vietnam, both of which had access to the sea and the naval power of the United States. ⚓

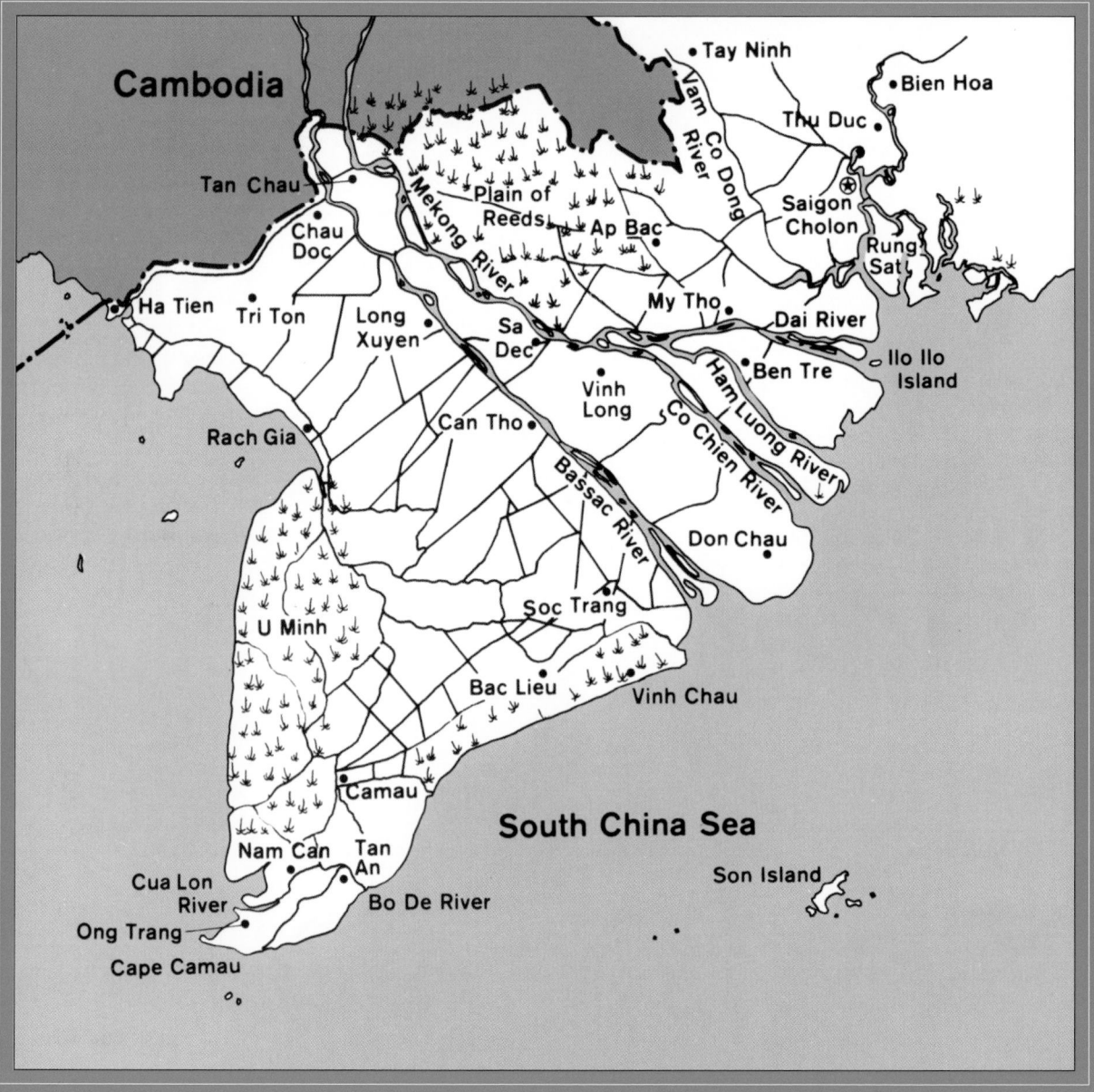

The Mekong Delta.

Even as Washington had focused on developments in Laos, the Military Assistance Advisory Group, Vietnam redoubled its efforts to create viable South Vietnamese armed forces. The MAAG's Navy section doubled in strength between 1959 and 1964, partly reflecting the growth in the Vietnam Navy from 5,000 officers and men to more than 8,000. By late 1964, the United States was supporting a Vietnamese naval arm of 44 seagoing ships and over 200 landing craft, patrol boats, and other vessels. The largest units in the VNN were Sea Force escorts (PCEs), motor gunboats (PGMs), large support landing ships (LSSLs), large infantry landing ships (LSILs), medium landing ships (LSMs), and tank landing ships (LSTs) that operated in the South China Sea and the Gulf of Siam.

The VNN inherited from the French not only combatants but a concept of river warfare built around the *dinassaut* or river assault division, which had provided the French with a measure of success against the Viet Minh. When operating with strong ground forces, the French *dinassaut* sometimes decimated Viet Minh guerrilla units prevented from escape by land or water.

Guided by the *dinassaut* concept, the Vietnamese formed river assault groups (RAGs) of armed and armored landing craft that transported troops, escorted convoys of rice boats, swept for mines, and provided gunfire support to ground units. The 102-man, 20-boat RAGs operated from bases at Saigon, My Tho, Vinh Long, Can Tho, and Long Xuyen. The RAGs were critical not only to the Vietnamese government's military control in the almost roadless

continued on page 42

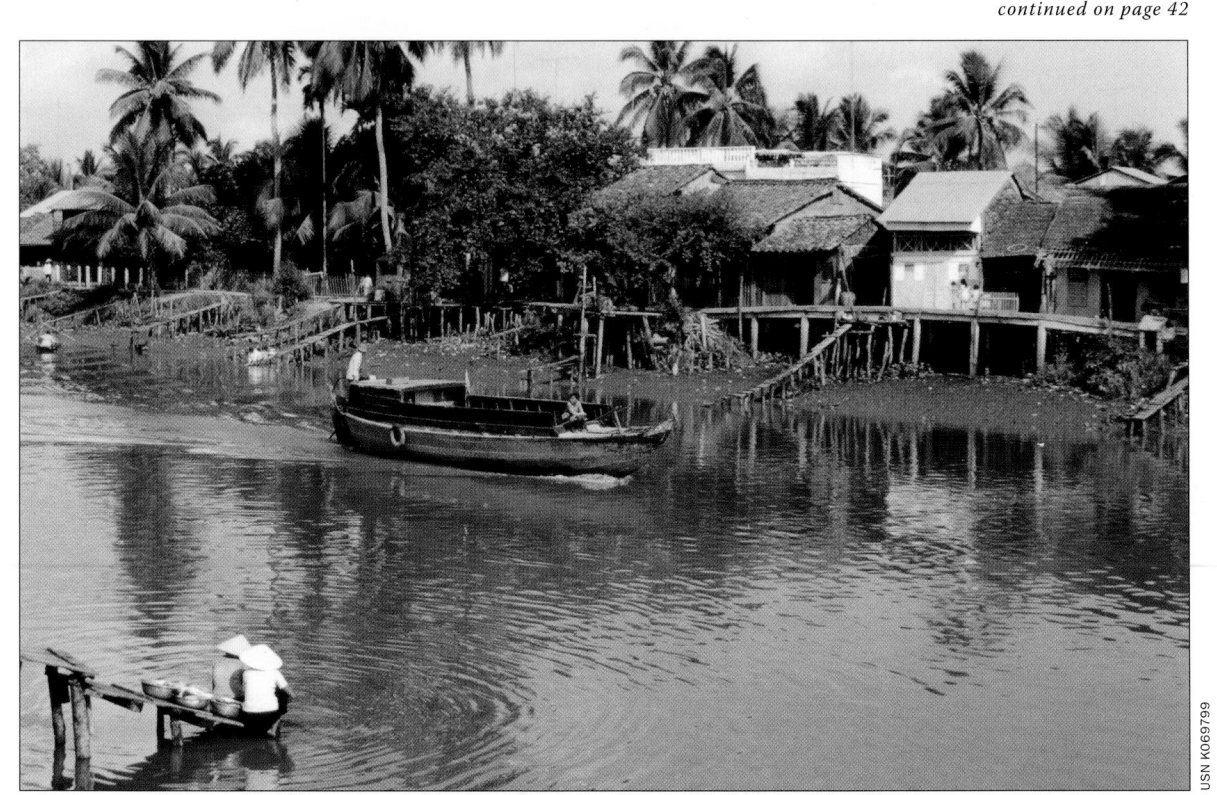

Life along a river in the Mekong Delta. The people who lived in this region, the most heavily populated in the country, depended on its myriad rivers and canals for their most basic needs. Control of these vital waterways was critical to the South Vietnamese government's survival.

USN K069799

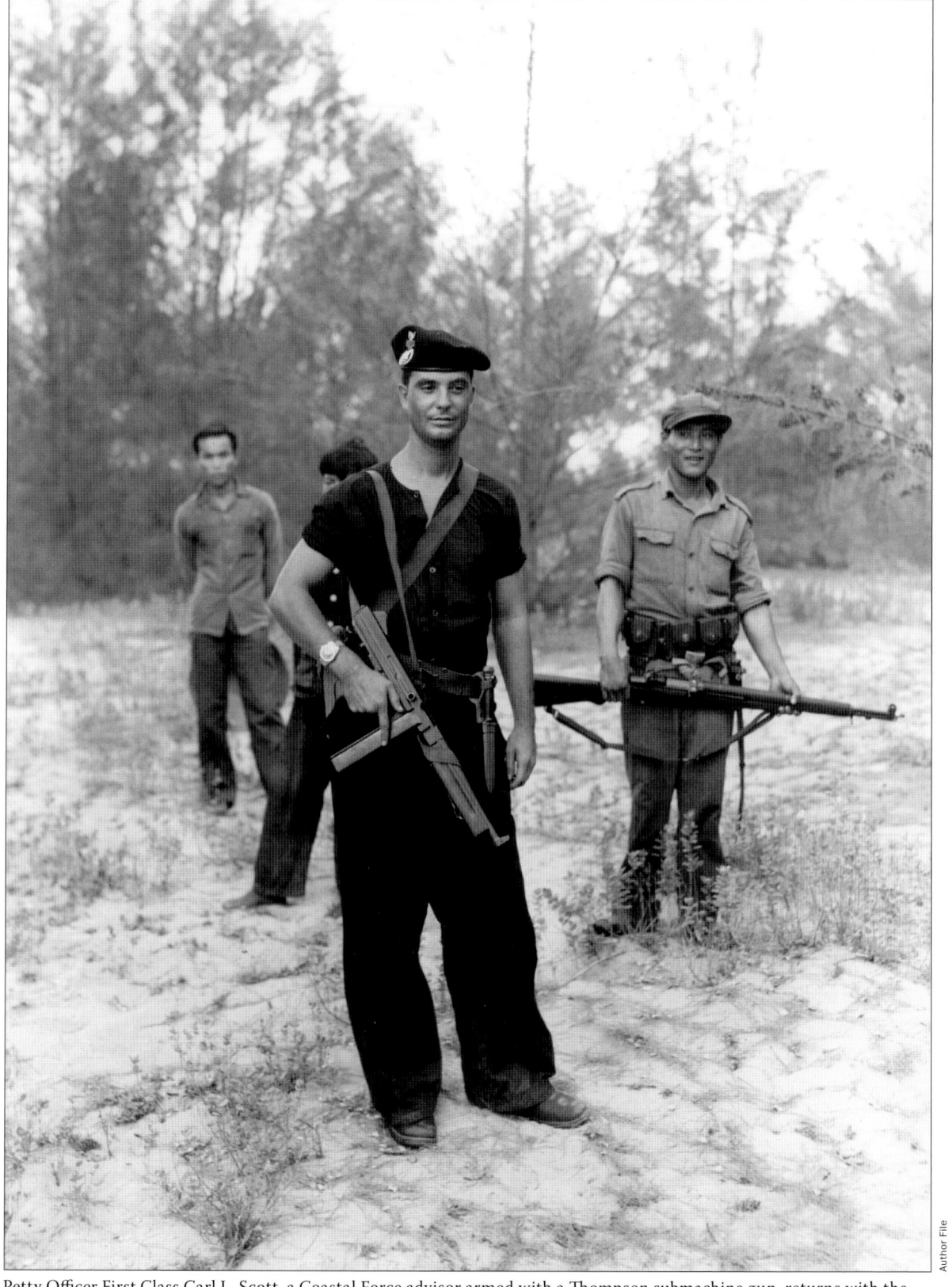

Petty Officer First Class Carl L. Scott, a Coastal Force advisor armed with a Thompson submachine gun, returns with the men of his unit from a raid against the Viet Cong.

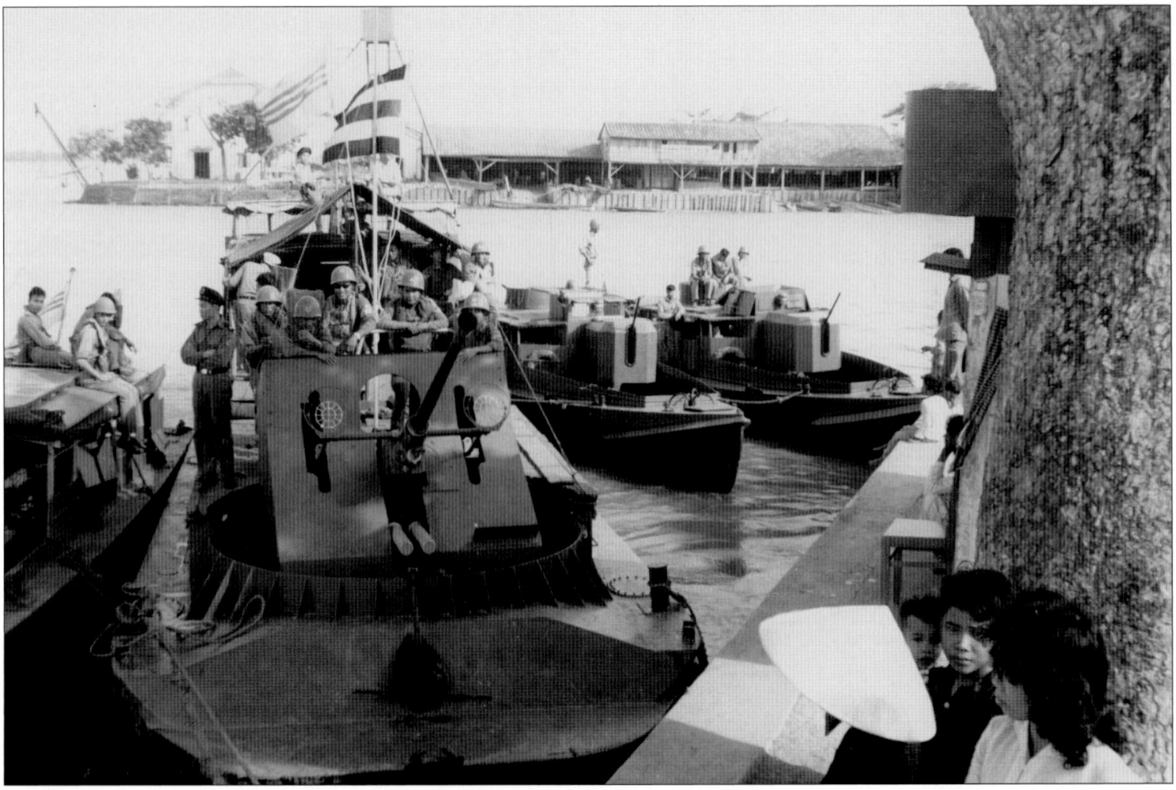
Author File

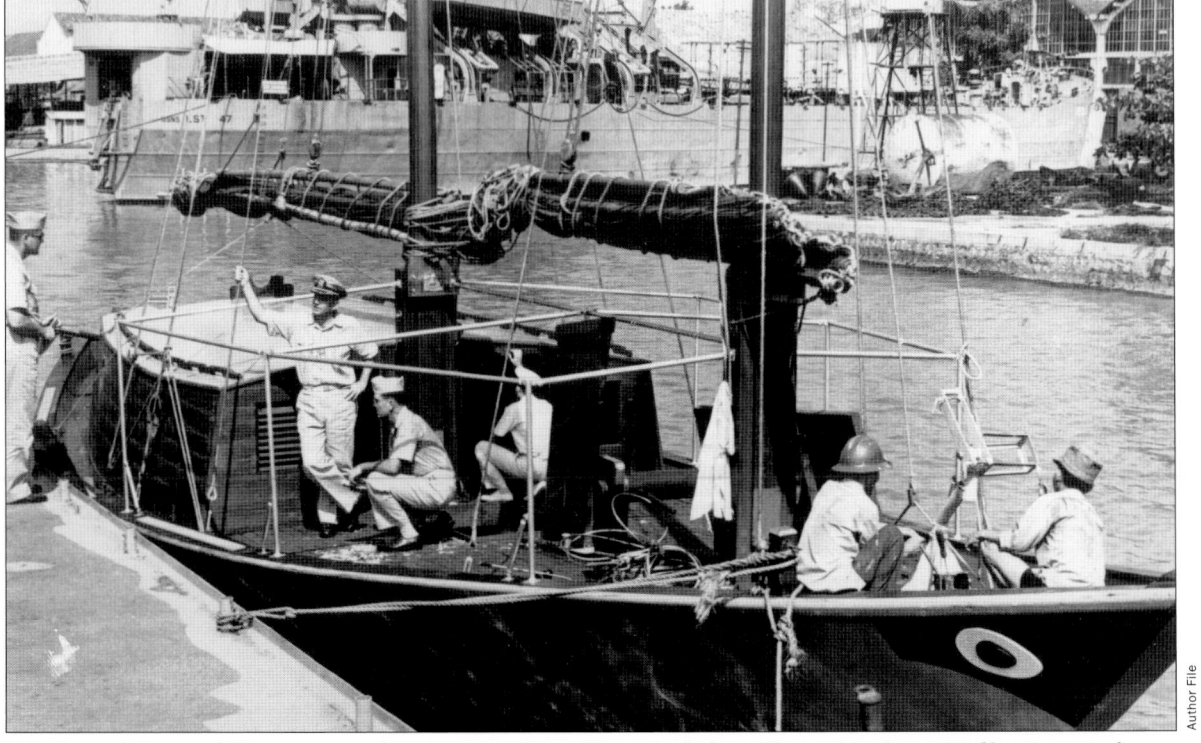

A converted LCM monitor and three STCAN patrol craft of the Vietnam Navy's 25th River Assault Group prepare to depart their base at Can Tho for an operation on the Bassac River.

Author File

U.S. Navy advisors and Vietnamese workers inspect a Coastal Force junk that will soon join the anti-infiltration patrol effort offshore.

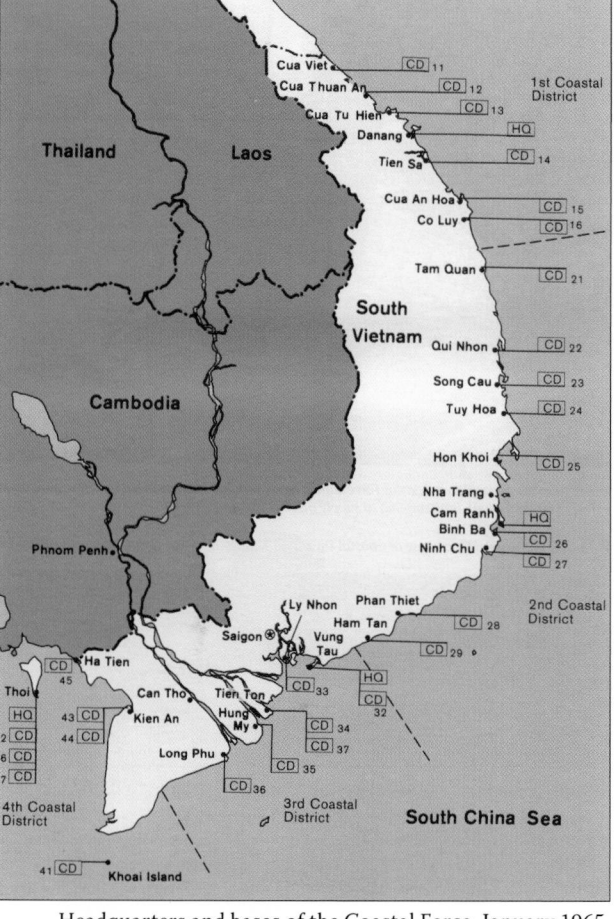

Headquarters and bases of the Coastal Force, January 1965.

From the end of the French Indochina War to 1964, the American naval advisors were most effective in facilitating the transfer to the VNN of ships, aircraft, and other equipment and establishing bases and supply depots. The *co vans*, as the Vietnamese referred to them, however, were much less effective at influencing their counterparts to adopt American operational and tactical approaches. Few naval advisors could speak Vietnamese or fully comprehend Asian culture. Having already led naval forces for years and expecting to fight for many more years, Vietnamese naval officers were less inclined than their short-term American counterparts to seek quick but potentially costly results on the battlefield.

Captain William Hardcastle, head of the Naval Advisory Group in 1964 and early 1965, recognized that his advisors were enthusiastic and dedicated to the mission but lacked practical experience. They came from a navy focused on defeating the Soviet fleet in major battles far out to sea, not working with small boats in the "green water" and "brown water" environs of South Vietnam. Despite this and other deficiencies, Hardcastle believed that his advisors would in time improve the operational effectiveness and fighting ability of the VNN.

There was then not much positive reinforcement for that rosy vision. The VNN was plagued with problems, including a lack of resources for training and operations, a secondary status in relation to the much larger Army of Vietnam, and poorly motivated personnel. Low pay and austere living conditions caused many Vietnamese sailors to desert.

But the greatest drawback to the development of the navy and the other South Vietnamese armed forces was the involvement of their officers in plots, coups, and other political intrigues. During much of this period, the Navy fared well because it sided with the winners. For instance, the naval service helped Diem suppress several religious sects in the mid 1950s. Captain Ho Tan Quyen, VNN Naval Deputy, backed Diem in the coup attempt of November 1960. When two rebel air force pilots attacked the Presidential Palace in February 1962, naval forces shot down one attacking plane, and Quyen offered to establish a command post in the navy yard for

Mekong Delta south of Saigon but to the political and economic well-being of the region.

The navy of the Republic of Vietnam, with the encouragement of American advisors, established another component—the paramilitary Coastal Force. The mission of that force was to patrol the 1,200-mile coast of South Vietnam in search of vessels trying to infiltrate arms, ammunition, couriers, and other special cargo from North Vietnam. The Coastal Force consisted of a fleet of 600 specially built wooden junks that operated from 28 austere bases established all along the South Vietnamese littoral. Vietnamese and American naval officers coordinated operations from coastal surveillance centers strategically positioned at Danang in the north, Cam Ranh on the central coast, Vung Tau southeast of Saigon, and An Thoi on Phu Quoc, a large island in the Gulf of Siam.

continued on page 46

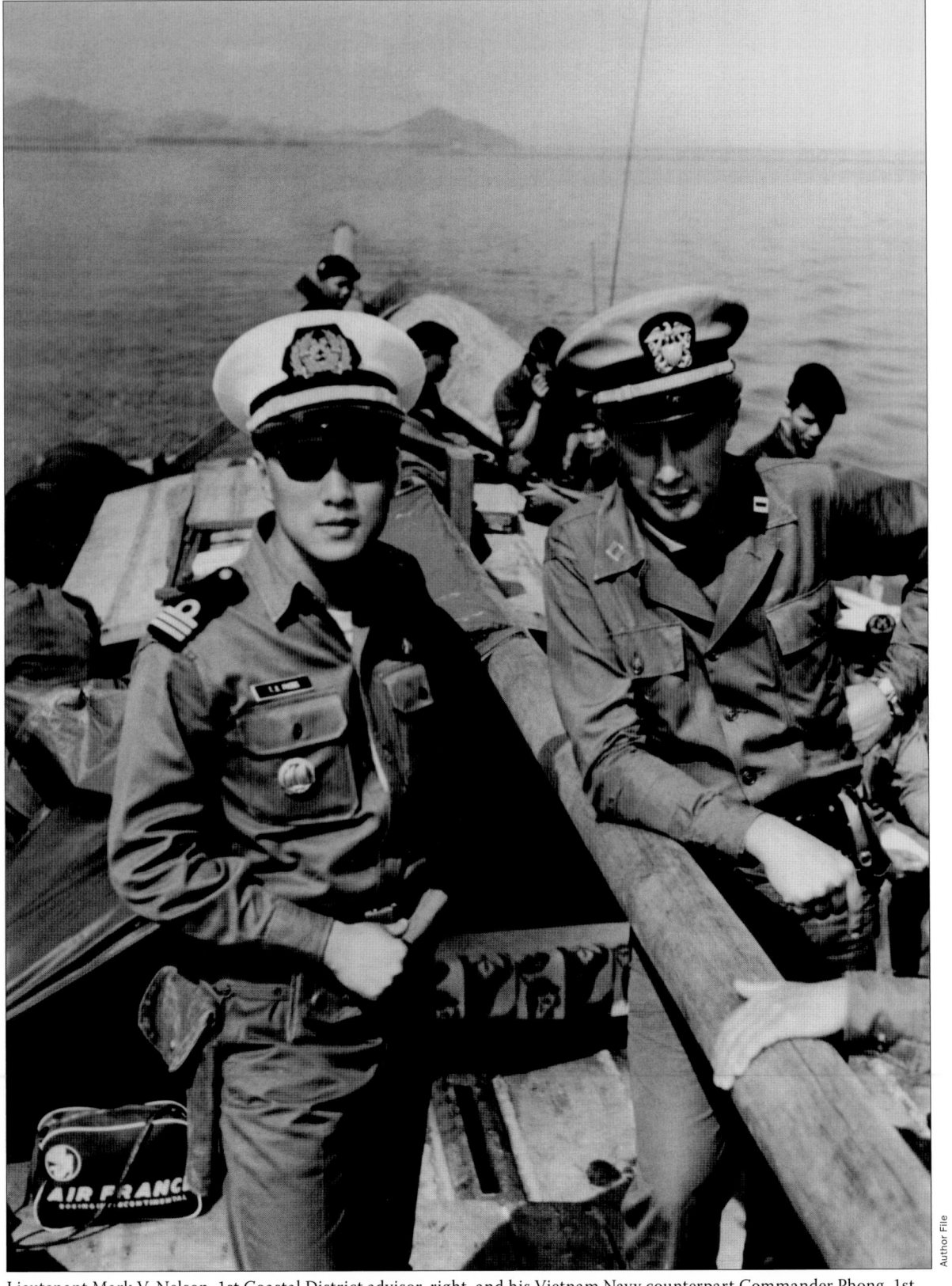

Lieutenant Mark V. Nelson, 1st Coastal District advisor, right, and his Vietnam Navy counterpart Commander Phong, 1st Coastal District commander, on board a junk off the northern coast of South Vietnam.

A Naval Advisor: Lieutenant Dale C. Meyerkord

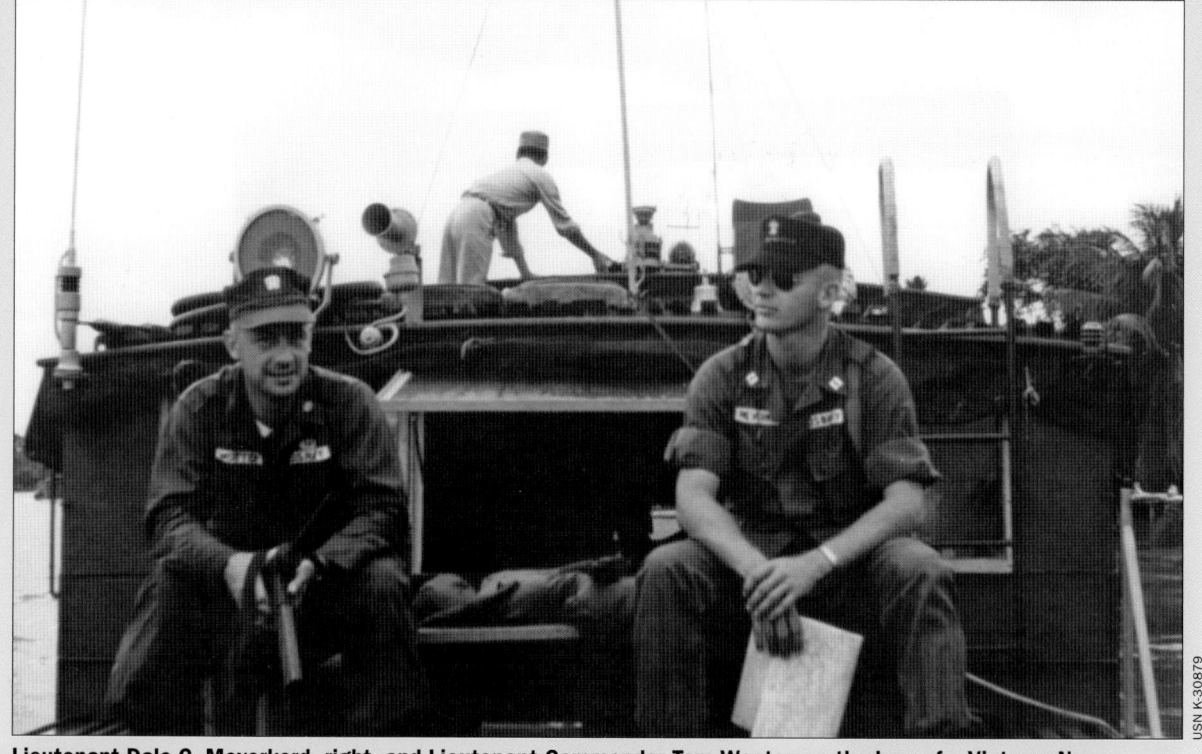

Lieutenant Dale C. Meyerkord, right, and Lieutenant Commander Tom Wooten on the bow of a Vietnam Navy combatant.

IN HIS INAUGURAL ADDRESS to the nation on 20 January 1961, President John F. Kennedy assured listeners worldwide that he and his fellow Americans would "pay any price, bear any burden, meet any hardship, support any friend, oppose any foe, in order to assure the survival and the success of liberty."

Navy Lieutenant Dale C. Meyerkord, like many of his compatriots, answered that clarion call and enlisted in the fight to defeat the Communist insurgency tearing apart the Republic of Vietnam. The 1960 graduate of officer candidate school told his mother that he had volunteered for Vietnam service because "a lot is going on there that will eventually change the world."

Once he had completed Vietnamese language training—finishing first in his class—Meyerkord was assigned as senior advisor to the Vietnam Navy's River Assault Group (RAG) 23 based at Vinh Long, deep in the heart of South Vietnam's Mekong Delta. The young officer and two Navy chiefs who comprised the small advisory detachment understood that the success of their mission would depend partly on their

ability to earn the support of the local population for the South Vietnamese navy. Meyerkord established good relations with area villagers; they appreciated his mastery of the Vietnamese language. He told them that the RAG would help protect them from Viet Cong guerrilla attacks and provide them medical and other government assistance.

Meyerkord and the other U.S. naval advisors in Vietnam were unique as individual human beings, the product of distinct backgrounds, and assigned to different South Vietnamese units, operational environments, and commanders, but there were common threads too. Most of the early advisors found their understanding of the Vietnamese language and culture inadequate for their assignment and had to learn on the job. Whether assigned to the VNN units on the coast, the major rivers, or the Mekong Delta border with Cambodia, the Americans often lived in rudimentary huts or "hootches." They had to endure the heat and humidity of tropical Vietnam and subsist on a diet of rice and vegetables, usually flavored with *Nuoc Mam*, a pungent

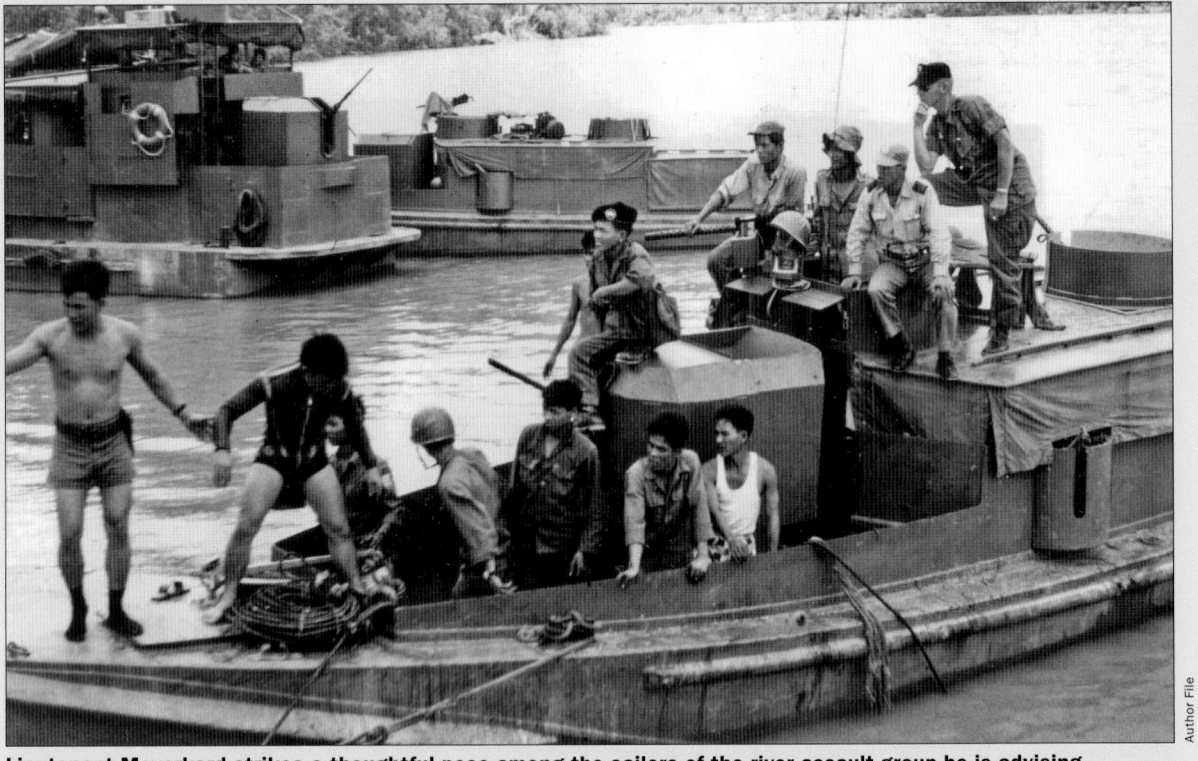

Lieutenant Meyerkord strikes a thoughtful pose among the sailors of the river assault group he is advising.

sauce made from fermented fish. Many American advisors found it a challenge to adapt the U.S. Navy's concepts of combat leadership, command and control, logistics, and maintenance to the VNN's more basic approaches. While less intent on seeking battle with the enemy than Meyerkord and other young, aggressive American advisors, Vietnamese officers and men rose to the occasion when necessary and fought with courage and determination.

Meyerkord's most pressing responsibility in late 1964 and early 1965, when the Communists mounted a serious, countrywide offensive against the government in Saigon, was to help RAG 23 defeat the enemy around Vinh Long. Meyerkord and the river assault group fought over 30 actions with Viet Cong forces in the period.

Lieutenant Meyerkord was the modern embodiment of hard-fighting naval warriors of the past. His radio call sign was, appropriately, "Hornblower" after C. S. Forrester's brave and daring fictional character. In numerous battles, Meyerkord displayed personal bravery, coolness under fire, and professional skill. In one action he helped direct artillery support, called in air strikes, and facilitated evacuation of wounded South Vietnamese sailors. When the commanding officer of RAG 23 was hit in another action, Meyerkord successfully directed the battle even though he was himself wounded.

In his final action, on 16 March 1965, Meyerkord positioned himself, as he always did, on the raised deckhouse of a South Vietnamese combat vessel— he believed an officer should inspire his men by example. Without warning, the enemy sprang a devastating ambush on the river assault group. Wounded, Meyerkord fired back at his assailants but he was struck by another round that mortally wounded him.

Lieutenant Dale C. Meyerkord, posthumously awarded the Navy Cross for his leadership, battle skill, and personal courage, was the first U.S. naval officer killed in action in South Vietnam. He would be an inspiration for the thousands of naval advisors who followed him. ⬎

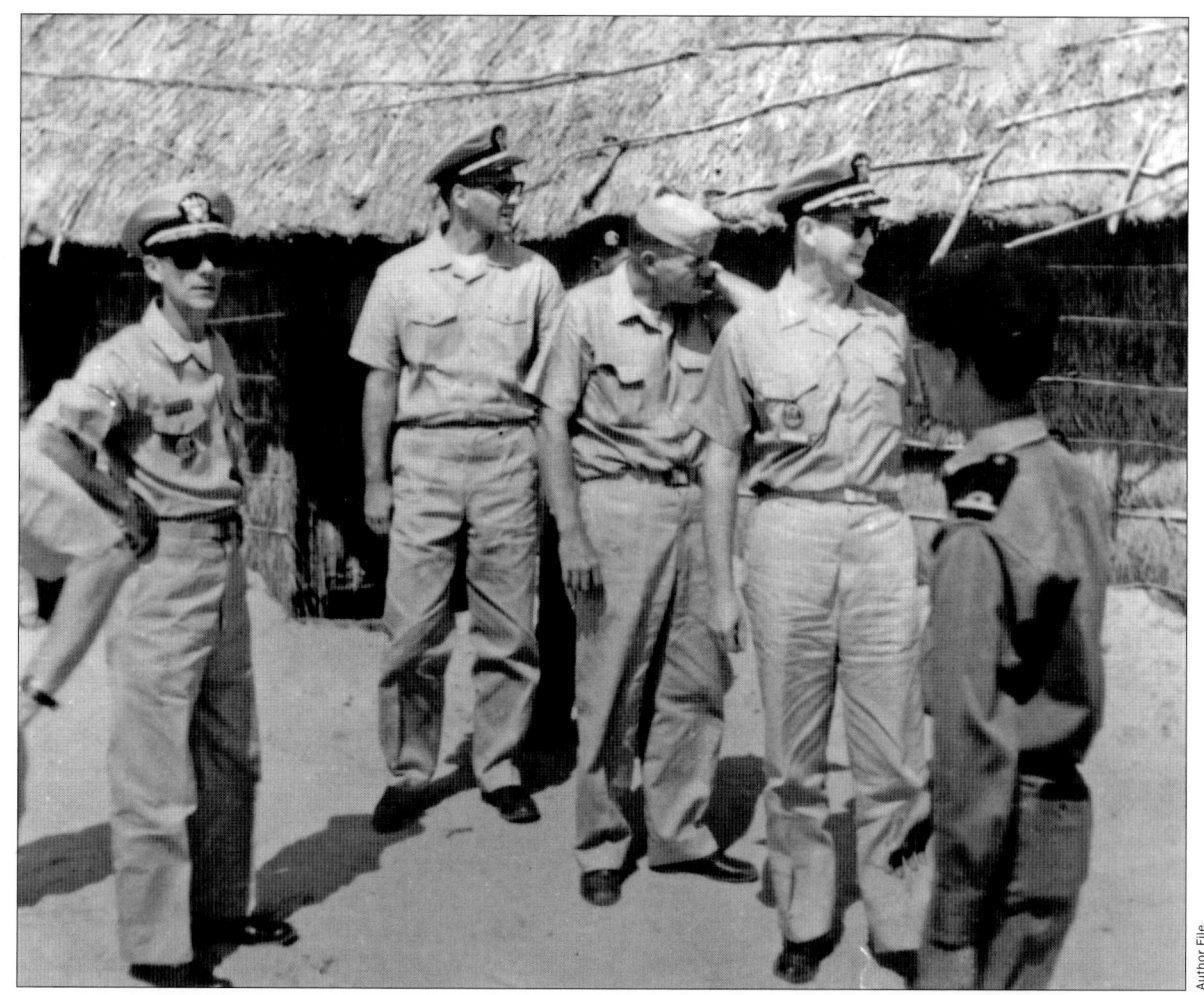

U.S. naval advisors inspect the base at An Thoi on the island of Phu Quoc in the Gulf of Siam. From left to right: Captain Joseph B. Drachnik, Chief of the Naval Advisory Group, Vietnam; Lieutenant Wesley A. Hoch, 4th Coastal District advisor; an unidentified U.S. naval officer; and Captain William H. Hardcastle, Drachnik's successor.

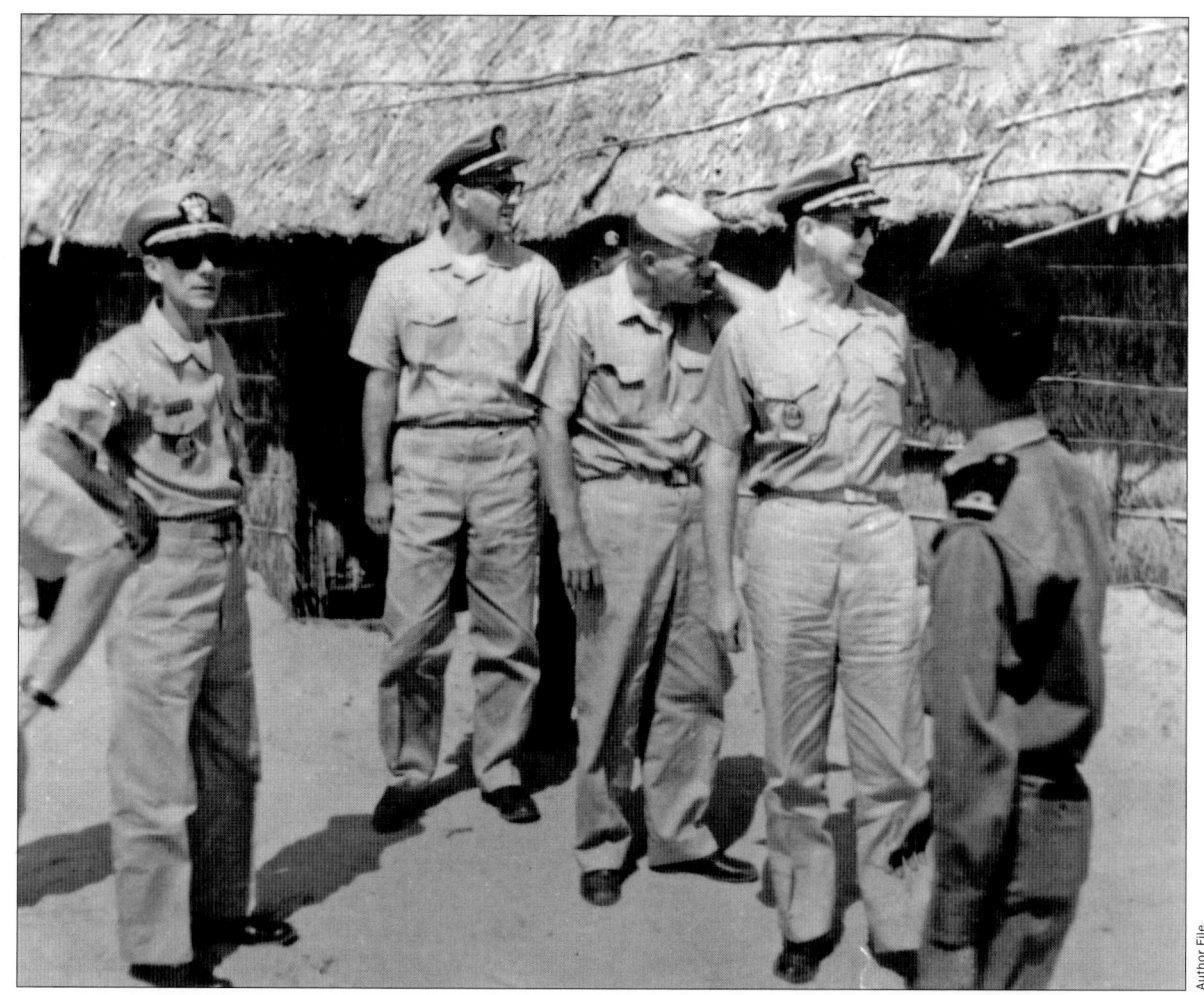

Author File

Diem. In recognition of his loyalty, Diem promoted Quyen to captain shortly thereafter. Hoping to enlist Quyen to the cause of overthrowing Diem on 1 November 1963, a naval officer involved in the plot invited to drive the captain to a party in honor of his birthday. En route, when Quyen refused to join the conspiracy, the officer put three bullets in the man's head and then drove to naval headquarters where he arrested the navy staff. In the aftermath of the coup that resulted in the assassination of Diem and his brother, the primary criteria for leadership of the navy became political reliability rather than operational skill or bravery in combat.

When Rear Admiral Henry S. Persons from the CINPAC staff inspected the VNN in November 1961,

he found many problems with the naval service. He determined that poor maintenance and repair prevented two-thirds of the patrol ships and half of the river vessels from conducting operations. He discovered that too many naval officers lacked combat experience, adequate professional preparation, and the drive to succeed as leaders. The enlisted force suffered from lack of adequate training. A major problem was the failure of the army-dominated Joint General Staff to devote sufficient resources to the navy.

Captain Phillip S. Bucklew, dispatched to South Vietnam early in 1964 by Admiral Felt, CINCPAC, found many of the same problems. He credited the Vietnamese naval service with making gains in some critical operational areas since 1961, but

concluded that much work remained to be done. By 1964, it was clear that the Communists were infiltrating guerrillas and supplies into the South from the sea and via the rivers, canals, and other waterways between South Vietnam and Cambodia. Bucklew was especially troubled by the VNN's inability to stem the flow of sampans laden with arms, ammunition, and supplies into the Mekong Delta region. He strongly urged Washington to increase material support and training of the Vietnamese navy to improve its operational performance along the coast and especially in the Mekong Delta. He advocated more robust coastal and river warfare units and the employment of barricades, curfews, checkpoints, and patrols. ⚓

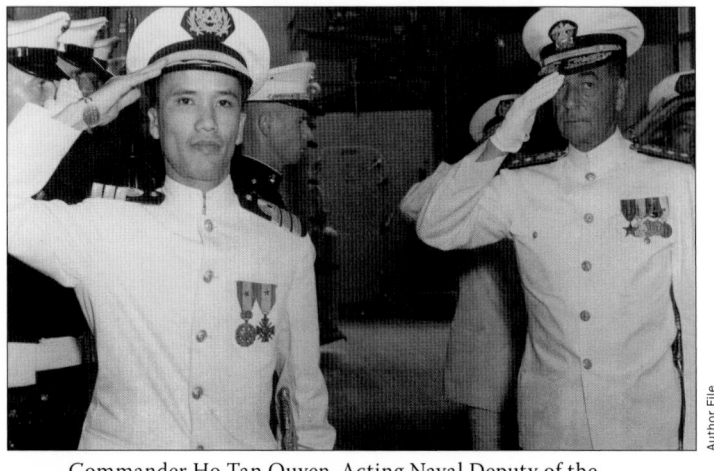

Commander Ho Tan Quyen, Acting Naval Deputy of the Vietnam Navy, left, and Rear Admiral Alfred G. Ward, Commander Cruiser Division 1, during an official function in October 1959. Quyen's loyalty to Diem ultimately led to the naval officer's death.

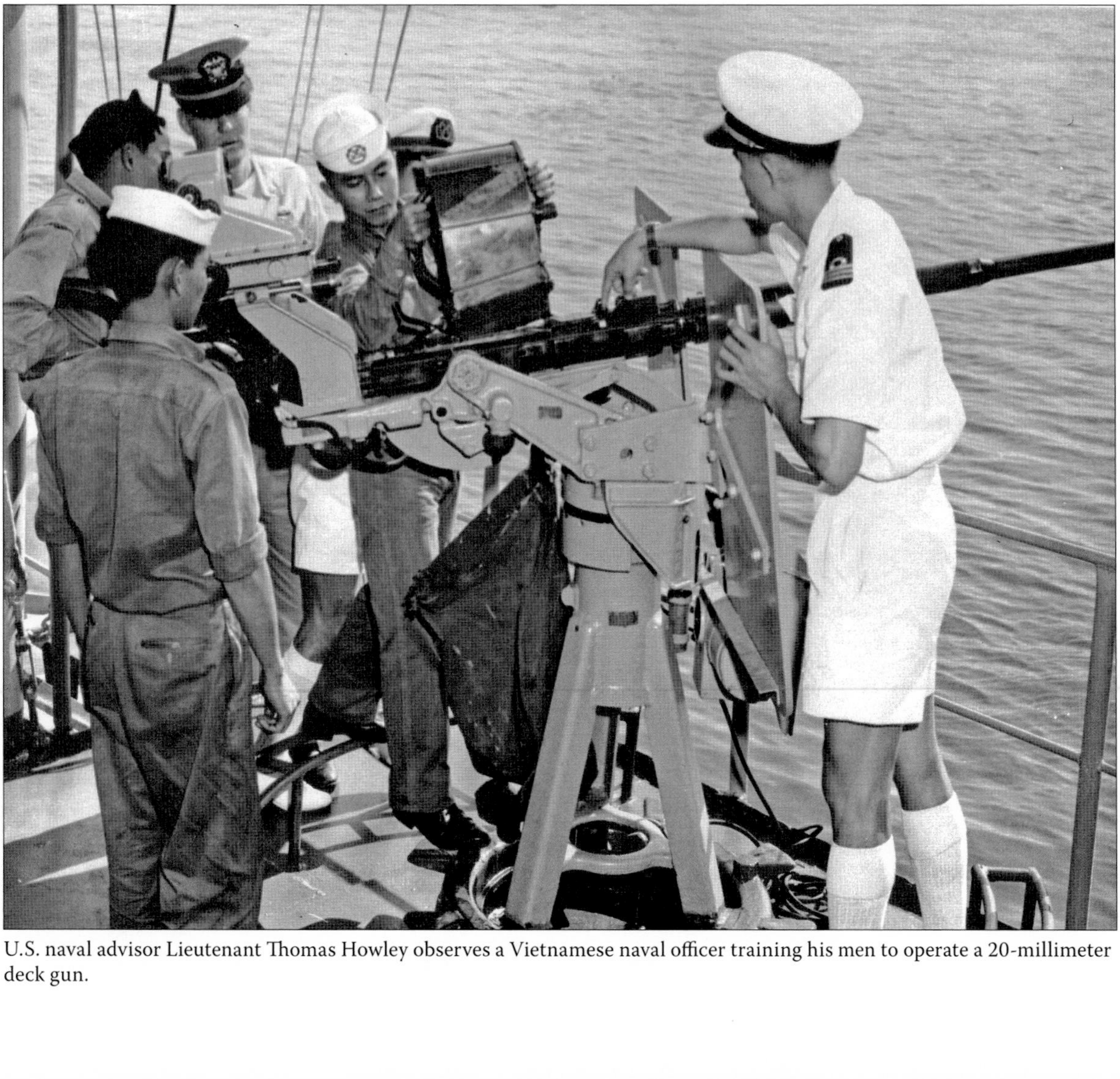

U.S. naval advisor Lieutenant Thomas Howley observes a Vietnamese naval officer training his men to operate a 20-millimeter deck gun.

SC-591961

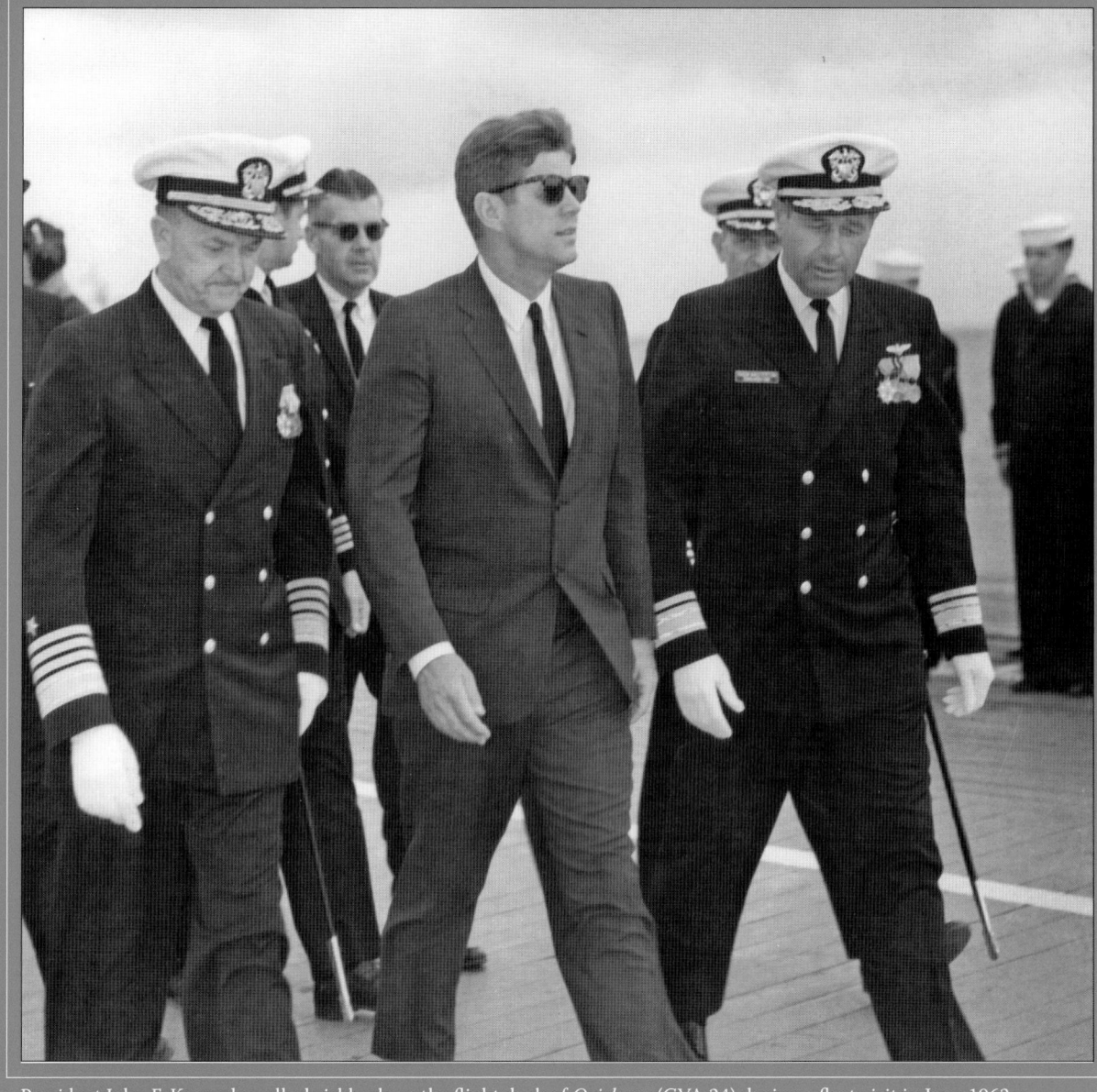

President John F. Kennedy walks briskly along the flight deck of *Oriskany* (CVA 34) during a fleet visit in June 1963. Kennedy was a strong advocate of counterinsurgency warfare as a response to Communist "wars of national liberation."

Although disappointed with the depth and pace of improvement of the VNN, in the early 1960s few American naval leaders or advisors were ready to give up. This was an era of boundless optimism in the power and influence of the United States. U.S. military leaders were confident that "counterinsurgency," their answer to the Communist world's "wars of national liberation," would strengthen America's Southeast Asian allies for the fight.

The counterinsurgency approach evolved from the U.S. national security establishment's Flexible Response concept of the late 1950s that called for measured and appropriate responses to Communist actions. For instance, a Soviet nuclear attack would be answered by U.S. nuclear retaliation, but the action of Viet Cong guerrillas to destabilize a rural district by killing local government officials would be countered by arming militia forces to defend the people and hunt the insurgents in the jungle.

Successes during the 1950s and early 1960s by the anticommunist governments in the Philippines and Malaya against insurgent movements suggested to American leaders that counterinsurgency warfare could be a valid antidote to the challenges in Indochina. British analyst Sir Robert Thompson and other experts shared with the Americans their views of which aspects of counterinsurgency warfare worked and which ones did not, based on the experience in Malaya.

Influenced by these success stories, the Kennedy administration wholeheartedly endorsed ambitious programs to develop and deploy to South Vietnam and other nations threatened by Communist insurgencies

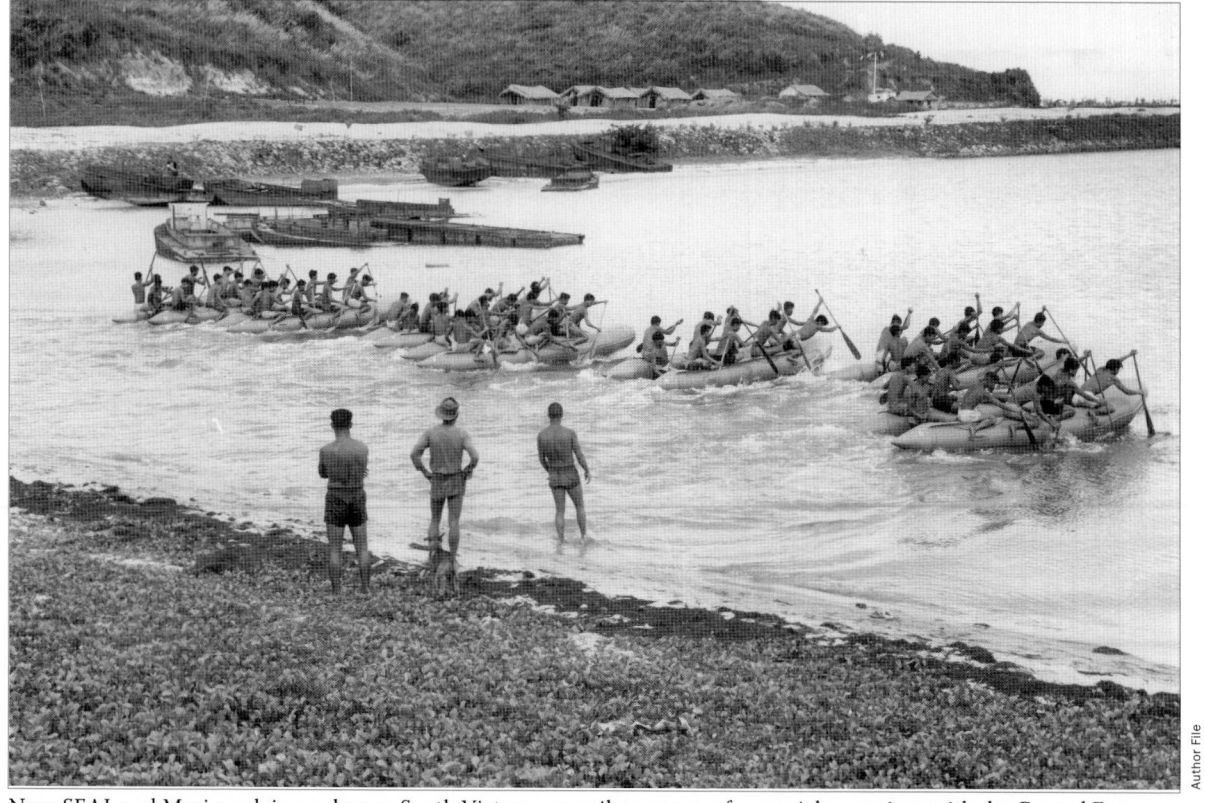

Author File

Navy SEAL and Marine advisors observe South Vietnamese sailors prepare for special operations with the Coastal Force.

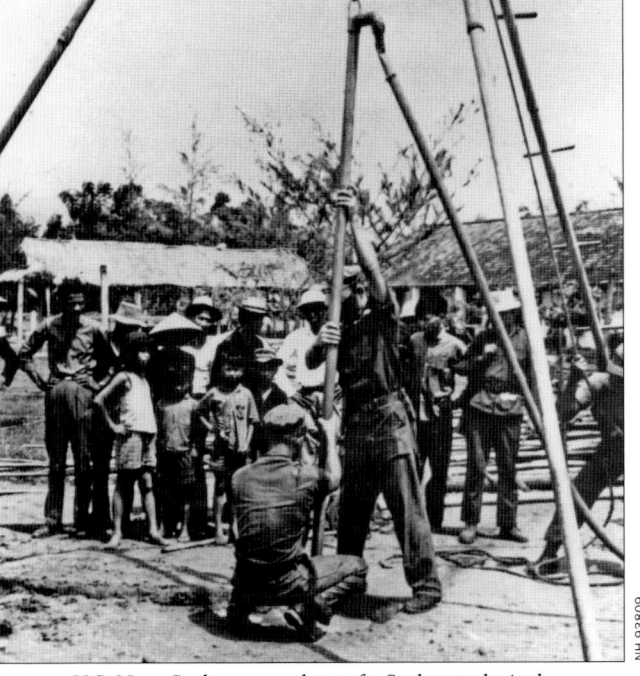

U.S. Navy Seabees, members of a Seabee technical assistance team, sink a well in a Vietnamese village as its inhabitants look on with anticipation.

military personnel trained to fight guerrillas and win the support of local peoples for their governments. The U.S. Army's Special Forces troops, the "Green Berets," soon became recognized symbols of America's counterinsurgency warfare establishment.

Admiral Arleigh Burke was the first Chief of Naval Operations (CNO) to push seriously for the development of Navy special forces suited to counterinsurgency warfare. Under his guidance, during 1961 the Navy studied the use of 60-man teams of naval warriors to operate at sea, in the air, and on land against Communist guerrillas and to train allied forces for special warfare. With the personal encouragement of President Kennedy, on 1 January 1962, the Navy established SEAL Team 1 in the Pacific Fleet and SEAL Team 2 in the Atlantic Fleet. During the next several years, SEALs deployed to Vietnam and worked to develop South Vietnamese naval commandos—LDNN (*Lien Doc Nguoi Nhia*).

The Navy also created specialized Seabee construction units to help the government of South

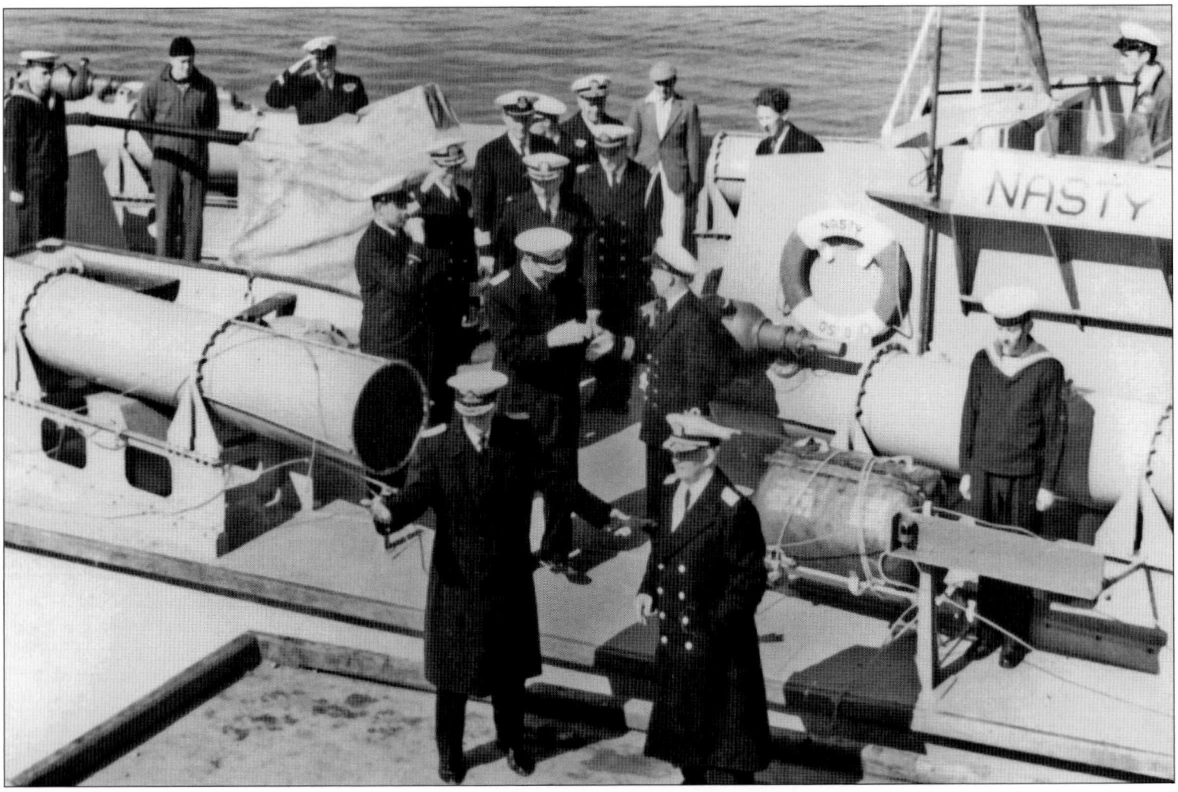

Chief of Naval Operations Admiral Arleigh Burke, right foreground, during an inspection of a Norwegian-built, *Nasty*-class special operations boat. Burke was instrumental in the development of enhanced naval special warfare forces and equipment.

Vietnam win the support of its people by building village fortifications, schools, hospitals, bridges, and roads. The units—Seabee Technical Assistance Teams, or STATs—also built fortified camps on the border with Cambodia for U.S. Army Special Forces A teams and affiliated Montagnard (hill tribesmen), Chinese, and Vietnamese irregular troops.

In this same vein, the Navy configured two of its Korean War–era motor torpedo boats for antiguerrilla warfare and bought from Norway six modern *Nasty*-class PT boats. The 80-foot-long *Nasty* boats, diesel-powered and fiberglass-hulled, were capable of 41-knot speeds. The American and Norwegian boats were classified fast patrol boats (PTFs), armed with 20- and 40-millimeter guns and recoilless rifles, and dispatched to the Far East. The PTF force was intended to bombard enemy coastal facilities and infiltrate saboteurs from the sea.

Finally, the naval service reconfigured submarines *Perch* (APSS 313) and *Sealion* (APSS 315) for special operations missions. The undersea vessels were readied to land SEALs, Green Berets, and South Vietnamese naval commandos behind enemy lines, gather intelligence, and rescue aviators shot down in hostile waters. ⚓

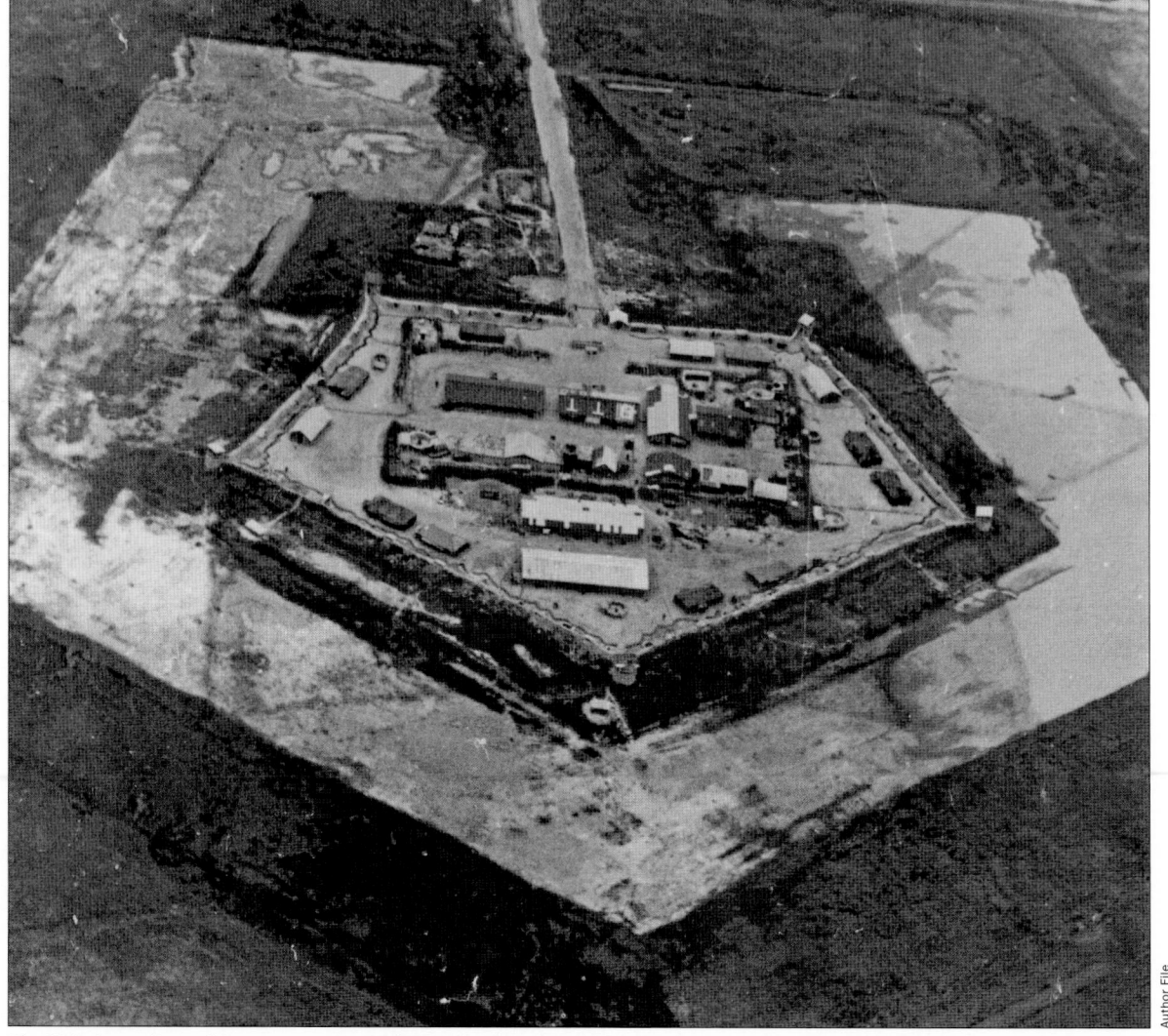

The U.S. Army Special Forces camp at Binh Thanh Thon, located in the Mekong Delta a few miles from Cambodia. Seabees helped build this and other camps from which special forces patrolled the border areas of South Vietnam.

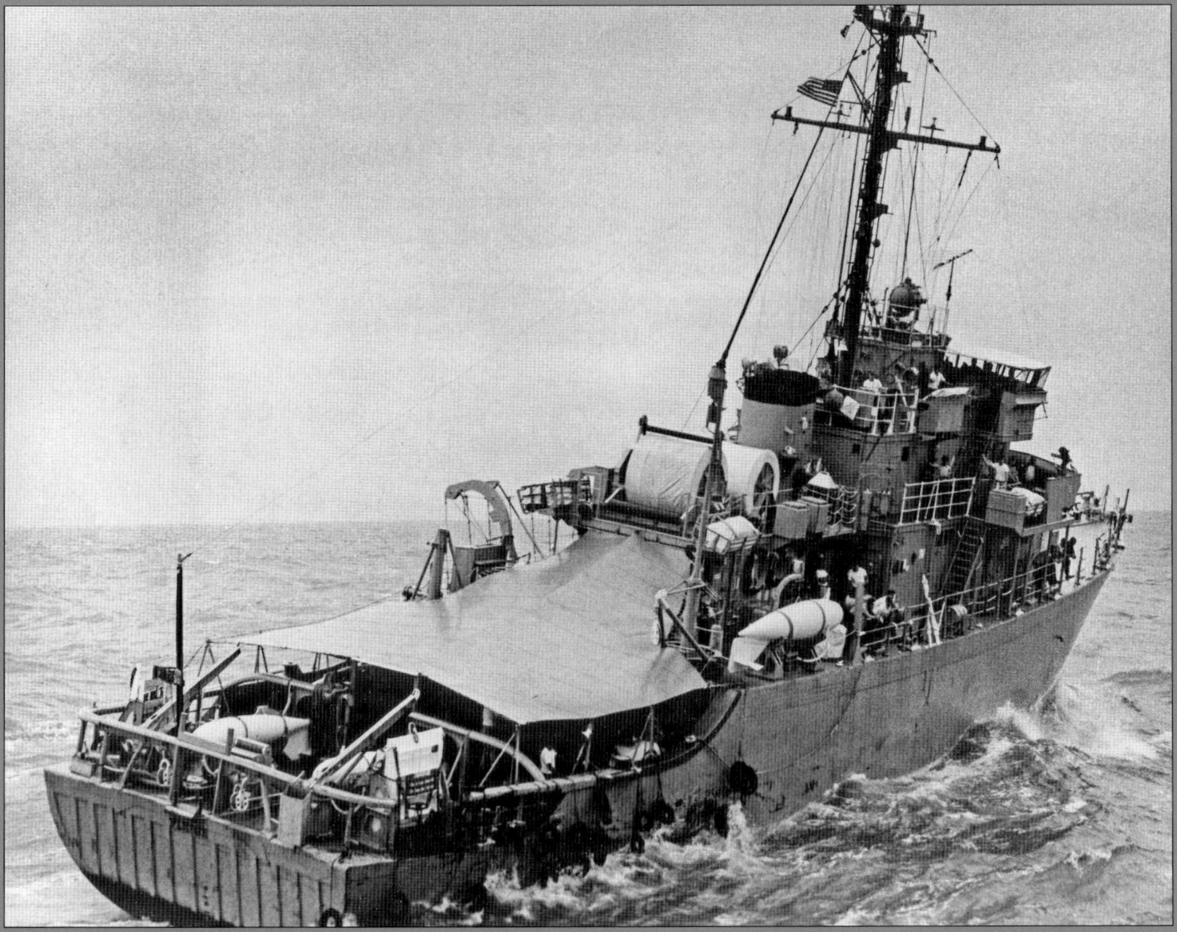

Author File

Ocean minesweepers like *Pledge* (MSO 492) formed the core of the U.S. Navy's anti-infiltration patrol east of the 17th parallel during 1961 and 1962.

The Navy has traditionally stressed that its ships, aircraft, and weapons should be capable of performing many different tasks, rather than single missions. Hence, when the Kennedy administration called for measures to combat the Communist insurgency in South Vietnam, U.S. naval leaders knew that conventional units could fill the bill in "limited partnership" with the Republic of Vietnam Armed Forces. In that vein, on 11 December 1961, *Core* (T-AKV 41), an aircraft ferry operated by the Navy's Military Sea Transportation Service, delivered to Saigon helicopters of the Army's 8th and 57th Transportation Companies (Light Helicopter). These units would immeasurably improve the mobility and reach of South Vietnamese ground forces. One month later aircraft ferry *Card* (T-AKV 40) deployed Army helicopters to Danang. In April 1962, Marine aviation units joined the fray when amphibious assault ship *Princeton* (LPH 5) deployed the 259 officers and enlisted men and 24 H-34D helicopters of Marine Medium Helicopter Squadron (HMM) 362 to Soc Trang, an old Japanese airstrip in the Mekong Delta. By the end of the long war in Vietnam, the helicopter would come to symbolize the American way of war.

Concerned that the North Vietnamese were infiltrating arms and other munitions into South Vietnam be sea, in December 1961 the U.S. Navy deployed ocean minesweepers and Martin SP-5B Marlin

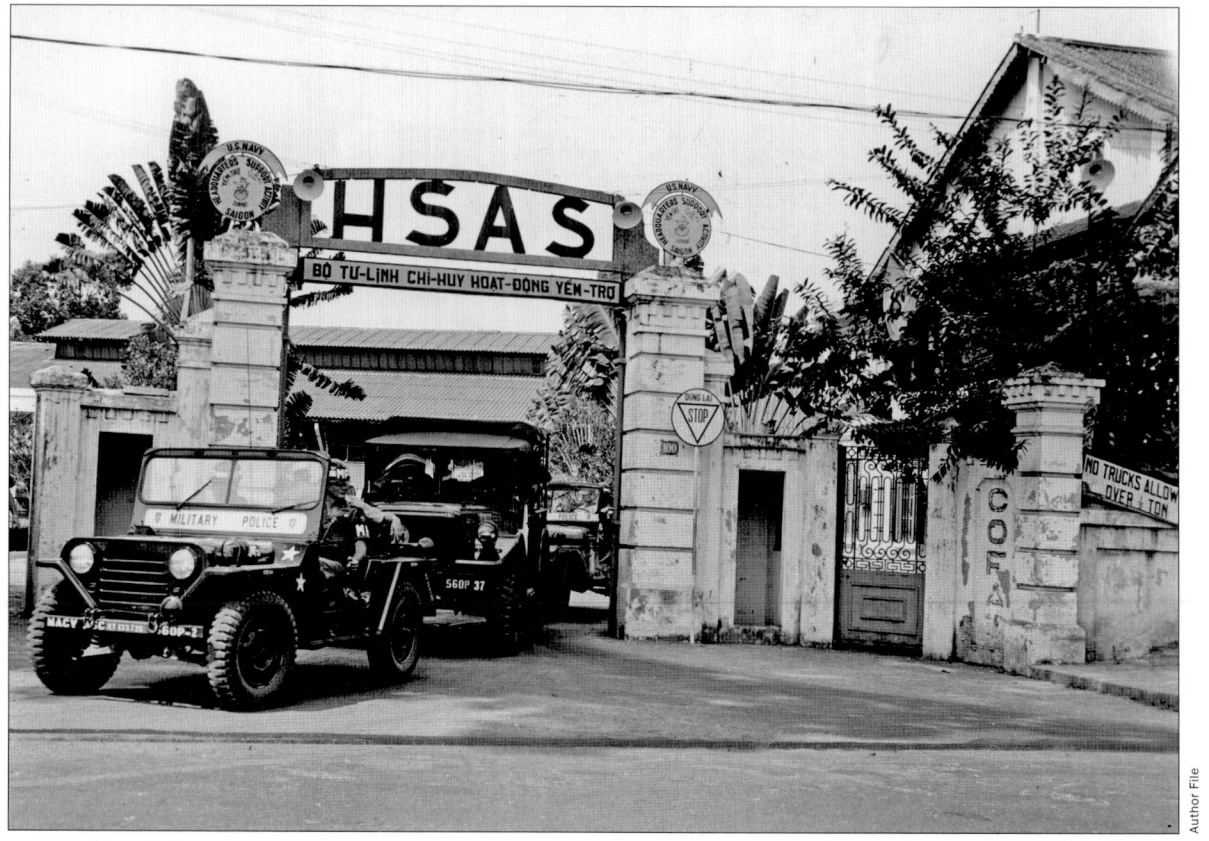

Author File

Army military police vehicles depart through the main gate of Headquarters Support Activity, Saigon. HSAS, a Navy administrative and logistical command, provided services to armed forces members, their families, and U.S. government civilians in South Vietnam during the early 1960s.

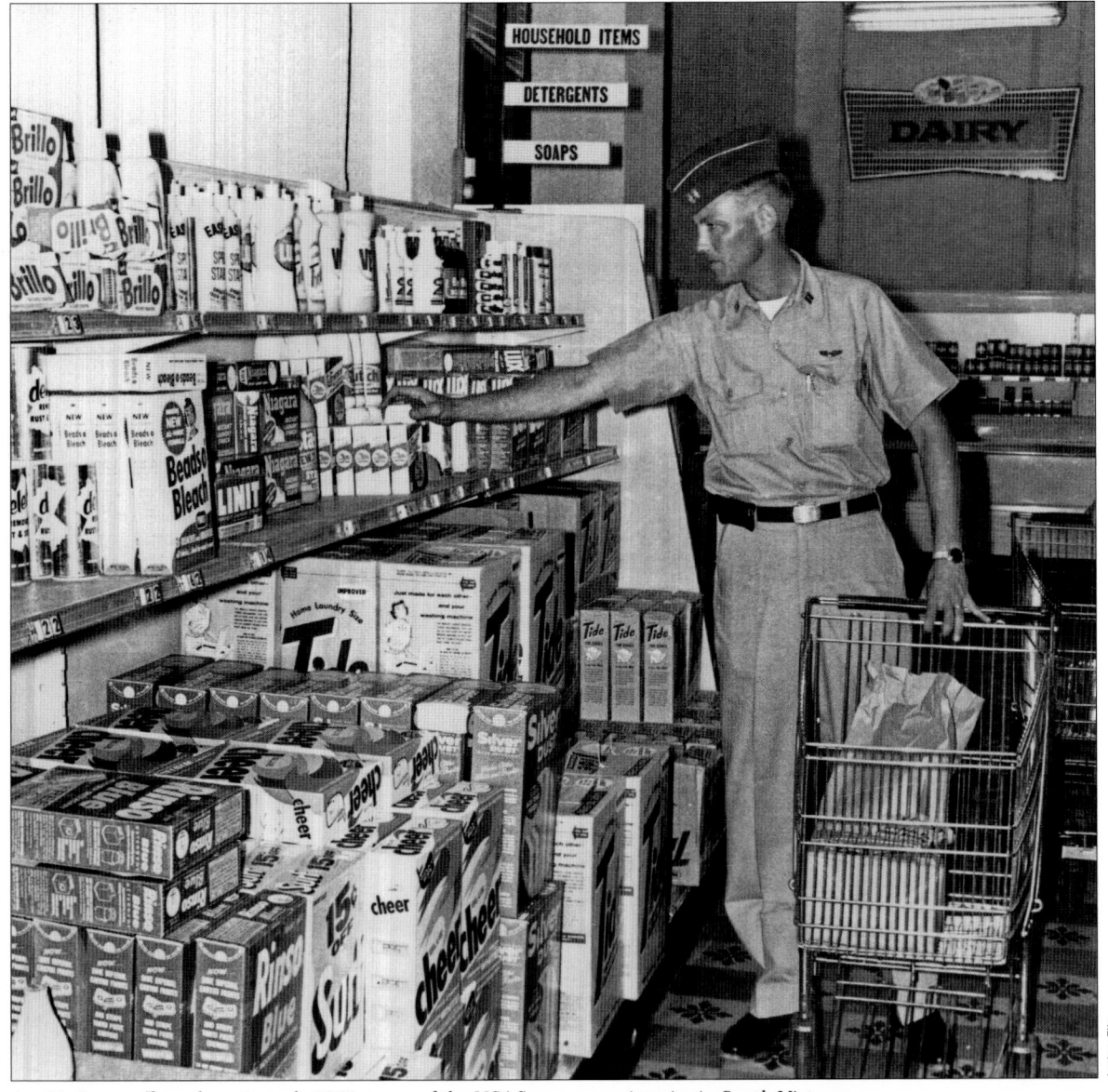

An Air Force officer shops in early 1965 at one of the HSAS-run commissaries in South Vietnam.

seaplanes in a joint USN-VNN surface and air patrol of the waters between the 17th parallel and the Paracel Islands. The two navies mounted a similar patrol in the Gulf of Siam; there the U.S. Navy employed destroyer escorts. The VNN received valuable training in open-ocean operations during the seven-month-long joint operation. But, despite stopping and searching thousands of suspicious vessels, the allied navies discovered no appreciable Communist infiltration. Ironically, soon after Washington ended the patrol

operation on 1 August 1962, Hanoi inaugurated a major seaborne infiltration program.

Even though the Navy ended its anti-infiltration patrol, U.S. conventional and special operations forces continued to flow into South Vietnam in the early 1960s. In keeping with a global division of labor among the American armed services, the Defense Department tasked the Navy with providing certain types of logistical and administrative support to U.S. personnel in the Republic of Vietnam. By the end of

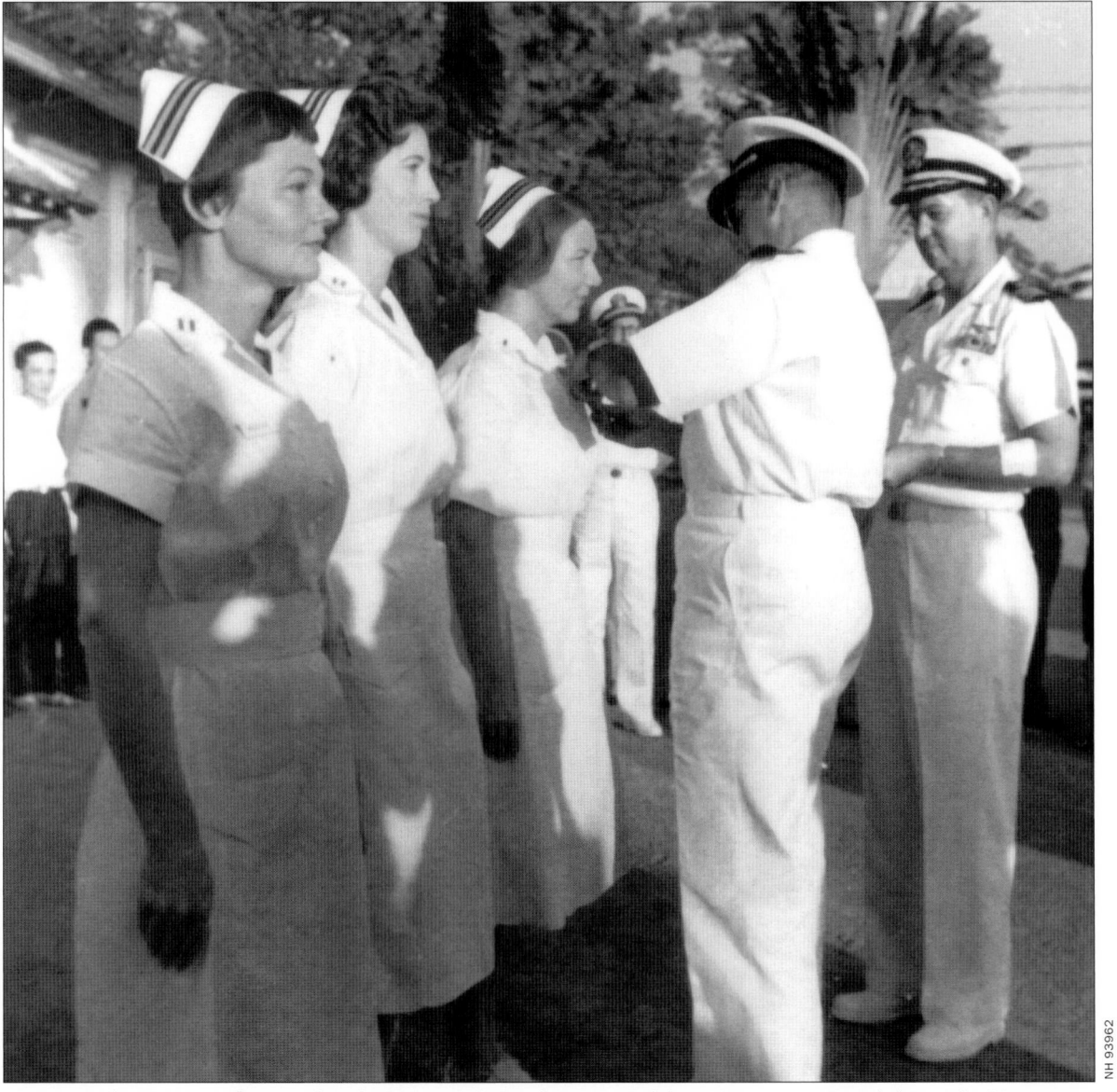

Captain Archie C. Kuntz, commander of HSAS, awards Purple Heart Medals to Navy nurses. From left to right: Lieutenant Barbara Wooster, Lieutenant Ruth A. Mason, and Lieutenant (jg) A. Darby Reynolds, who were injured in the bombing of the Brink Hotel Bachelor Officers Quarters on Christmas Eve, 1964.

1964, when there were 23,000 American military personnel and 2,700 U.S. government civilians in South Vietnam, the Navy's Headquarters Support Activity, Saigon (HSAS) was the primary command for their in-country support. The 600 personnel who staffed HSAS provided medical and dental services at the Saigon Station Hospital; arranged rest and recuperation (R&R) flights, sponsored USO shows, oversaw in-country exchange stores, transported supplies throughout the country, and managed 32 quarters for transient officers and enlisted personnel. Members of the Navy Nurse Corps carried out their vital services at the Saigon Station Hospital in an environment fraught with danger. Throughout 1964, Viet Cong assassinations and bombings rocked Saigon. As a reflection of this reality, Captain Archie C. Kuntz, commander of HSAS, awarded three Navy nurses Purple Heart medals for wounds they received while caring for U.S. servicemen at the Brink Bachelor Officers Quarters, bombed on Christmas Eve. ⚓

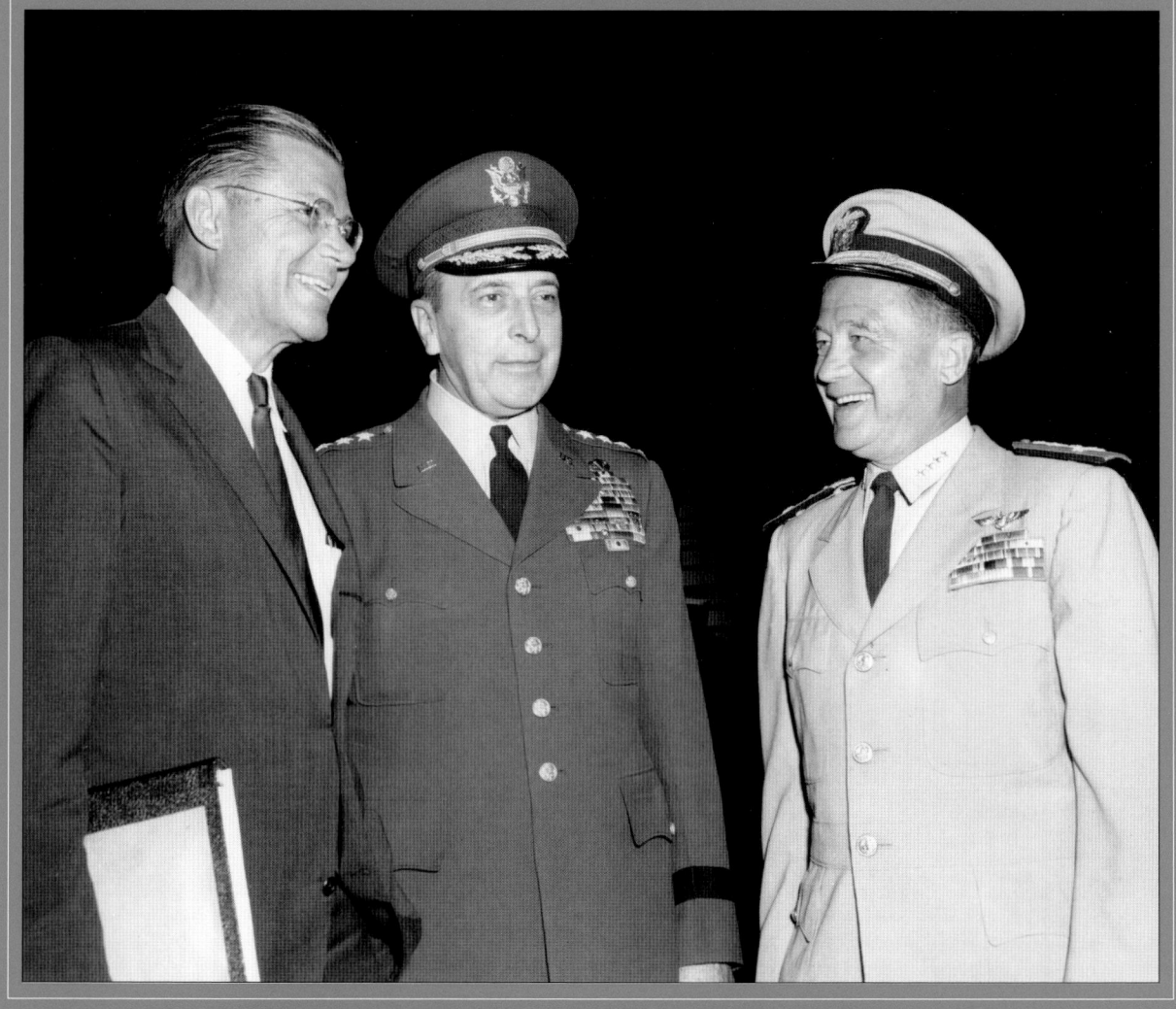

Secretary of Defense Robert S. McNamara converses with General Lyman L. Lemnitzer, Chairman of the Joint Chiefs of Staff; and Admiral Harry D. Felt, Commander in Chief, Pacific.

By 1964 it was clear to many American leaders that the counterinsurgency campaign and limited American military operations would not discourage Hanoi from its sponsorship of the war in South Vietnam. Following the assassination of Diem and his brother Nhu, the Communists launched devastating attacks against the armed forces of South Vietnam, seized control of much of the countryside, and increasingly targeted American military compounds and advisors.

Key Navy flag officers proposed various military operations by U.S. forces to temper aggressive North Vietnamese behavior. They considered coastal raids, sabotage, harassment of shipping, small-scale amphibious landings, mining of ports, coastal blockade, aerial interdiction of the Ho Chi Minh Trail, and even air strikes against the Democratic Republic of Vietnam. In calling for these operations, Admiral Claude Ricketts, Vice Chief of Naval Operations, observed that if the protection of South Vietnam necessitated "escalation of the war into North Vietnam, then that must be done, because it is from North Vietnam that the vast majority of the guerrillas are coming."

There was hardly consensus about the wisdom of these actions, however, even among military officers. Admiral Felt feared that a U.S. closure of North Vietnam's ports to oceangoing commerce would prompt Chinese air attacks on the blockading fleet. President Johnson and his chief civilian advisors were equally concerned about the prospect of Chinese or even Soviet intervention. They also feared that hostile acts against the North would stimulate the Communists to increase pressure on the already beleaguered South Vietnamese government and society.

To limit the risk of major escalation but still increase pressure on Hanoi, U.S. leaders decided to focus on North Vietnamese forces operating in Laos, especially along the Ho Chi Minh Trail. By 1964, the 600-mile-long trail had become a major transit route for Communist troops and material heading for South Vietnam. Close to 5,000 North Vietnamese and Pathet Lao troops defended the trail that included bridges, way stations, and primary and secondary roadways. Porters carrying backpacks filled with supplies and pushing bicycles loaded down with hundreds of pounds of explosives, ammunition, and weapons pressed forward over

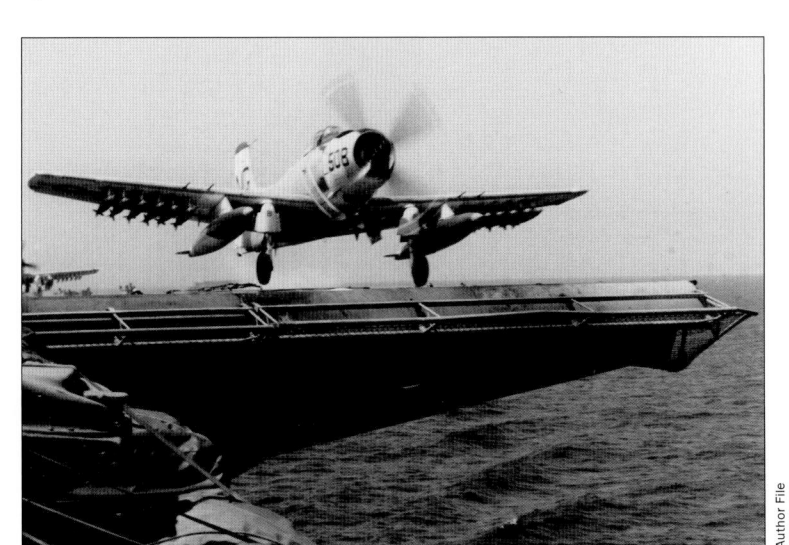

An armed A-1 Skyraider launches from aircraft carrier *Ranger* (CVA 61). The great fuel and armament capabilities of the propeller-driven planes made them valuable assets in search and rescue missions.

passageways hacked from the jungle. The porters were mountain tribesmen involuntarily pressed into duty and Communist troops. Fighting disease, starvation, physical exhaustion, and torrential monsoons that often swept in from the South China Sea, the trail porters delivered their precious cargos to Communist forces in South Vietnam—or perished in the effort.

On 17 May 1964, the JCS directed Admiral Felt to initiate low-level "reconnaissance/show of force" flights by Air Force planes based in South Vietnam and Navy planes from aircraft carrier *Kitty Hawk*

57

continued on page 60

Escape from Laos

ONE OF THE MOST MEMORABLE episodes during the early days in the Southeast Asian war was the shootdown and escape from Communist captivity in Laos of Navy Lieutenant Charles F. Klusmann.

The young officer was assigned to Light Photographic Squadron 63 on board aircraft carrier *Kitty Hawk*, deployed to the South China Sea in June of 1964 as part of Operation Yankee Team. The operation's objective was twofold: demonstrate U.S. resolve to oppose Communist actions in Laos by a military show of force and gather low-level intelligence on North Vietnamese forces operating in that mountainous, jungled country. Between 21 May and 9 June 1964, Navy carrier and Air Force land-based reconnaissance planes completed 130 flights over the Plain of Jars and the southern panhandle of Laos.

On 6 June 1964, *Kitty Hawk* launched Lieutenant Klusmann's RF-8A photorecon-naissance plane for one more mission, this one over an area of central Laos controlled by Laotian Communists—the Pathet Lao. The Americans nicknamed the area "lead alley" because there were so many antiaircraft weapons positioned there. While making a low-level pass over one site, Klusmann's plane was hit by fire from a 37-millimeter antiaircraft gun and soon became uncontrollable. The naval aviator ejected from his crippled plane and para-chuted to the ground, all the while under enemy fire. He injured his knee on landing but managed to radio his compatriots for help. Rescue planes soon arrived on the scene but because of heavy Communist ground fire could not retrieve the downed flyer.

Pathet Lao troops swarmed around the pilot, restrained him, and marched him off to internment. At an isolated jungle camp, his captors physically and psychologically abused him, denied him adequate food, and compelled him to sign a paper attacking U.S. policy in Asia. After some time, the Pathet Lao moved Klusmann to another location where pro-American Laotian and Thai soldiers were being held. With the help of fellow prisoners, the Navy lieutenant tried but failed to dig a hole under the wall of their hut. Since the guards didn't discover this attempt at escape, however, the men tried again.

Almost three months after his capture, Klusmann and five other prison-ers silently slipped out of the camp and into the jungle before the Communist guards raised the alarm. Three of the men went in one direction to an unknown fate. Looking for food, a fourth escapee unwisely entered a village that happened to be filled with Pathet Lao troops and probably did not survive this encounter with the agitated enemy. Three days after their flight from the Communist prison camp, the American lieutenant and his last companion stag-gered into friendly lines.

Lieutenant Klusmann was one of only a few American aviators to escape from captivity in Laos for the remainder of the long war in Southeast Asia. Because of the loss of "face" with Klusmann's successful escape and evasion, the Communists in Laos came down especially hard on American avia-tors who had the misfortune to fall into their hands in later years. ⚓

Laotian Panhandle

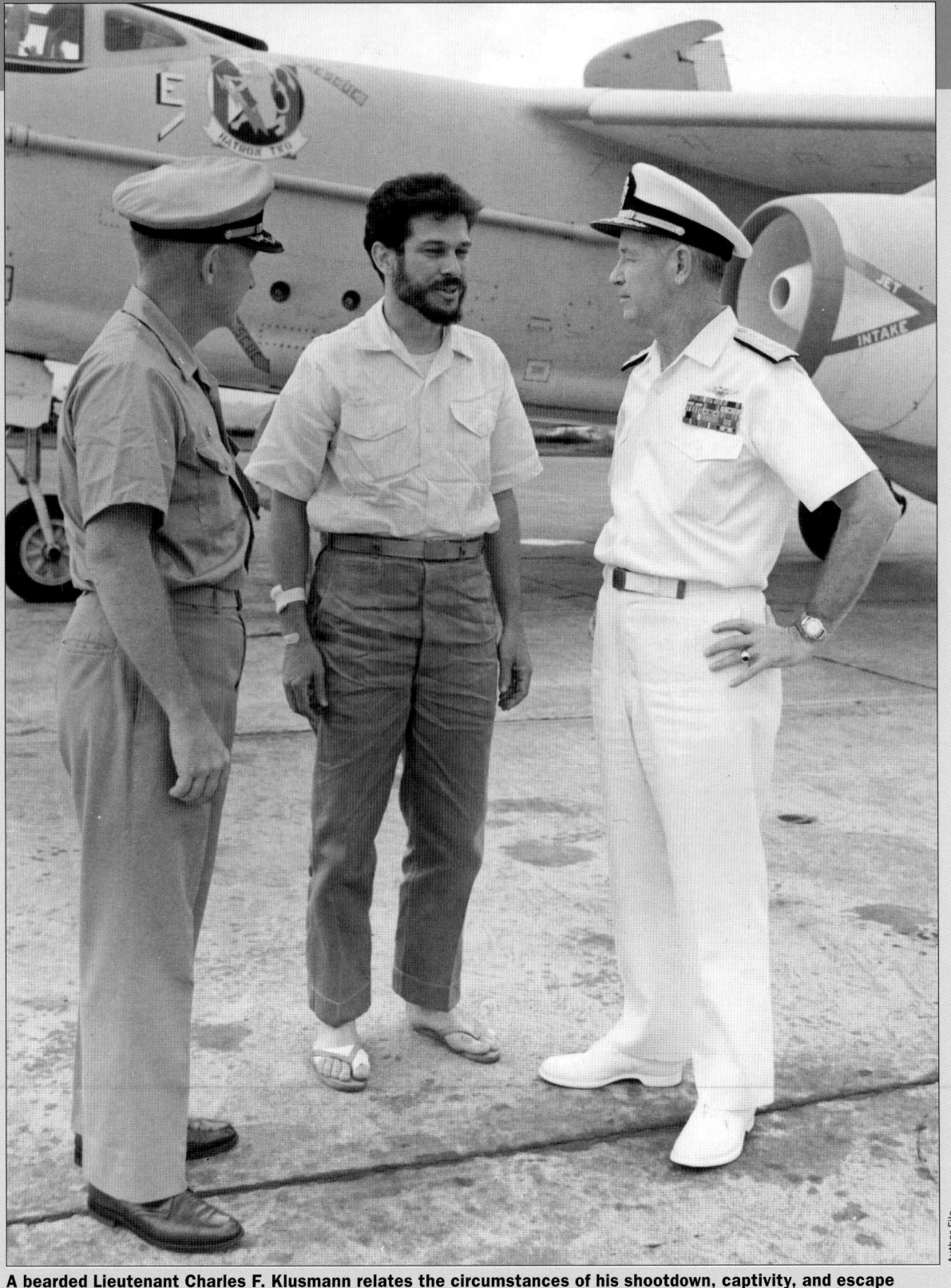

A bearded Lieutenant Charles F. Klusmann relates the circumstances of his shootdown, captivity, and escape to Admiral Ulysses S. Grant Sharp, Commander in Chief, Pacific, left, and Vice Admiral Roy L. Johnson, Commander Seventh Fleet, September 1964.

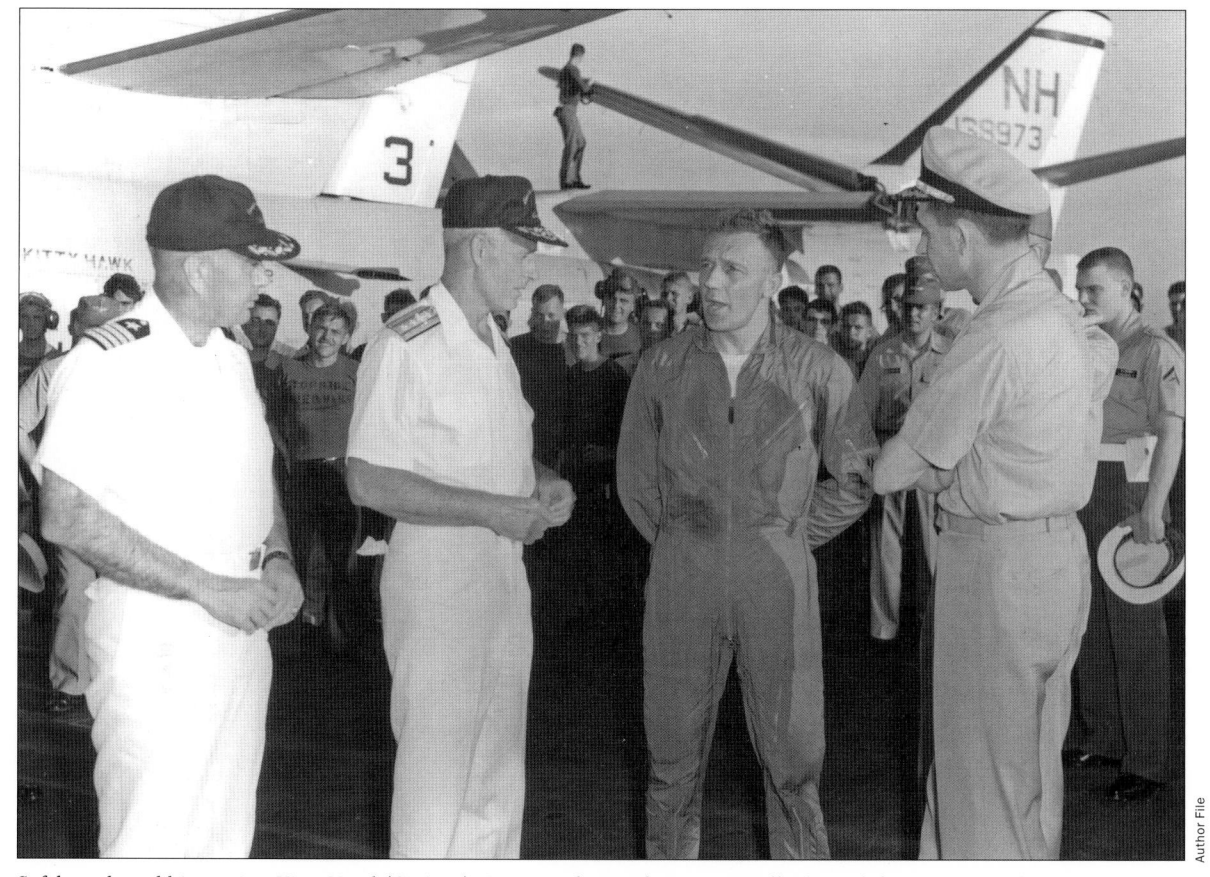

Safely on board his carrier, *Kitty Hawk* (CVA 63), Commander Doyle W. Lynn tells the task force commander, Rear Admiral William F. Bringle, second from left, and other attentive listeners how he survived his shootdown and recovery.

(CVA 63) positioned at soon-to-be famous Yankee Station in the South China Sea. In Operation Yankee Team, the American air units photographed Communist military activity in the Plain of Jars area and along the infiltration routes through the "panhandle" of southern Laos.

The Communist reaction was not long in coming. On 6 June, antiaircraft fire downed an RF-8A Crusader reconnaissance plane piloted by Lieutenant Charles F. Klusmann of *Kitty Hawk*'s Light Photographic Squadron 63. In response to the shootdown, Secretary of Defense Robert S. McNamara ordered that subsequent reconnaissance missions be escorted by fighter aircraft and authorized them to retaliate against hostile antiaircraft sites. On 7 June, three *Kitty Hawk* F-8D Crusaders escorting a photoreconnaissance plane carried out just such an attack on an antiaircraft position in the Plain of Jars, but enemy gunners damaged the jet flown by

Commander Doyle W. Lynn of Fighter Squadron 111, forcing him to eject and parachute to earth. He landed safely in the jungle south of Xieng Khouang in central Laos and hunkered down for the night.

Better prepared than they had been after Klusmann's shootdown, American search and rescue (SAR) coordinators immediately dispatched to the scene four propeller-driven A-1H Skyraiders that had been in a standby pattern over Danang, South Vietnam. Task Force 77 sent another four Crusaders and an A-3B Skywarrior, the latter plane to facilitate communications and pick up Lynn's distress signals. Homing in on these electronic emissions and guided further by the pilot's radio directions and flares, the rescuers located him the next morning. An H-34 Sea Horse helicopter sped to the scene and tried to lower its rescue cable through the forest canopy but found the trees there too tall. Finally, discovering a small clearing nearby, the SAR team directed Lynn

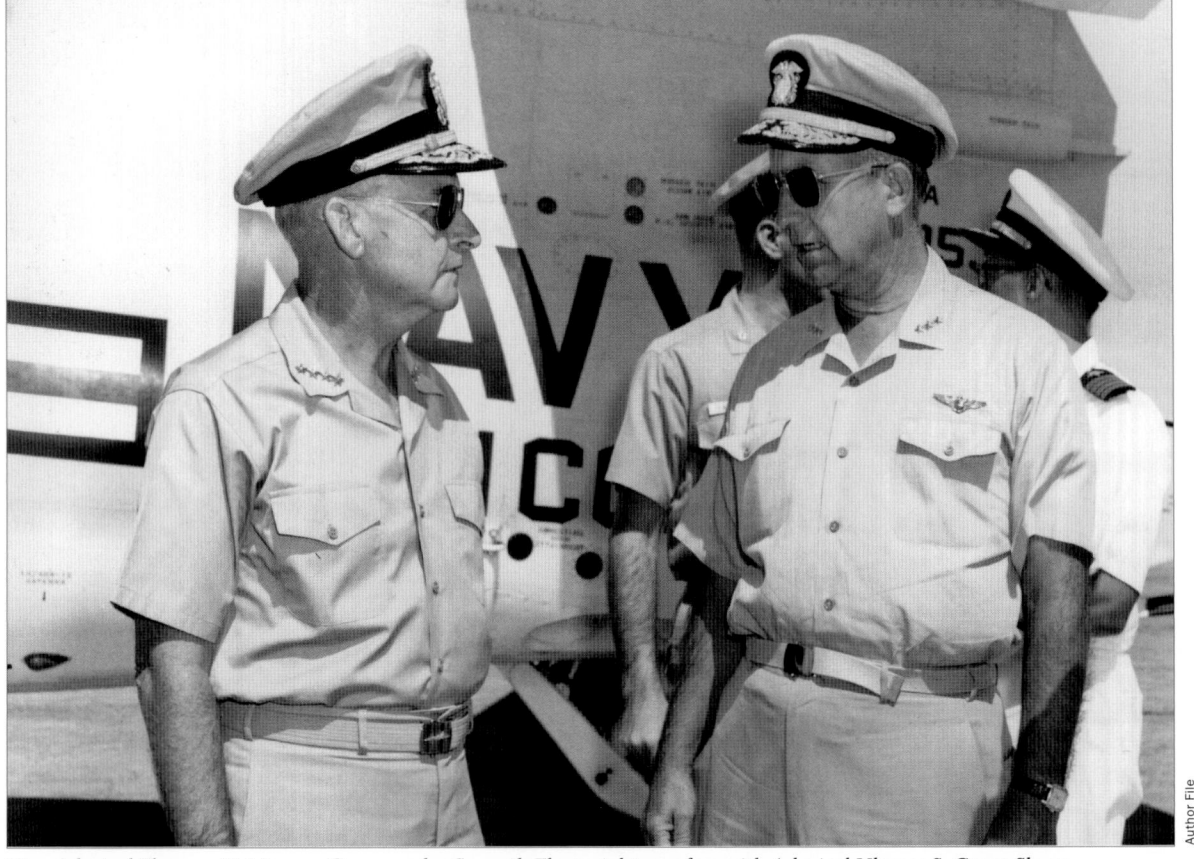

Vice Admiral Thomas H. Moorer, Commander Seventh Fleet, right, confers with Admiral Ulysses S. Grant Sharp, Commander in Chief, U.S. Pacific Fleet, in early 1964.

there, swooped down to retrieve him, and whisked the tired but grateful naval aviator to safety. Enraged by Klusmann's escape and Lynn's aerial rescue, however, the Pathet Lao guerrillas established such tight and brutal control over their prisoners that only a few other men made it out of the Laotian jungle alive in later years.

These early operations in Laos revealed what would become the norm during the Vietnam War: civilian leaders in Washington orchestrating military operations in faraway Southeast Asia. By using the advanced communications equipment of the Pentagon's National Military Command Center, developed to manage America's nuclear readiness posture, Secretary of Defense McNamara could issue specific operational orders to commanders in the field. Admiral Thomas H. Moorer, Commander Seventh Fleet, complained privately to the Chief of Naval Operations, Admiral David L. McDonald:

"[O]ur total capability has not been utilized and . . . we have been restricted as to the number of sorties, have been directed as to the specific type camera to use and have had late changes in target assignments." For instance, after Lynn's loss, McNamara criticized naval commanders for how they positioned aircraft for the mission and how they armed the planes.

Frustrated by the loss of the two jets, Washington ordered future reconnaissance missions to be conducted from above 10,000 feet, well out of range of enemy antiaircraft guns. The JCS also insisted on prior approval of operation plans that would stipulate the purpose, duration, aircraft involved, tactical formation, altitude, and route to the target for each mission. This cautious application of force considerably reduced not only the risk to pilots and aircraft during the rest of 1964, but also the value of the intelligence gained, and it certainly did not send the desired signal of menace to the Hanoi regime. ⚓

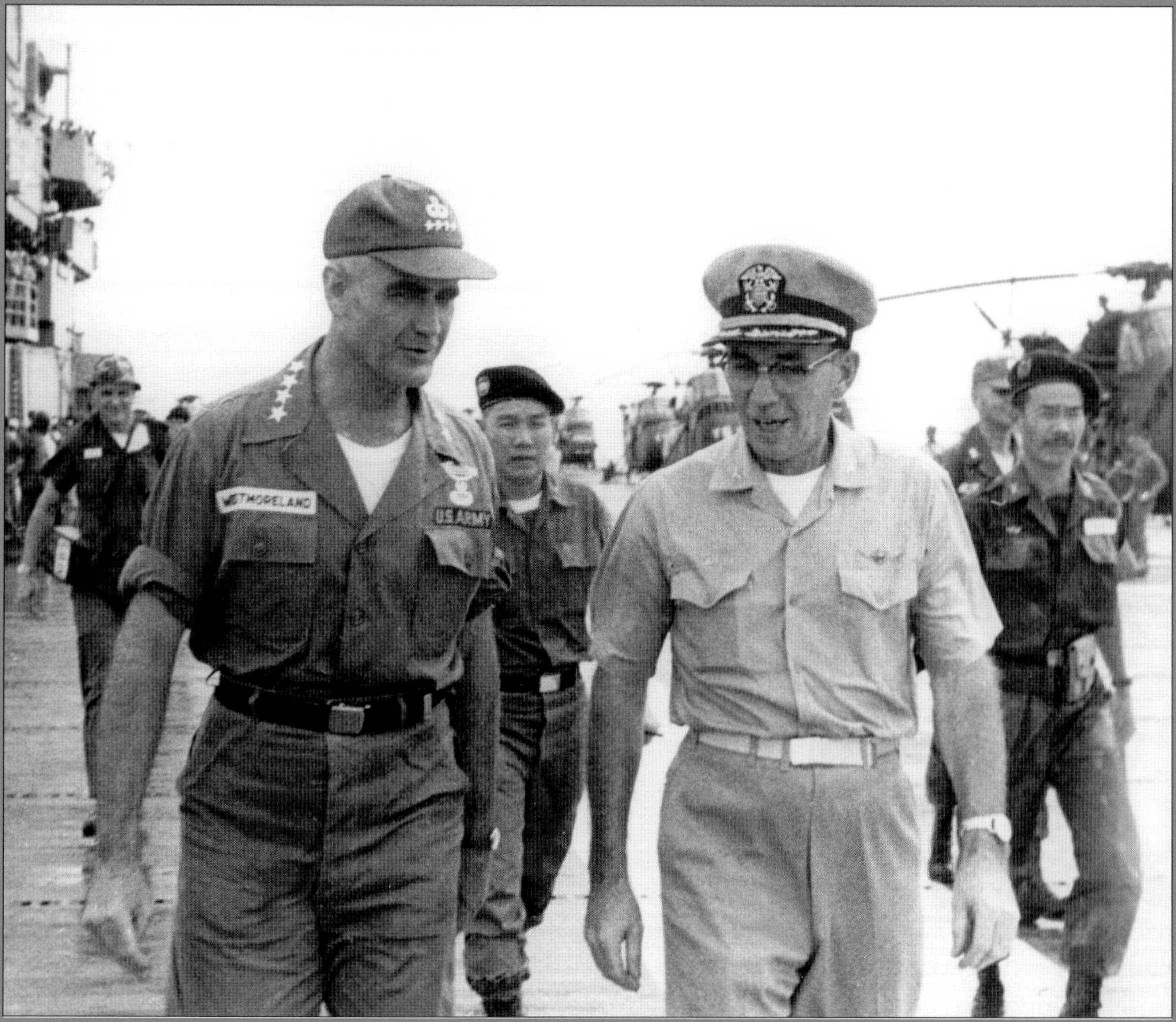

General William C. Westmoreland, Commander U.S. Military Assistance Command, Vietnam, left, listens to Captain Paul J. Knapp, commanding officer of amphibious assault ship *Princeton* (LPH 5), during a visit to the warship off South Vietnam.

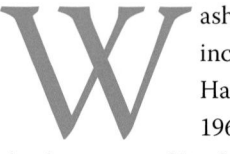

Washington also decided to increase military pressure on Hanoi from the sea. In January 1964, Admiral Moorer authorized the destroyers of his fleet's Desoto Patrol to conduct "all-source intelligence" collection operations closer to the littoral of North Vietnam than ever before.

Since the inauguration of the Desoto Patrol in 1962, U.S. naval vessels had been instructed to approach no closer than 12 nautical miles to China, North Korea, and North Vietnam, a distance generally recognized as the extent of these nations' sovereignty. Early in 1964, however, the State Department ruled that since Hanoi had made no official pronouncement regarding North Vietnam's territorial waters, the U.S. government considered the earlier French three-mile limit to remain in effect.

Moorer lifted the previous injunction against U.S. warships steaming closer than 20 miles to North Vietnam and other Asian Communist countries. The Seventh Fleet commander enabled his destroyer commanders to operate as close as four miles from coastal islands of the DRV. He also agreed to provide General Paul D. Harkins, Commander U.S. Military Assistance Command, Vietnam (COMUSMACV), in Saigon with intelligence that would facilitate raiding and sabotage operations by South Vietnamese commandos on the North Vietnamese coast as part of Operation 34 Alpha (34A). For eleven days during February and March of 1964, U.S. destroyer *John R. Craig* (DD 885) moved along the DRV and PRC coastlines in the Gulf of Tonkin gathering intelligence. Moorer scheduled another patrol for late July.

In the meantime, the maritime operations of the 34A program suffered numerous setbacks. The Communists defeated or frustrated one South Vietnamese sabotage mission after another. A prime factor in these failed operations was the lack of good intelligence on the enemy. General William C. Westmoreland, Harkins' successor, asked the Navy to provide him with better intelligence on North

Vietnamese naval vessels, ground forces, and radar sites along the coast. He was particularly interested in enemy activity around the islands of Hon Me, Hon Nieu, and Hon Matt where the South Vietnamese intended to operate at the end of July. The new CINCPAC, Admiral Ulysses S. Grant Sharp, who had moved up from command of the Pacific Fleet, called for a Desoto Patrol mission with the "primary purpose of determining DRV coastal patrol activity."

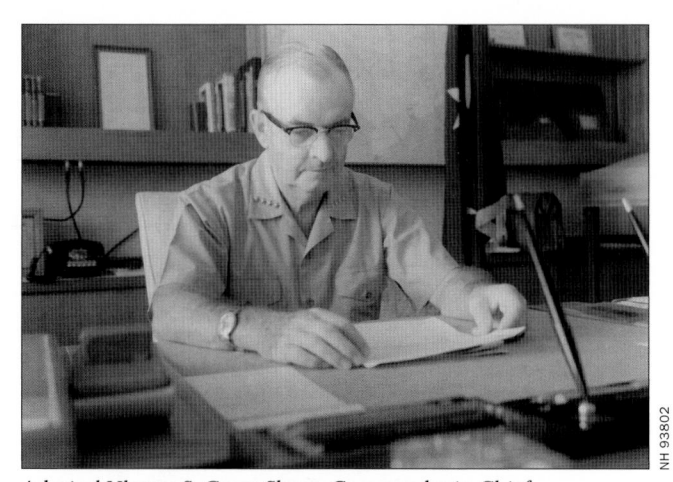

Admiral Ulysses S. Grant Sharp, Commander in Chief, Pacific, in his Pearl Harbor headquarters.

Concerned that North Vietnamese defenses had become too robust for commando raids ashore to succeed, McNamara and military leaders directing the 34A maritime operations opted instead for bombardment missions from the sea. At the end of July, South Vietnamese-crewed *Nasty*-class PTFs followed this new approach when they shelled a gun emplacement, a communications tower, and related buildings on Hon Me and Hon Nieu.

As the four PTFs returned to their base at Danang from that mission on the morning of 31 July, they passed by *Maddox* (DD 731), a *Sumner*-class destroyer, taking on fuel from a Navy oiler east of the Demilitarized Zone between North and South Vietnam. The warship, with mission commander Captain John J. Herrick on board, then steamed

63

continued on page 66

34 Alpha Maritime Operations

TO CONVINCE THE HANOI GOVERNMENT that its sponsorship of the insurgency in South Vietnam could be costly, in the early 1960s U.S. leaders pressed for clandestine sabotage operations against North Vietnam. Admiral Harry D. Felt, Commander in Chief, Pacific Command, called for striking the enemy close to home in order to upset "some Communist apple carts." Felt argued that if such operations resulted in the destruction of railroads, bridges, power plants and other vulnerable targets, the Communists might be restrained from carrying out bombings, assassinations, and like actions in the South. Chief of Naval Operations Admiral George W. Anderson agreed that a "campaign of harassment" against North Vietnam could pay dividends for U.S. policies in Southeast Asia.

The first effort launched by the U.S. government, a CIA program employing motorized junks and other craft was a bust. Successfully operating relatively small, slow, and lightly armed vessels in the often-rough waters off North Vietnam proved too difficult. Directing maritime operations was not a strength of the CIA.

Hence, in 1962 the Defense Department instructed the Navy to reactivate two gasoline-powered motor torpedo boats, mothballed in Philadelphia, for potential operations in Southeast Asia. Secretary of Defense Robert S. McNamara also tasked the Navy with purchasing from Norway two *Nasty*-class fast patrol boats. All the boats were classified as fast patrol boats or PTFs.

As the boats were being readied, Admiral Felt had his staff draw up a plan for clandestine operations against North Vietnam that they identified as CINCPAC Operation Plan 34. The MACV staff in Saigon developed their own plan for operations against North Vietnam, and because they borrowed liberally from the CINCPAC document, they labeled it Operation Plan 34 Alpha. Convinced by the turmoil in South Vietnam following Ngo Dinh Diem's

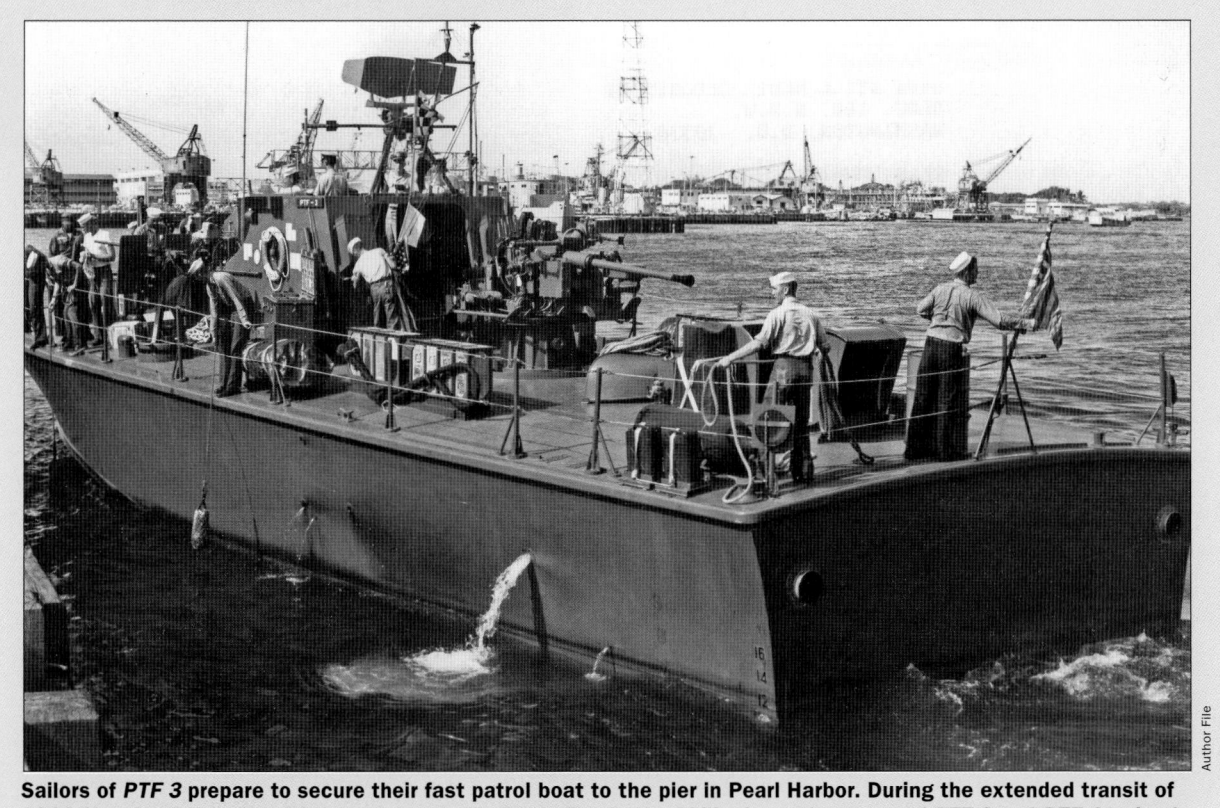

Sailors of *PTF 3* prepare to secure their fast patrol boat to the pier in Pearl Harbor. During the extended transit of 1963 from Norfolk to San Diego and eventually Subic Bay in the Philippines, the crews of *PTF 3* and *PTF 4* trained and prepared their boats for special operations in Southeast Asia.

assassination that some new action was needed to restrain Hanoi, on 16 January 1964 President Lyndon Johnson approved the start of 34A.

Eight days later, MACV established the Special Operations Group (later Studies and Observations Group)—MACSOG—to run the 34A program, even its maritime aspects. Directly responsible for those maritime operations was the U.S. Naval Advisory Detachment deployed to Danang. The naval contingent in Danang consisted of Navy officers and men who maintained and repaired the PTFs, and other Sailors and Marines who trained the Vietnamese commandos and boat crews that would operate in North Vietnam. The enemy knew through their intelligence sources of this American involvement in the 34A program.

Plagued by delays in transportation of the boats to South Vietnam (due to stays of varying length in Norfolk, San Diego, Pearl Harbor, and Subic Bay), mechanical problems, and refitting of armament (removal of the forward 40-millimeter guns from the *Nastys* and addition of 81-millimeter mortars and 50-caliber machine guns), the first operation finally kicked off from Danang in mid February.

On 16 February, the PTF force landed South Vietnamese commandos on the coast of North Vietnam with the object of destroying Swatow patrol craft at Quang Khe. The clandestine sabotage operation failed to accomplish this and later missions in the spring, prompting the U.S. Ambassador to the Republic of Vietnam, Henry Cabot Lodge, to note that the 34A actions "might be good training but were certainly having no effect on Hanoi." The 34A maritime force registered modest success in June when saboteurs destroyed a storage building and a bridge in southern North Vietnam. On 1 July, two PTFs landed commandos who leveled a reservoir pump house with recoilless rifle fire. The team had to fight its way back to the beach, losing two men, but aided by 40-millimeter and 20-millimeter fire from the PTFs managed to re-embark for the return trip to Danang.

Faced with increasing enemy resistance and coastal defenses, MACSOG leaders decided that future 34A operations should emphasize quick-in, quick-out coastal bombardments by the PTFs. The first of these missions took place on the night of 30–31 July when four PTFs shelled military buildings on the islands of Hon Me and Hon Nieu. North

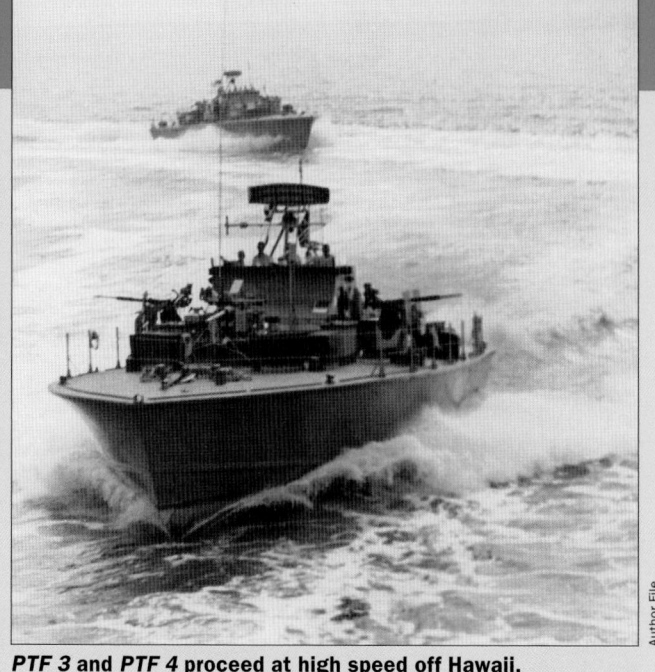

PTF 3 and **PTF 4** proceed at high speed off Hawaii.

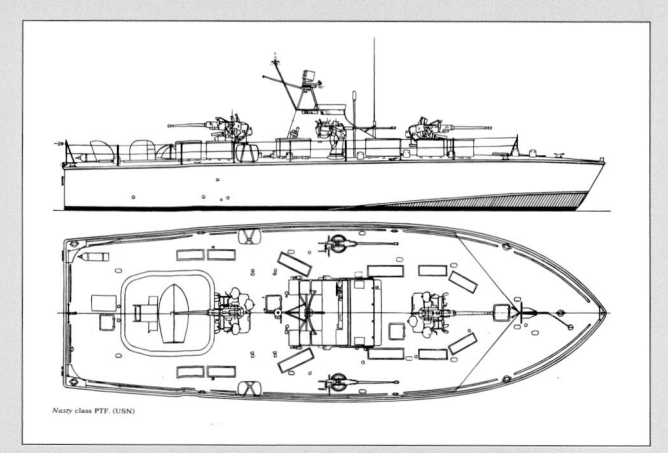

PTF diagram, from Norman Friedman, *U.S. Small Combatants: An Illustrated Design History* (Naval Institute Press, 1987).

Vietnamese shore fire wounded four of the South Vietnamese raiders, but enemy patrol boats could not catch up with the fast PTFs as they retired to Danang.

It was hardly surprising then that North Vietnamese naval vessels attacked U.S. destroyer *Maddox* when that ship steamed past this hornet's nest around Hon Me and Hon Nieu on 2 August, touching off the seminal Tonkin Gulf incident of 1964. The 34A maritime operation would continue for years afterward to harass the enemy on the coast of North Vietnam, with limited success. ⚓

65

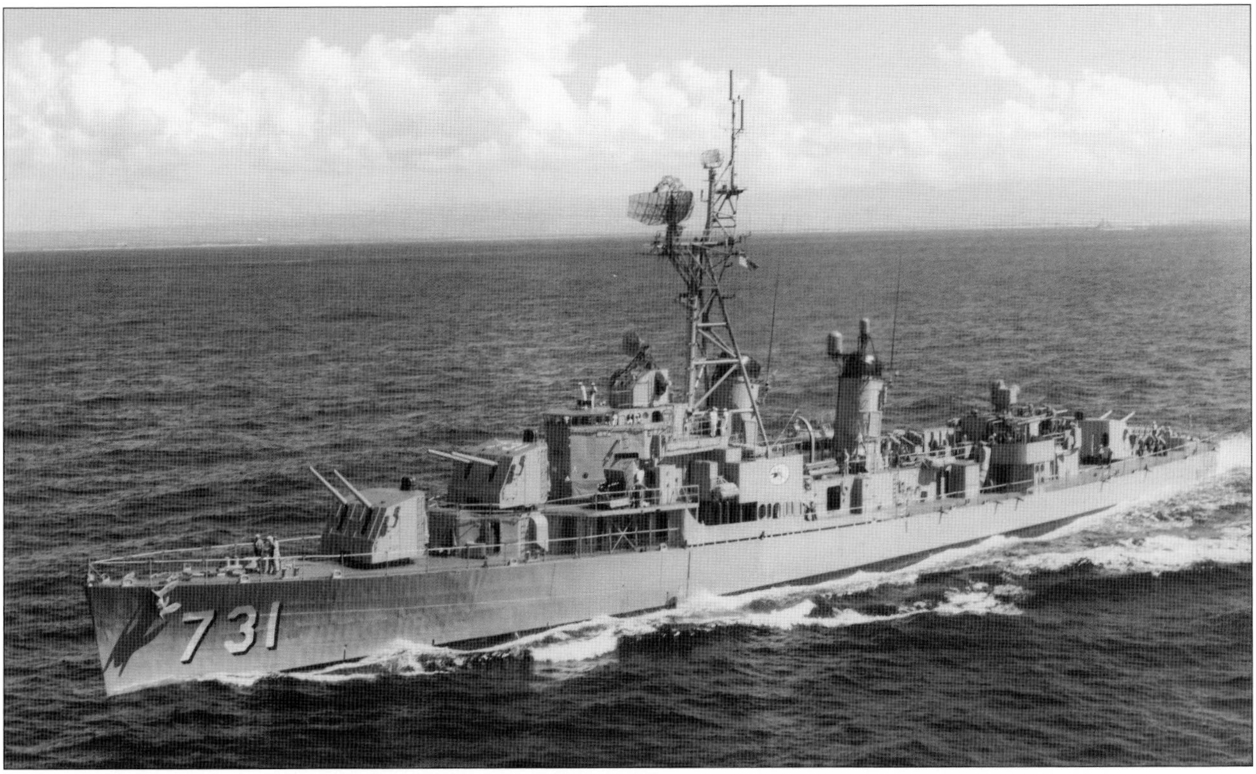

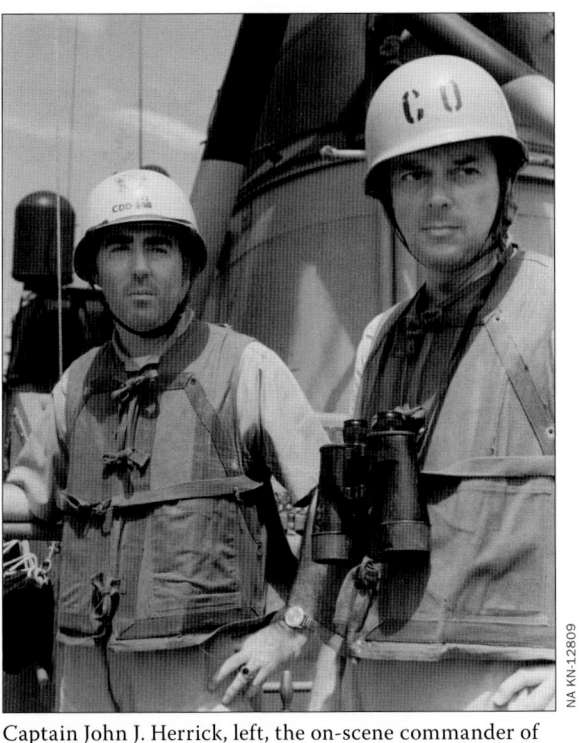

Destroyer *Maddox* (DD 731) three months prior to her rendezvous with destiny in the Gulf of Tonkin.

Author File

Captain John J. Herrick, left, the on-scene commander of the Desoto Patrol in the Gulf of Tonkin during late July and early August 1964, and Commander Herbert L. Ogier, commanding officer of *Maddox*.

NA KN-12809

along a predesignated track off the coast of North Vietnam gathering photographic, electronic, hydrographic, and other intelligence. In the evening on 1 August, *Maddox* reached a position five miles southeast of Hon Vat, a small islet close to Hon Me. This was the closest point the destroyer came to North Vietnamese territory during the entire mission. The North Vietnamese monitored the U.S. intelligence-gathering patrol but took no action against it.

In the early morning hours of 2 August 1964, however, a communications-interception team operating on board *Maddox* picked up a transmission from North Vietnamese naval headquarters directing fleet units to prepare for battle and ordering the concentration of forces near Hon Me. Determined not to abort the mission, however, the U.S. naval command ordered Herrick to continue his patrol. Beginning at 1500 (H time, or Saigon time), as *Maddox* headed away from the coast in a northeasterly and then southeasterly direction, her surface-search radar picked up high-speed contacts attempting to close with the destroyer. At 1530, the

ship's commanding officer, Commander Herbert L. Ogier, sounded general quarters, and soon afterward Captain Herrick alerted U.S. naval headquarters of an impending attack and requested air support.

By 1600, three Soviet-made North Vietnamese P-4 motor torpedo boats, moving at 50-knot speeds, had closed to 9,800 yards off the destroyer's starboard quarter. While continuing on their hostile approach, the P-4s made no attempt with radio, signal flags, lights, flares, or other means to communicate their intent to the American ship. When three warning shots from one of the warship's weapons failed to deter the North Vietnamese, at 1608 *Maddox* opened fire in earnest with her 5-inch and 3-inch guns. The enemy boats turned to port, launched torpedoes, fired their 14.5 millimeter guns, and withdrew astern of the destroyer. The North Vietnamese attackers failed to put a torpedo into the

destroyer, but one round from a deck gun punctured the ship's superstructure.

Gunfire from *Maddox* shot up one of the boats, killing its commander, and soon afterward four *Ticonderoga* (CVA 14) F-8 Crusaders, one of them piloted by Commander James B. Stockdale, a future vice admiral and Medal of Honor recipient, arrived overhead. The jets raked the boats with 5-inch Zuni rockets and 20-millimeter cannon fire, leaving one dead in the water and burning from the stern. Although badly damaged, the P-4s managed to make it back to the North Vietnamese coast. *Maddox* retired to the mouth of the Gulf of Tonkin and a rendezvous with the *Forrest Sherman*-class destroyer *Turner Joy* (DD 951).

President Johnson announced that the destroyer patrol would resume and that the DRV would incur "grave consequences" if the Communists made

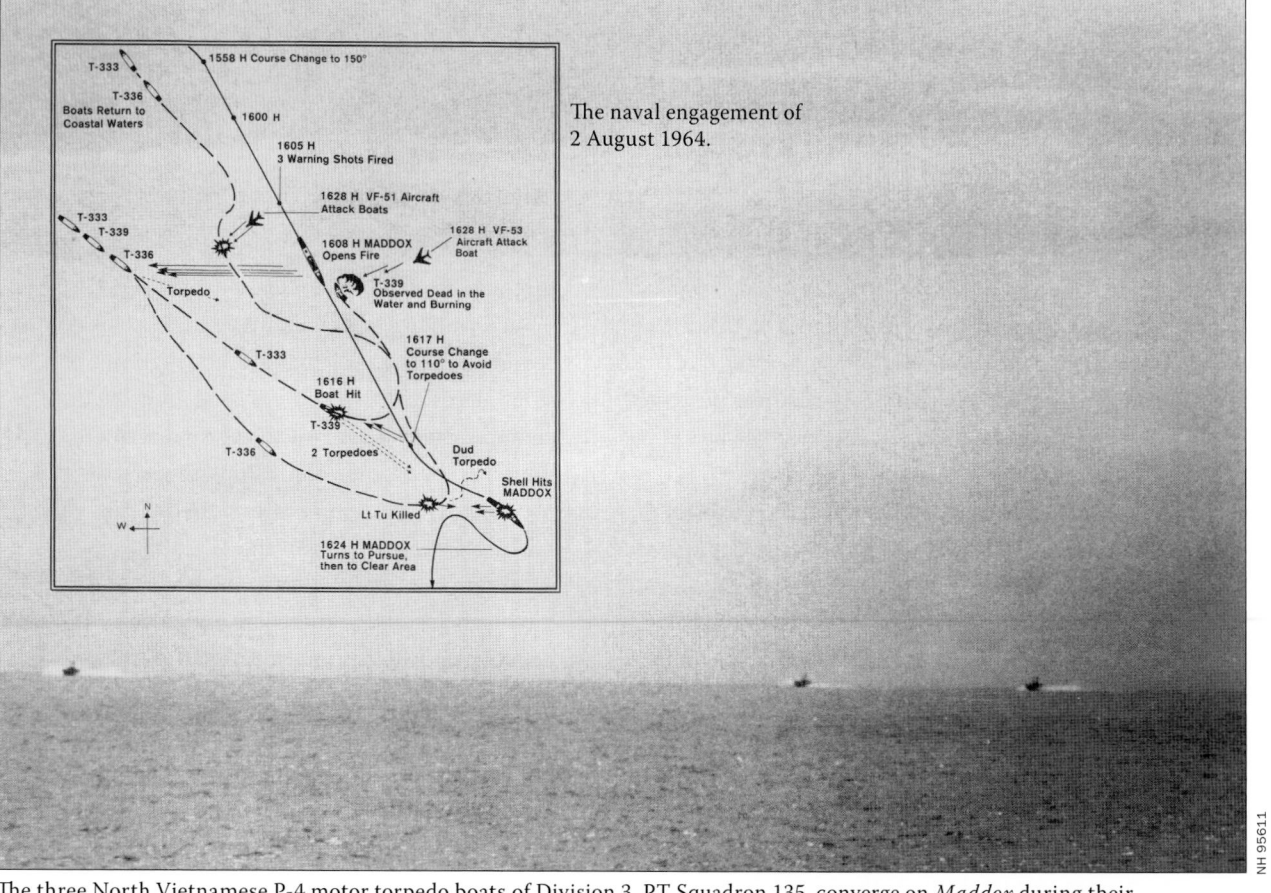

The naval engagement of 2 August 1964.

The three North Vietnamese P-4 motor torpedo boats of Division 3, PT Squadron 135, converge on *Maddox* during their attack on the American destroyer.

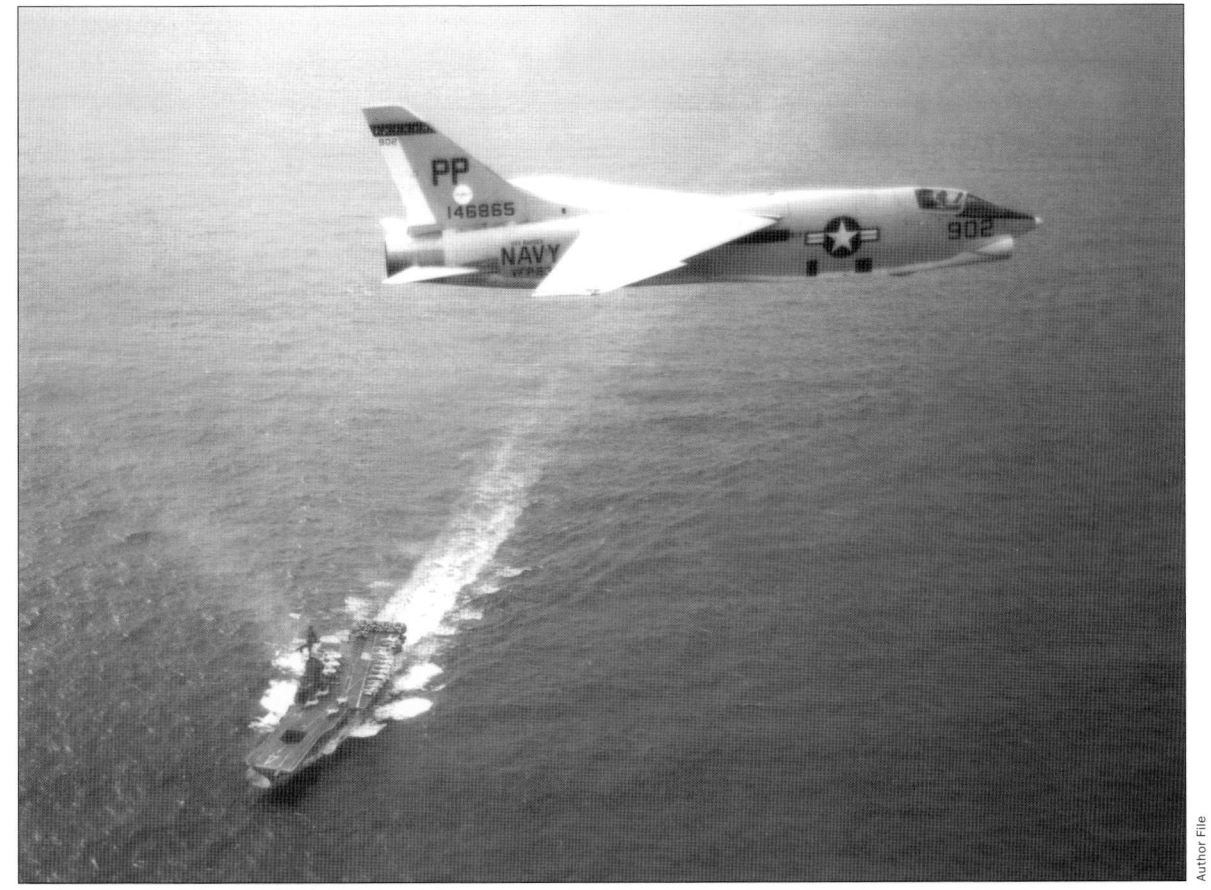

An RF-8A Crusader aerial reconnaissance plane flies over carrier *Ticonderoga* (CVA 14) in the Gulf of Tonkin.

another aggressive move against U.S. forces. Admiral Moorer, the Pacific Fleet commander, undeterred by the attack on *Maddox* and determined to "assert [the] right of freedom of the seas," a long-held tenet of U.S. foreign policy, ordered Herrick to continue the patrol off North Vietnam. *Maddox*, accompanied by *Turner Joy*, headed back into the gulf on 4 August.

Beginning at 2041 on the dark, overcast night of 4 August, radars on *Maddox* and *Turner Joy* picked up high-speed contacts to the northeast. Captain Herrick ordered the ships to move away from what he thought were surface vessels with hostile intent. At 2239, when one contact was tracked as close as 7,000 yards, Herrick directed *Turner Joy* to open fire. For the next two hours the U.S. ships, soon joined by aircraft, maneuvered to avoid what the Americans believed were enemy fast attack craft launching torpedoes against them. At the end of the confused nighttime episode, the destroyers reached the

entrance of the gulf and the safety of the fleet drawn up there.

U.S. military and civilian leaders began receiving reports of a North Vietnamese attack from the ships and from other sources soon after the first contacts. Herrick sent one message that questioned the accuracy of some of his ships' reports, but this information only temporarily slowed the decision-making process in Hawaii and Washington.

Additional information from Herrick and from intelligence stations in the Far East, however, convinced President Johnson and his chief civilian and military advisors that Hanoi's navy had again attacked American warships in international waters. The wealth of information available from national and naval intelligence sources and from naval operating forces then and for years afterward persuaded many objective observers that the North Vietnamese had attacked the two destroyers.

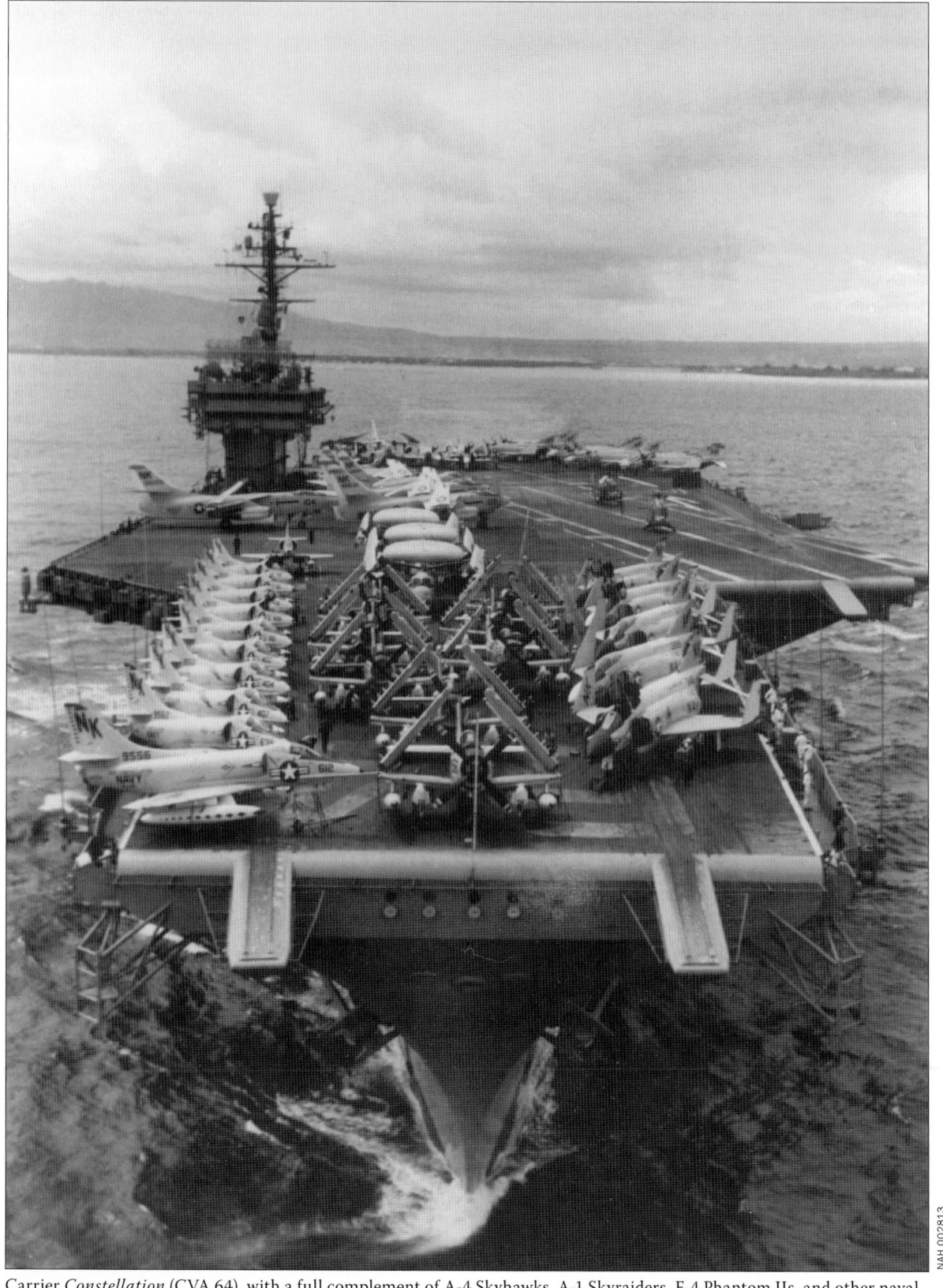

Carrier *Constellation* (CVA 64), with a full complement of A-4 Skyhawks, A-1 Skyraiders, F-4 Phantom IIs, and other naval aircraft, heads for combat action off North Vietnam.

NAH 002813

It is now virtually certain, however, that North Vietnamese naval vessels did not attack American destroyers on the night of 4 August 1964. The National Security Agency misinterpreted intercepted North Vietnamese radio transmissions suggesting an attack; key eyewitnesses on the ships and in aircraft overhead that night later changed their minds about spotting attacking craft; and the Navy's reports of the operation revealed that some of the information gathered was imprecise or contradictory. Moreover, the Vietnam War has been over for 30 years and no archival records or personal accounts have surfaced in Vietnam to refute Hanoi's unchanged assertion that its forces did not attack *Maddox* and *Turner Joy* that night.

Knowing that the Communists had indeed attacked *Maddox* on 2 August in broad daylight, however, and persuaded that a similar action had occurred two days later, President Johnson ordered U.S. forces to execute retaliatory air strikes—soon named Operation Pierce Arrow—against North Vietnam at 0800 local time on 5 August. With operational problems and little time to prepare for the mission, aircraft carriers *Ticonderoga* and *Constellation* could not launch their planes in time. Just after noon on 5 August, however, *Ticonderoga* launched F-8 Crusaders, A-4 Skyhawks, and a RF-8A photoreconnaissance plane that joined with A-1H Skyraiders already in the air. These units headed for the oil storage facility at Vinh. Other planes from *Ticonderoga* set a course for Quang Khe.

Less than an hour later, *Constellation* sent Carrier Air Wing 14 squadrons aloft. Separate groups of propeller-driven A-1 Skyraiders carrying huge loads of ordnance headed for their targets at Hon Gay and Lach Chao. Later *Constellation* launched Skyhawk and Phantom II jets that quickly caught up with the A-1s en route to their targets.

For the first time in the long Vietnam War, the Navy's carrier air arm projected its power ashore. A strike force of Crusaders, Skyhawks, and Skyraiders under Commander Stockdale roared across the coast near Ha Tinh and headed for Vinh. The carrier force flew among the hills that dotted the area to evade North Vietnamese radar and antiaircraft defenses.

In a well-planned maneuver, Commander Wesley L. McDonald's Attack Squadron (VA) 56 Skyhawks approached Vinh through a valley, while the dive-bombing A-1H "Spads" climbed for altitude before descending on the target. The Crusaders flew along the coast and then turned in toward Vinh at the river entrance to the city. No alarm was raised as the squadrons converged on the fuel tank farm there.

At 1330, the Crusaders roared over the red-tiled roofs of Vinh and let loose with their rockets and 20-millimeter guns against enemy antiaircraft positions, as did A-4 Skyhawks that emerged from the valley. Their way cleared of potential enemy opposition, the slower A-1H Skyraiders of VA-52 and other Skyhawks now dove on the 14 fuel tanks at the facility. Twenty-eight thousand pounds of bombs and Zuni rockets slammed into the target area. The fenced enclosure erupted in fire and smoke that rose thousands of feet in the air.

Minutes after this attack, the carrier force moved on to the nearby Ben Thuy naval base to sink or damage four North Vietnamese naval vessels. That same day, other *Ticonderoga* aircraft returned to Vinh to complete destruction of the tank farm and sank another pair of combatant craft at Ben Thuy.

The Crusaders attacking Quang Khe to the south also achieved surprise. The F-8s of Fighter Squadron (VF) 53, discovering enemy vessels at anchor or attempting to put to sea, holed five boats and sank another with their guns and rockets.

At 1540, *Constellation*'s VA-144 Skyhawks reached Hon Gay where they pounced on Swatow gunboats and other craft in the harbor. From shoreside positions and from the naval vessels, enemy antiaircraft gunners opened up against at the aerial intruders.

Lieutenant (jg) Everett Alvarez, piloting an A-4, made one pass over the target area and when he returned for another, North Vietnamese antiaircraft fire crippled his Skyhawk. Before his plane crashed, Alvarez ejected from the cockpit and parachuted safely to earth. His squadronmates radioed an Air Force HU-16 amphibian aircraft standing by on SAR alert. When he learned that Communist troops were closing on Alvarez's position, however, the on-scene commander called off the rescue attempt. The North

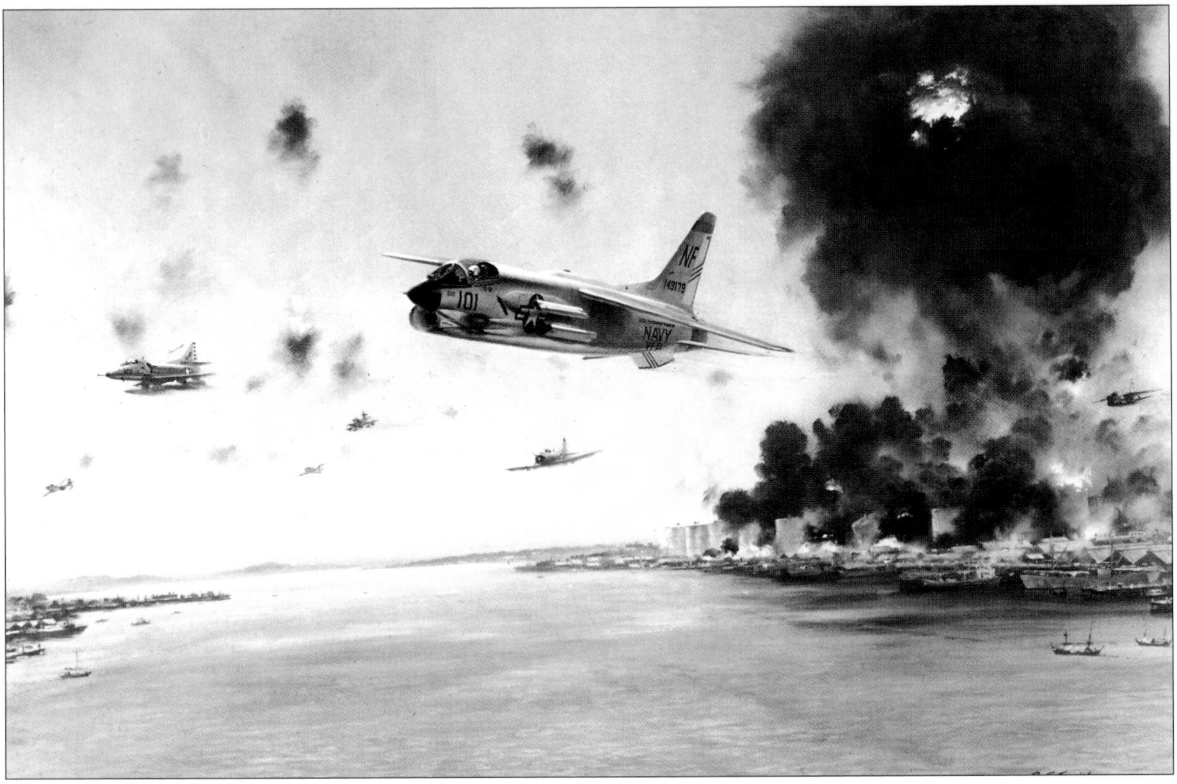

U.S. Naval Institute, Courtesy Sharlyn Marsh

Operation Pierce Arrow by R. G. Smith.

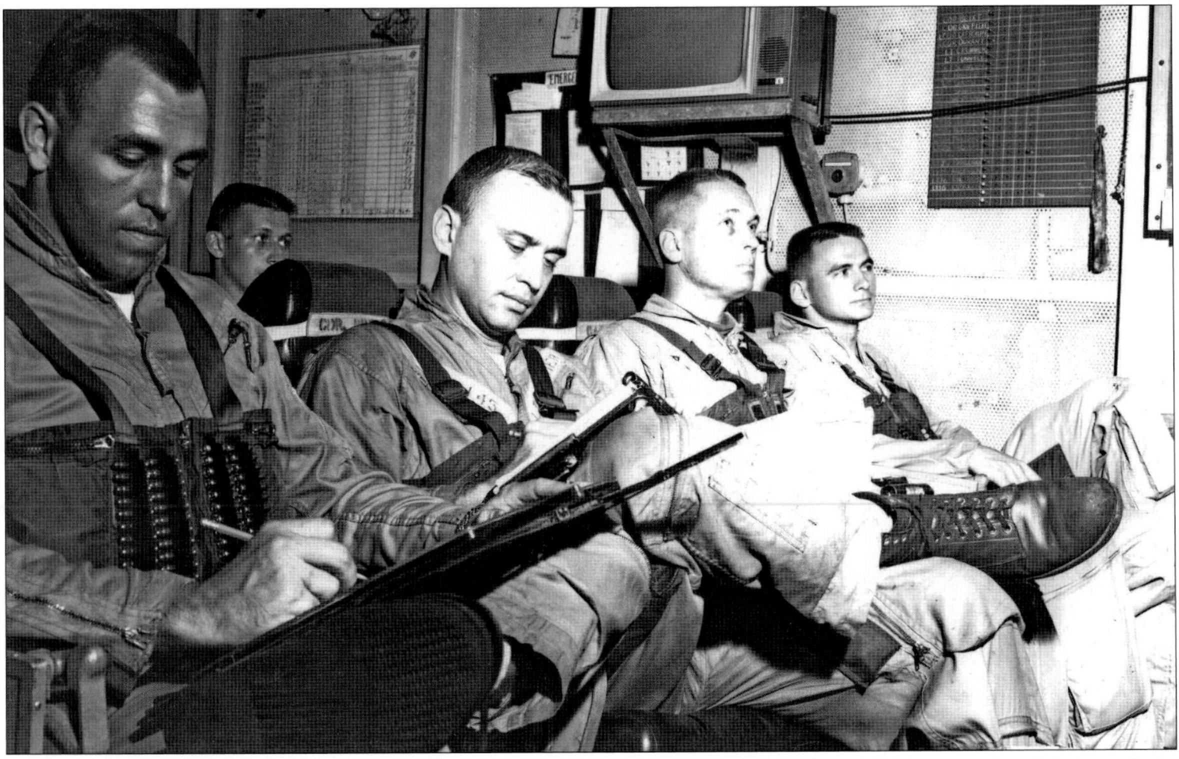

Author File

Lieutenant James S. Hardie, far right, and his squadronmates of *Constellation*'s Attack Squadron 145 get briefed about their mission in Operation Pierce Arrow.

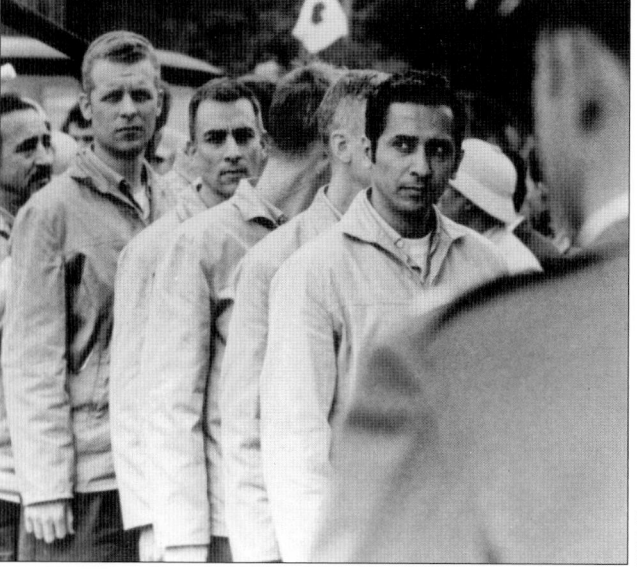

Lieutenant (jg) Everett Alvarez Jr., right, during his release from captivity in North Vietnam in 1973, eight years after he was shot down during the Pierce Arrow strike of 5 August 1964.

Vietnamese troops marched the American pilot off to a prison cell. Until his release from captivity in 1973, the dedicated naval aviator endured long years of isolation and torture at the hands of his cruel captors.

Meanwhile, the A-1 Skyraiders of VA-145 arrived at Hon Gay and immediately joined the hunt for enemy naval vessels. When the piston-driven planes departed the scene, they left behind a half-dozen shot-up and burning Swatows and other craft.

En route to the Lach Chao estuary, the Skyhawks and Skyraiders of Carrier Air Wing 14 spotted five North Vietnamese naval vessels near Hon Me island and immediately pushed over to attack them. The enemy fought back; antiaircraft fire from one of the boats severely damaged the A-1 flown by Lieutenant James S. Hardie. The determined officer continued his attack run, nursed his shot-up plane back to *Constellation*, and made a successful emergency landing on the carrier.

One of his shipmates was not so fortunate. Antiaircraft fire from one of the boats shot down the Skyraider piloted by Lieutenant (jg) Richard C. Sather. He was the first naval aviator to be killed in the Vietnam War. Not until 1985 did the Communists return his body to the United States.

Despite these losses to the strike formation, the Americans damaged all five enemy craft and left several dead in the water.

The Pierce Arrow retaliatory strike did serious damage to North Vietnamese naval forces. The 67 U.S. carrier aircraft that took part in the operation sank seven enemy naval vessels, severely damaged another ten, and put holes in all but three of the Swatow gunboats or PT boats in the North Vietnamese navy.

In addition to ordering the Pierce Arrow retaliation, the White House encouraged the United States Congress to take appropriate action. Convinced that North Vietnam had carried out a deliberate attack on American naval forces on 2 and 4 August, Congress approved a resolution proposed by the Johnson administration. On 7 August, the Senate, by a vote of 88 to 2, and the House of Representatives, in a unanimous vote, passed the Tonkin Gulf Resolution. This measure enabled Johnson to employ the U.S. armed forces in the defense of the Republic of Vietnam and the other noncommunist nations of Southeast Asia. In essence, it served as the legal basis for fighting the Vietnam War.

The Tonkin Gulf incidents, however, worried Johnson that events in Southeast Asia might be spiraling out of control. Hence, in spite of recommendations from Admiral Sharp and other military leaders that the United States maintain pressure on Hanoi, the administration lowered the military presence off North Vietnam. Washington postponed or cancelled most of the 34A maritime operations along the North Vietnamese coast for the rest of 1964.

The last Desoto Patrol in the Gulf of Tonkin, which involved a two-day cruise by destroyers *Morton* (DD 948) and *Richard E. Edwards* (DD 950) on 17 and 18 September, approached no closer than 20 miles to North Vietnam. The destroyers opened fire on high-speed contacts on the night of the 18th and reported having been attacked, but without conclusive proof, Washington questioned the validity of the report and cancelled further operations. Thus, from a military standpoint, the Tonkin Gulf incidents of August did not spark immediate escalation of the conflict in Southeast Asia. ⚓

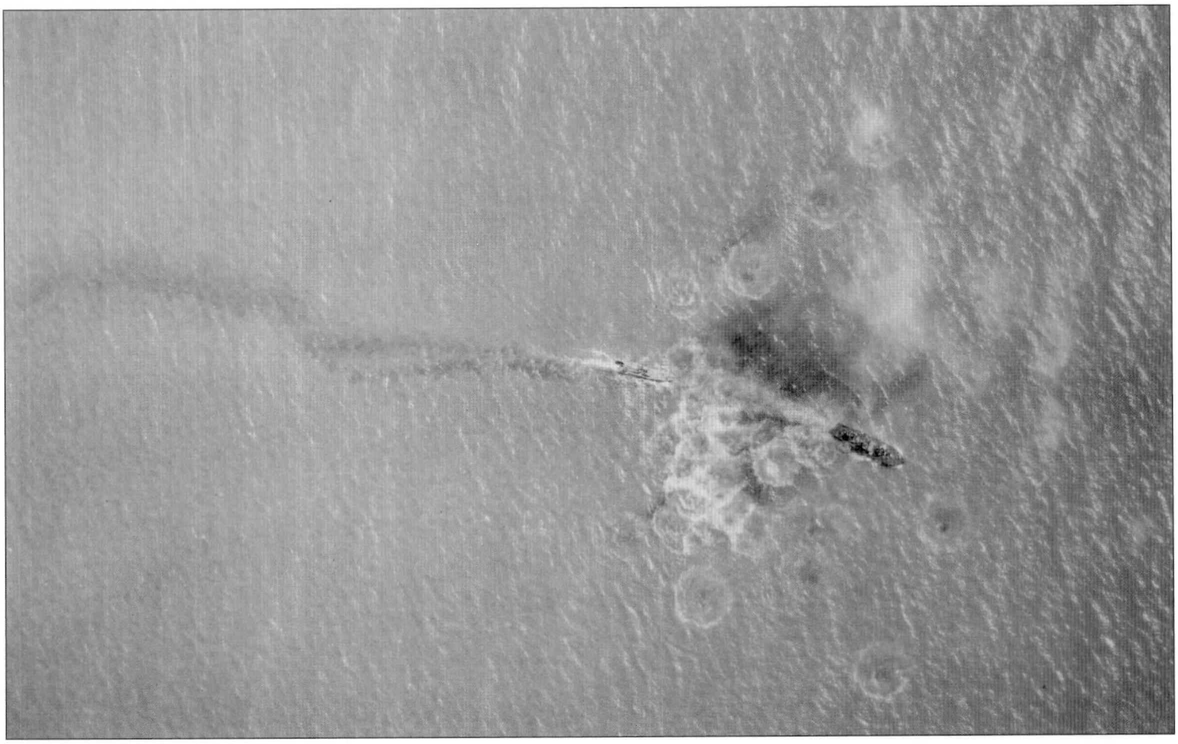

NH 95612

A Swatow and a trailing P-4 torpedo boat under attack by *Constellation* aircraft near the Lach Chao Estuary off North Vietnam on 5 August 1964.

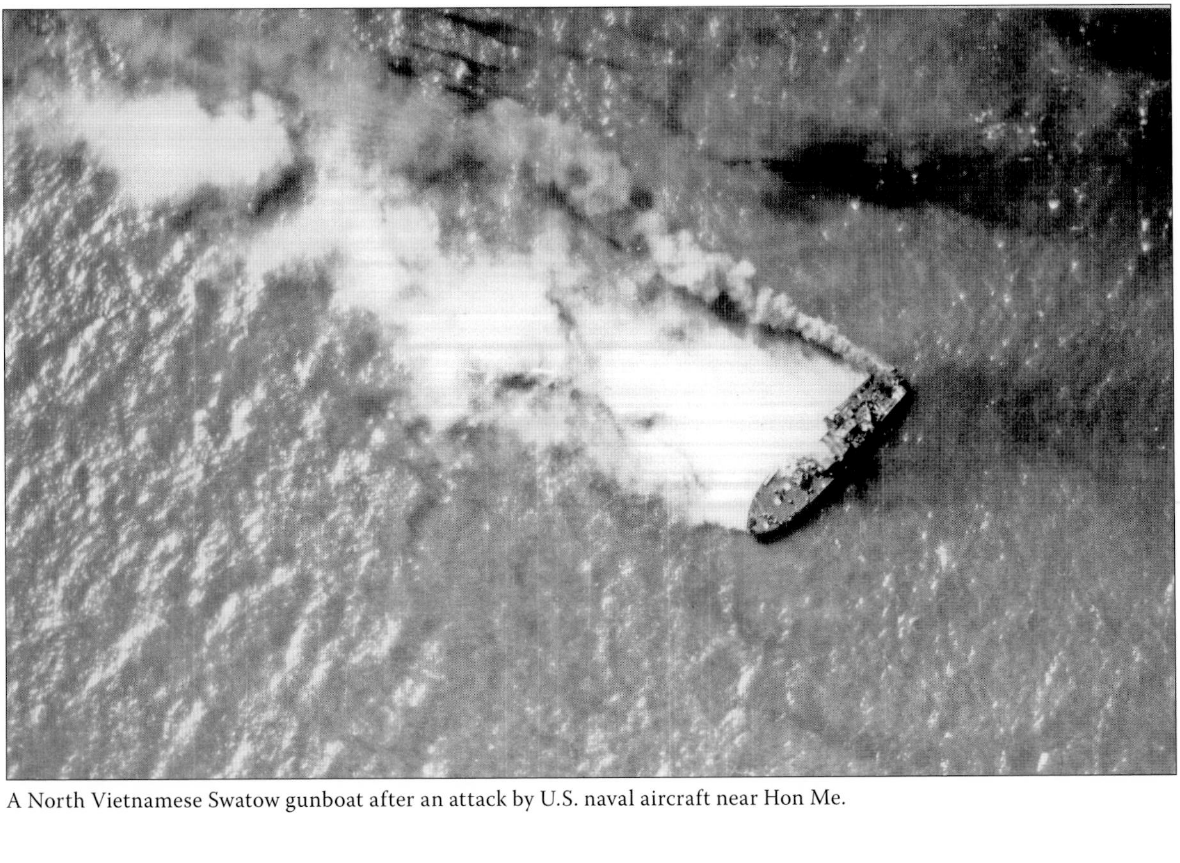

NH 95613

A North Vietnamese Swatow gunboat after an attack by U.S. naval aircraft near Hon Me.

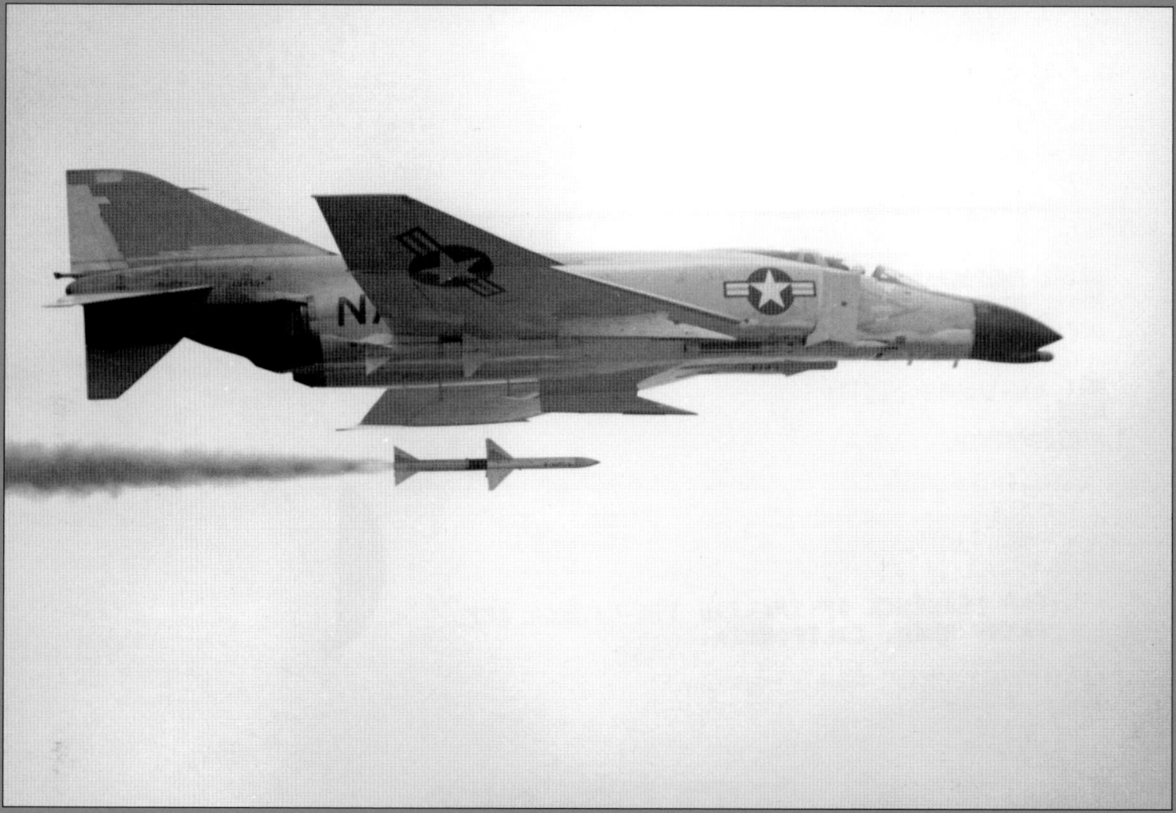

NA KN-10093

An F-4 Phantom II, based at Point Mugu Naval Air Station, California, fires a Sparrow III air-to-air missile in preparation for combat operations in Southeast Asia.

ohnson also drew back from actions in South Vietnam that might further inflame the region. On 1 November 1964, the day before the U.S. presidential election, Viet Cong forces shelled an American barracks at Bien Hoa Air Base in the Republic of Vietnam, killing 4 men and wounding 72 others. The President rejected a JCS call for reprisal strikes against North Vietnam. Similarly, Johnson disapproved plans to bomb North Vietnam when Communists carried out a sabotage attack on Saigon's Brink Hotel on Christmas Eve, killing or injuring more than a hundred Americans, Australians, and Vietnamese. Focused on making his Great Society domestic program a success, Johnson cast about for some way to preserve the Republic of Vietnam while preventing the outbreak of a full-scale war in Southeast Asia.

Increasingly convinced that overt conflict with Vietnamese Communists could not be avoided, the U.S. military redoubled efforts to prepare forces for combat in Indochina. In the six months after the Tonkin Gulf crisis, the Navy reinforced the Seventh Fleet with 15 ships (one attack carrier, three submarines, ten destroyer types, and one LST) and planned to send another ten. The Navy's Military Sea Transportation Service dispatched passenger, cargo, and tanker ships to the Western Pacific, reactivated ships in the National Defense Reserve Fleet, and chartered U.S. and foreign merchantmen. The Navy also doubled the number of aircraft in the fleet replacement pool and deployed a P-3 Orion patrol squadron to the Philippines. Fleet ordnance facilities in the United States shipped improved Sidewinder and Sparrow air-to-air missiles, the new antiradar Shrike air-to-

ground missile, modernized 20-millimeter cannon, and huge stocks of bombs to the operating theater. Seabee battalions enlarged fuel storage complexes and built additional ammunition magazines, warehouses, hangars, and ship berthing facilities at U.S. Navy installations on Guam, Okinawa, and especially Subic Bay in the Philippines. Naval intelligence commands updated information on potential enemy forces and target sites in North Vietnam.

If the Navy needed another reason to get ready for combat in South Vietnam, it was supplied on 16 February 1965. That morning, a U.S. Army officer flying his helicopter along the coast of central South Vietnam suddenly spotted a large, camouflaged vessel perpendicular to the shore. Cargo was being unloaded and stacked on the beach at Vung Ro, an isolated bay on the rocky coast. The pilot immediately radioed

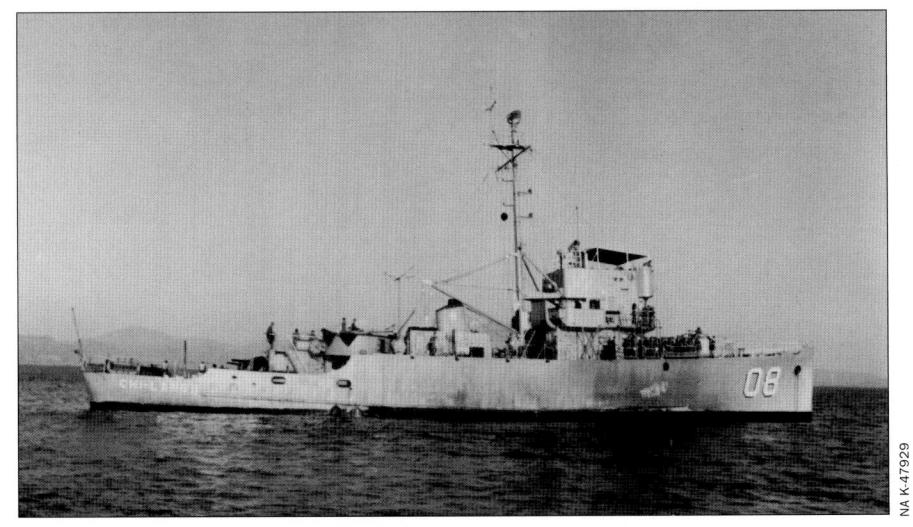

Vietnam Navy escort *Chi Lang II* (HQ 08).

his sighting to Lieutenant Commander Harvey P. Rodgers, the senior advisor to the South Vietnamese 2nd Coastal District headquartered in Nha Trang, who in turn notified the coastal district commander, Lieutenant Commander Ho Van Ky Thoai.

Thoai dispatched South Vietnamese A-1H Skyraiders to the bay where their bombs capsized

75

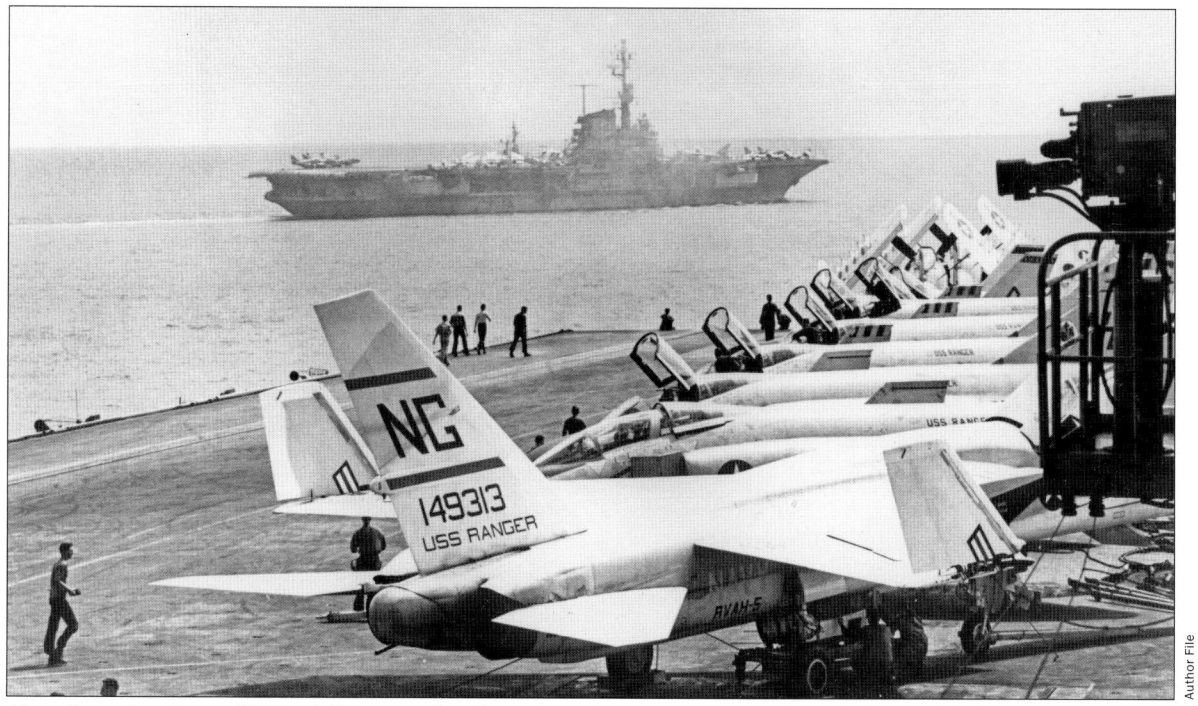

Aircraft carriers *Ranger* (CVA 61) (foreground) and *Coral Sea* (CVA 43) operating at Yankee Station in March 1965.

and sank the ship. Additional air strikes pummeled the stores on the beach the next day, but not until 1100 on 19 February were South Vietnamese escort *Chi Lang II* (HQ 08), medium landing ship *Tien Giang* (HQ 405), and submarine chaser *Tuy Dong* (HQ 04) able to overcome command indecision and enemy small-arms fire to land their embarked troops and naval commandos.

What the soldiers and naval commandos, the latter accompanied by U.S. naval advisor Lieutenant Franklin W. Anderson, discovered in the wrecked ship and piled up on shore ended a long-running debate among U.S. military and intelligence officials. The allies recovered from the 130-foot North Vietnamese ship and from shore sites 100 tons of Soviet- and Chinese-made war material such as 3,500 to 4,000 rifles and submachine guns, one million rounds of small-arms ammunition, 1,500 grenades, 2,000 mortar rounds, and 500 pounds of explosives. For years many American analysts had doubted that the Communists were using the sea to supply their forces in the South. Even though it is now clear that Hanoi had developed a major seaborne infiltration program as early as 1963, not

until the Vung Ro event were American leaders enlightened. The Seventh Fleet commander, Vice Admiral Paul P. "Brick" Blackburn, observed that the Vung Ro find was "proof positive." He and General Westmoreland called for a major U.S.-Vietnamese anti-infiltration patrol operation.

The Vung Ro event was one more indication that the nature of the conflict in Southeast Asia was entering a new phase of direct American military involvement. Admiral Moorer, the Pacific Fleet commander, observed to Admiral McDonald, Chief of Naval Operations, "[I]t seems clear that our national policy towards SVN is shifting from one in which we attempted to maintain an 'advisory' image in SVN to one of active and overt U.S. participation." He told McDonald that his fleet was "on the scene with the capability and . . . are ready to go." He suggested his units could provide the South Vietnamese with powerful support in the form of shore bombardment, aerial minelaying, submarine reconnaissance, SEAL activities, over-the-shore logistical support, sealift, and air strikes against Viet Cong guerrilla concentrations. He informed the CNO that "unless you feel to the contrary, I will push in this direction." The

continued on page 80

Author File

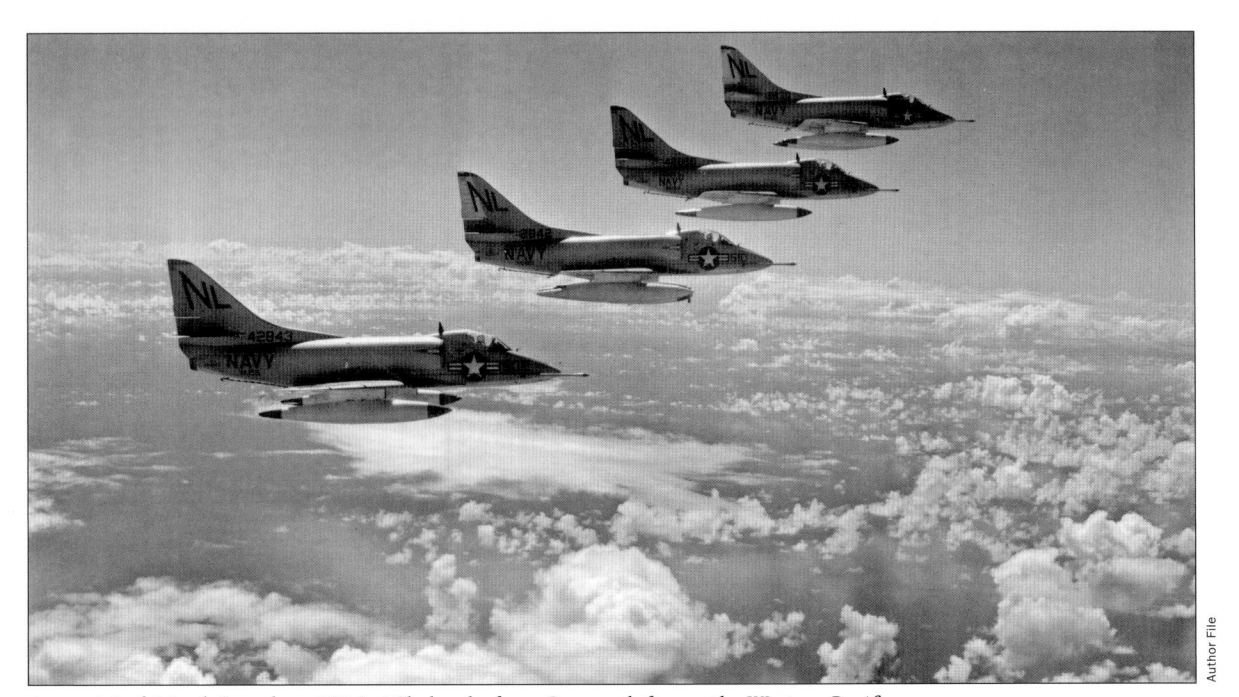

A quartet of Attack Squadron 155 A-4 Skyhawks from *Ranger* aloft over the Western Pacific.

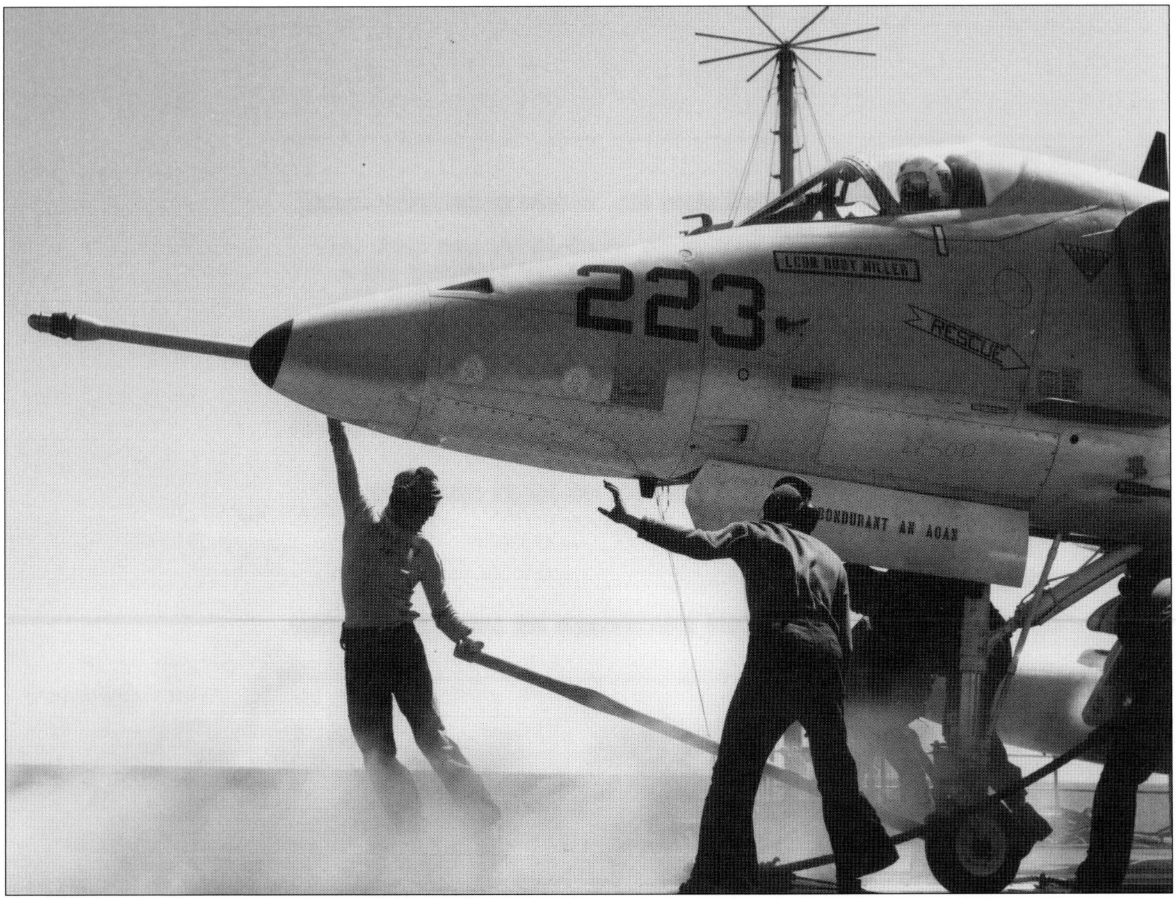

Author File

Deck crewmen of carrier *Ranger* ready an A-4 Skyhawk attack plane for a strike against North Vietnam.

Task Force 77

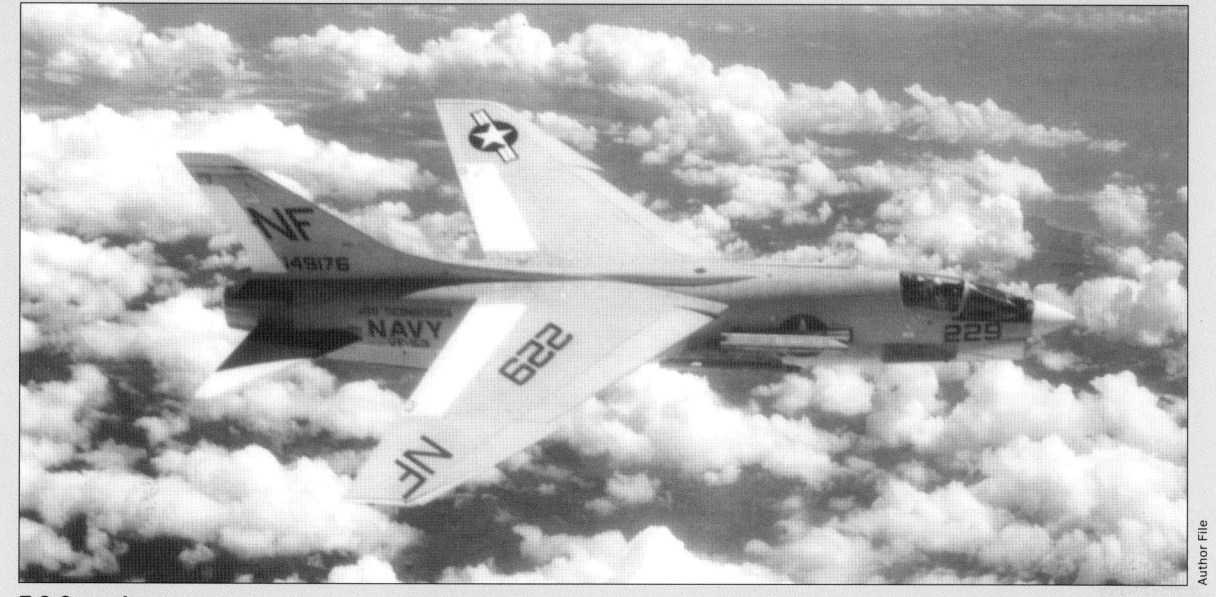

F-8 Crusader.

THE SEVENTH FLEET'S Attack Carrier Striking Force, Task Force 77, was the cutting edge of U.S. naval power confronting North Vietnam throughout the war.

The aircraft carriers of the task force operated from waters at the mouth of the Gulf of Tonkin between the coast of Vietnam and the Chinese island of Hainan. This operating area—Yankee Station— became one of the most recognizable names of the Vietnam War.

Each carrier's air wing consisted of two fighter squadrons, three attack squadrons, and smaller fixed-wing aircraft and helicopter detachments. The larger ships, the *Forrestal*-class carriers, operated sometimes close to 100 aircraft, while the smaller World War II–era, *Essex*-class ships had a complement of about 70 planes. During these early years of the war, the F-8 Crusader and F-4 Phantom II served as the Navy's primary fighter planes, while the A-4 Skyhawk and propeller-driven A-1 Skyraiders handled the lion's share of strike operations. Mainstays of the Yankee Team reconnaissance missions flown in Laos were the RF-8A Crusader, RA-3B Skywarrior, and RA-5C Vigilante. E-2 Hawkeyes provided the large "alpha strike" aircraft groups with airborne command control, early warning, and communications support. Sikorsky SH-3 Sea King and Kaman UH-2 Sea Sprite helicopters, along with U.S. Air Force aircraft, stood by during carrier strikes on North Vietnam to rescue aircrews shot down ashore and at sea.

These planes carried a lethal arsenal of bombs, rockets, missiles, and guns. Strike aircraft dropped 250-, 500-, 1,000-, and 2,000-pound general-purpose bombs ("iron bombs)," napalm bombs, and magnetic sea mines and fired 5-inch Zuni and 2.75-inch "Mighty Mouse" rockets. Rounding out the weapons suite were Shrike air-to-surface missiles for taking out enemy radars, Bullpup glide bombs, and television-guided Walleye bombs. For air-to-air combat, naval aircraft employed the deadly Sidewinder and Sparrow missiles and 20-millimeter machine guns.

Essential to the hitting power and the air, surface, and subsurface defense of the ships in Task Force 77 were its assigned cruisers and destroyers. Normally one cruiser and two to four destroyers defended each carrier. The surface warships maintained a protective ring around the carriers and by mid-1965 would be bombarding targets ashore in North Vietnam in Operation Sea Dragon. The 8-inch and 6-inch guns on these ships were as vital to the fleet's projection of power ashore in Vietnam as they had been in World War II and Korea.

In short, Task Force 77 packed a considerable punch that U.S. leaders were prepared to employ and did employ in the growing conflict with North Vietnam. ⚓

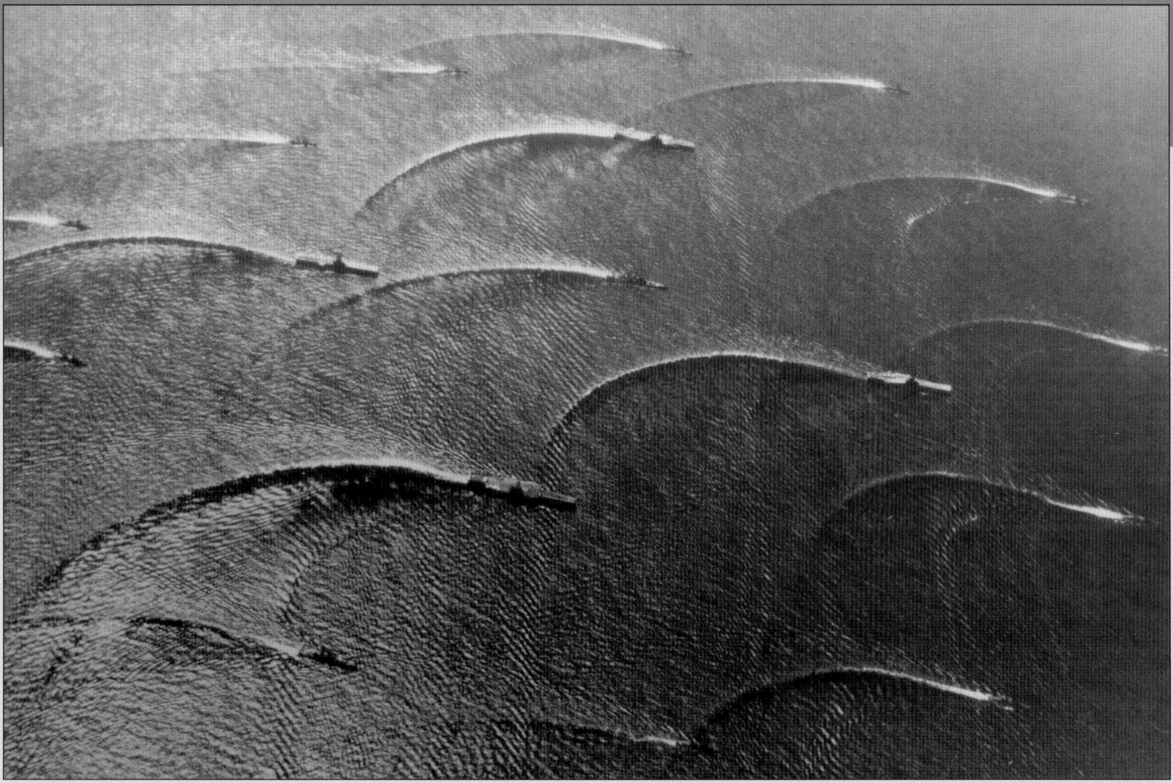

A quartet of aircraft carriers surrounded by the cruisers and destroyers of Task Force 77 steam through the South China Sea early in 1965.

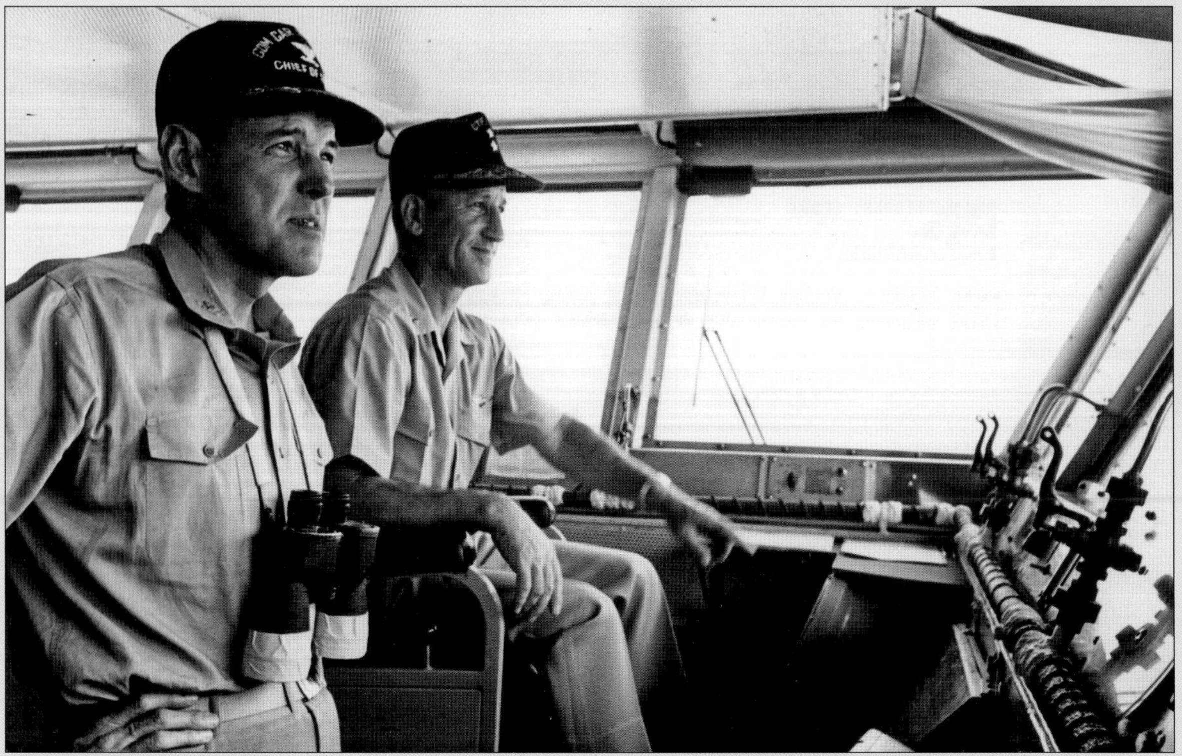

Rear Admiral Henry L. Miller, Commander Task Force 77, right, and his chief of staff coordinate operations from the bridge of carrier *Ranger*.

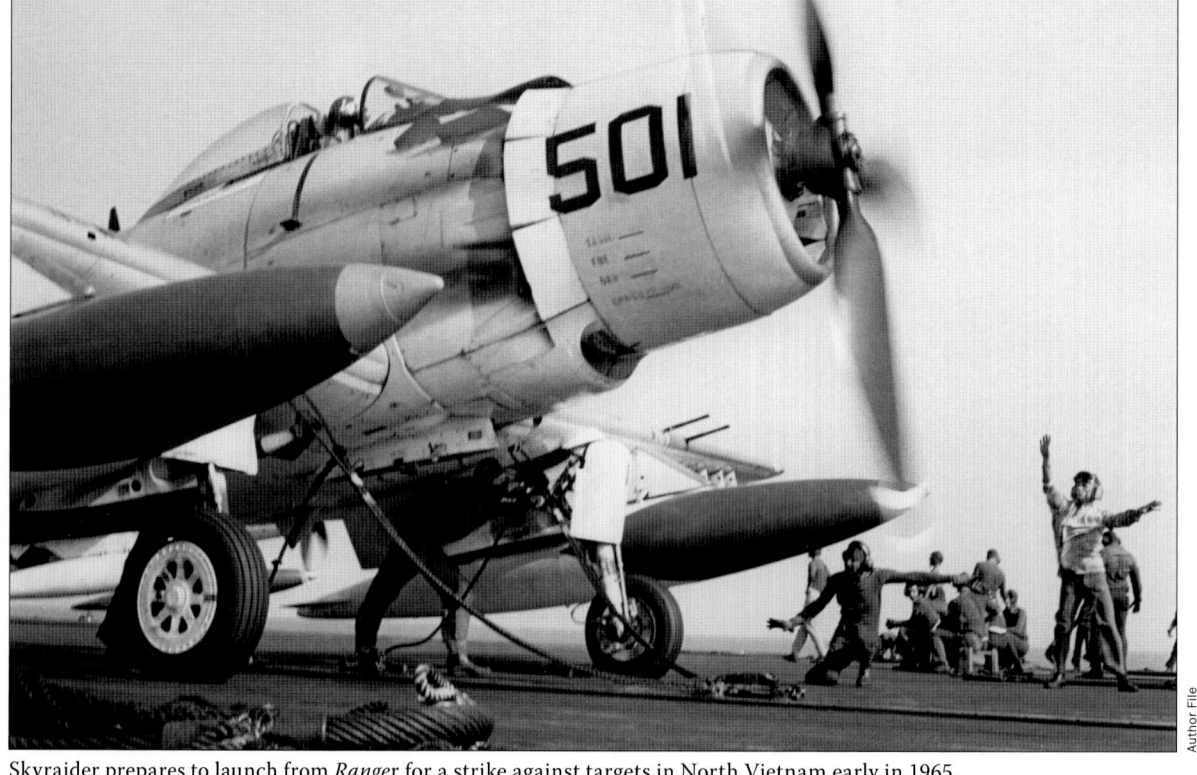

Skyraider prepares to launch from *Ranger* for a strike against targets in North Vietnam early in 1965.

Navy's top leader did not dissuade his Pacific Fleet commander.

Even before U.S. officials considered stopping Communist infiltration by sea, they had taken action to interfere with the Communist supply lines that wound through eastern and southern Laos. On 17 December 1964, A-1H Skyraider attack planes protected by F-4B Phantom fighters and followed by RF-8A photoreconnaissance planes from carrier *Ranger* (CVA 19) executed the first Navy "armed reconnaissance" mission of the joint Navy–Air Force Operation Barrel Roll. The planes were directed to attack Communist supply trucks and, if they found none, bomb preselected storage buildings, antiaircraft emplacements, and other military sites. The primary object of this program, however, was a political one—to convince the Communists that the United States would use armed force to frustrate their designs on Indochina.

When American leaders concluded that the Communists probably suffered little from these limited operations, they directed the U.S. forces to cut enemy supply lines at key transportation bottlenecks or "chokepoints." The Mu Gia Pass, which crossed the rugged Truong Son range bordering North Vietnam and Laos, was the target of the first attack. On 28 February 1965, Skyraiders and Skyhawks from *Coral Sea* (CVA 43) executed a massive strike on Mu Gia Pass, followed by an early March attack by *Hancock* planes. These attacks with delayed-action and other bombs cratered the roadways and hindered repair operations, but did not perceptibly slow the truck traffic. By the end of March, carrier planes had carried out half of the 43 Barrel Roll missions with 134 strike, 28 flak suppression, 56 combat air patrol, 32 aerial photographic, and 25 escort sorties. However, few American leaders believed that the operation had been or would be effective in discouraging North Vietnam from pursuing its objectives in South Vietnam or Laos.

Indeed, Hanoi upped the ante when Communist forces mortared an American advisors' cantonment in Pleiku, South Vietnam, on 7 February 1965, killing eight Americans and wounding 109 others.

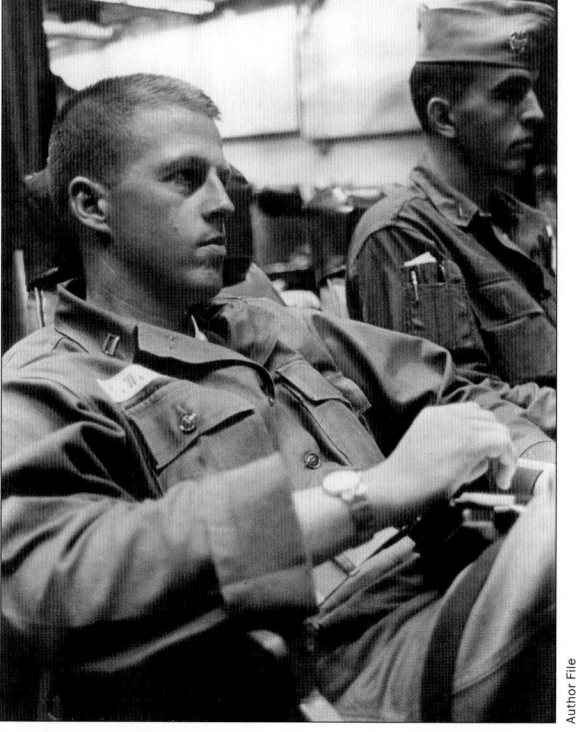

Lieutenant William T. Majors, rescued by an Air Force SAR plane after he bailed out of his stricken plane over the Gulf of Tonkin in February 1965, gets briefed in his squadron's ready room for another combat mission several weeks later.

In response to this attack, the President finally authorized another retaliatory strike against North Vietnam—the first since the Pierce Arrow operation in August 1964. Johnson approved a one-time, tit-for-tat reprisal strike by Navy, Air Force, and South Vietnamese air force units on enemy barracks. That same day *Ranger*, *Hancock*, and *Coral Sea* dispatched aircraft for strikes on the barracks at Vit Thu Lu and Dong Hoi, both just north of the Demilitarized Zone. *Ranger*'s attack on Vit Thu Lu was scrubbed because of heavy clouds over the target. The weather was little better at Dong Hoi, but the massed air units of the other two carriers bore in on the compound, home of North Vietnam's 325th Infantry Division.

A 29-plane strike formation from *Coral Sea* approached the target under a low cloud ceiling at 500 knots. The A-4 Skyhawks of attack squadrons VA-153 and VA-155 hit the barracks with rockets and 250-pound bombs. Ready in February as they had not been in August of 1964, North Vietnamese

antiaircraft gunners threw up a curtain of fire from 37-millimeter guns, automatic weapons, and small arms ashore and from Swatow gunboats in the Kien River. Some of this fire hit Lieutenant Edward A. Dickson's Skyhawk but he bravely continued his attack. Soon after, the young naval aviator punched out of his crippled plane, but his parachute failed to open and he plunged to his death.

Right behind *Coral Sea*'s formation came *Hancock*'s Carrier Air Wing 21. The 17 Skyhawks of VA-212 and VA-216 dropped their ordnance on already burning and smoking camp facilities as F-8 Crusaders suppressed fire from enemy antiaircraft sites.

Completing the mission, RF-8A reconnaissance aircraft rolled in to photograph the scene for naval intelligence analysis. The results were unimpressive. The attack had destroyed or damaged only 22 of the 275 buildings in the camp.

Hardly deterred by the American attack, the Communists sent their own message to Washington. On 10 February, Viet Cong guerrillas sabotaged the American barracks in Qui Nhon, a port city on the central coast of South Vietnam. The explosion resulted in more dead and maimed Americans. The U.S. response was not long in coming.

The next day, Task Force 77 launched a massive one-day strike labeled Flaming Dart II. Under Commander Warren H. Sells, a force of 99 planes from *Ranger*, *Hancock*, and *Coral Sea* were tasked with destroying the enemy barracks at Chanh Hoa, while U.S. Air Force and South Vietnamese air force units were directed to hit similar facilities at Vu Con. The Skyraiders and Skyhawks from the ships delivered tons of bombs and rockets to the target area at Chanh Hoa as F-8E Crusaders and F-4B Phantoms rocketed and strafed enemy antiaircraft positions. A total of 33 Crusaders, Phantoms, and Skyraiders protected the attack force should North Vietnamese MiGs based near Hanoi challenge the mission.

Although MiGs did not interfere with the operation, enemy antiaircraft gunners damaged a *Coral Sea* A-4C, forcing the pilot to make an emergency landing at Danang. Unused bombs still positioned on the wings exploded when the pilot landed at Danang, destroying the aircraft; the pilot

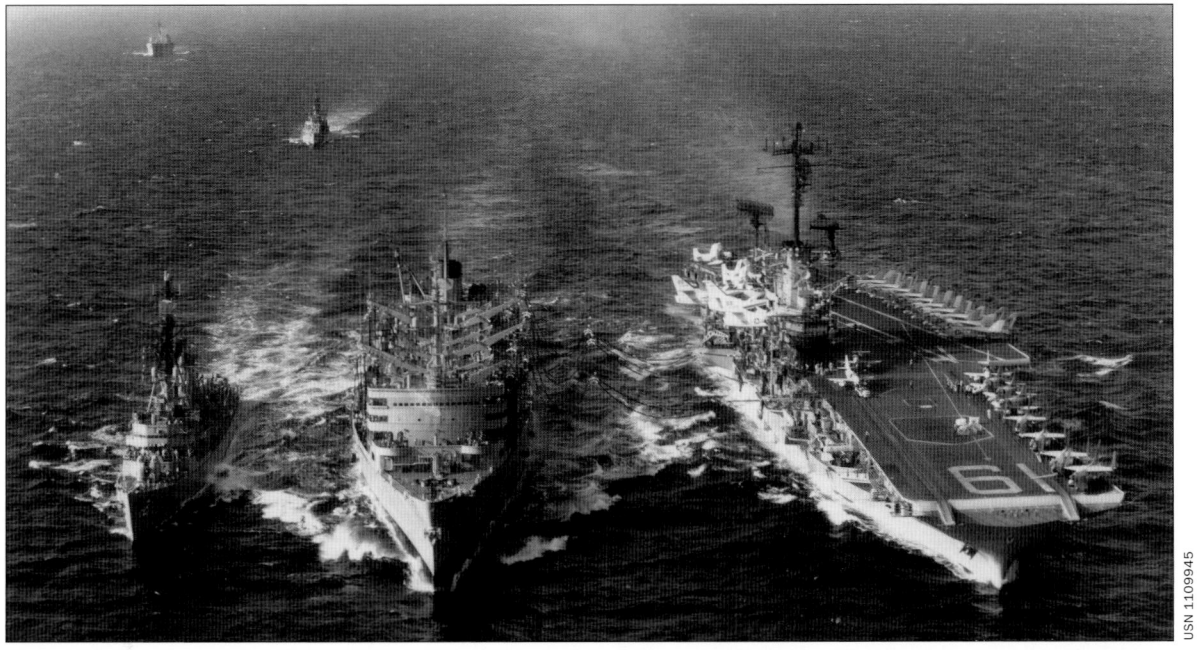

Carrier *Hancock* and guided missile destroyer *Robinson* (DDG 12) take on fuel from fast combat support ship *Sacramento* (AOE 1) as two other naval vessels bring up the rear in the South China Sea early in 1965. For the next ten years, the U.S. Navy would be heavily committed to combat operations in Southeast Asia.

survived. The pilot of another damaged plane, Lieutenant William T. Majors of VA-153, reached the sea, radioed that he was "feet wet," and bailed out. He was soon rescued by an Air Force HU-16. Unable to reach the sea, where SAR units stood by to pluck naval aviators from the water, Lieutenant Commander Robert H. Shumaker of VF-154 ejected from his stricken Crusader over Chanh Hoa. Communist troops swarmed over the landing site, took the American aviator into custody, and dispatched him to Hanoi where he joined Lieutenant Alvarez in captivity.

Even though Flaming Dart II destroyed or damaged one-third of the barracks buildings at Chanh Hoa, few civilian or military leaders in Washington believed the one-time strike would cause the Communists to abandon their goals in South Vietnam.

By now, U.S. leaders were convinced that only a systematic and sustained bombing campaign against strategically vital targets in North Vietnam would compel Ho Chi Minh to forego his campaign to unify Vietnam under the banner of the Communist Party. Hence, on 2 March 1965, three weeks after Flaming Dart II, the U.S. and South Vietnamese

air forces opened the Rolling Thunder bombing campaign, and on 15 March, the Navy joined in with strikes by massed aircraft from Task Force 77 carriers *Hancock* and *Ranger*. Rolling Thunder would continue for more than three years.

By mid-March of 1965, it was clear to the Johnson administration that the Communist leaders in Hanoi, unrestrained and indeed encouraged by their comrades in Beijing and Moscow, were determined to achieve their objectives in Indochina by force of arms. Despite counterinsurgency actions in South Vietnam, carrier deployments into the South China Sea, 34A operations along the coast of North Vietnam, Desoto Patrols, Yankee Team and Barrel Roll operations in Laos, and retaliatory strikes against targets in North Vietnam, Communist activity continued. Armed with an increasing amount of sophisticated Chinese and Soviet weaponry, large units of the North Vietnamese army were deploying into South Vietnam for a final showdown with the South Vietnamese armed forces and their American patrons.

The stage was now set for a full-blown war that would challenge the fortitude of the American people and the U.S. Navy. ⚓

The Author

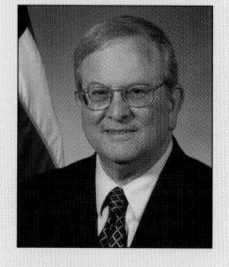

Edward J. Marolda has served as the Acting Director of Naval History and the Chief of the Histories and Archives Division of the Naval Historical Center, designated in December 2008 as the Naval History and Heritage Command. Dr. Marolda has written a number of books on the U.S. Navy's modern experience in Southeast Asia, including *From Military Assistance to Combat, 1959–1965*, vol. 2 in the official series The United States Navy and the Vietnam Conflict; *By Sea, Air, and Land: The United States Navy and the War in Southeast Asia; Aircraft Carriers*, no. 4 in the Bantam series The Illustrated History of the Vietnam War; and *Operation End Sweep: A History of Minesweeping in North Vietnam*. He inaugurated and then served as series editor for the Command's commemorative booklets on the Navy in Korea and the follow-on anthology *The U.S. Navy in the Korean War* (Naval Institute Press, 2007). A lecturer on military and naval history, he is also coauthor of *Shield and Sword: The United States Navy and the Persian Gulf War* (Naval Institute, 2001) and author of an illustrated history of the Washington Navy Yard. He holds degrees in history from Pennsylvania Military College (BA), Georgetown University (MA), and George Washington University (PhD).

Acknowledgments

As the author of this commemorative work and coeditor of The U.S. Navy and the Vietnam War series, I am especially grateful to Rear Admiral Jay A. DeLoach, USN (Ret.), Director of Naval History and Heritage, and his predecessor Rear Admiral Paul E. Tobin, USN (Ret.), for their unstinting support of this project. Equally deserving of our thanks are Admiral James L. Holloway III, USN (Ret.), Vice Admiral Robert Dunn, USN (Ret.), and Captain Todd Creekman, USN (Ret.), distinguished leaders of the Naval Historical Foundation who enthusiastically endorsed this effort to recognize the service and sacrifice in Vietnam of our Sailors and the Navy's vital contribution.

Dr. Malcolm Muir Jr. of the Virginia Military Institution, Dr. David Winkler of the Naval Historical Foundation, and Dr. John Sherwood of the Naval History and Heritage Command's Histories and Archives Division reviewed the manuscript and provided insightful advice on its content and presentation. Many more of my colleagues at the Command, too numerous to single out, provided historical support and assisted in the selection of photographs and art. We are grateful to Sharlyn Marsh, the daughter of R. G. Smith, for permission to use her father's paintings in illustrating this work.

Sandy Doyle, my coeditor, was clearly instrumental in bringing this first booklet to fruition and establishing the format and presentation for the series that will reward its readers for years to come.

For permission to reproduce images of R. G. Smith's paintings, please contact SharlynMarsh@aol.com.

Suggested Reading

Hooper, Edwin B., Dean C. Allard, and Oscar P. Fitzgerald. *The Setting of the Stage to 1959.* The United States Navy and the Vietnam Conflict, vol. 1. Washington: Naval Historical Center, 1976.

Marolda, Edward J. *By Sea, Air, and Land: An Illustrated History of the U.S. Navy and the War in Southeast Asia.* Washington: Naval Historical Center, 1994.

Marolda, Edward J., and Fitzgerald, Oscar P. *From Military Assistance to Combat, 1959–1965.* The United States Navy and the Vietnam Conflict, vol. 2. Washington: Naval Historical Center, 1986.

Moyar, Mark. *Triumph Forsaken: The Vietnam War, 1954–1965.* London: Cambridge University Press, 2006.

Schreadley, Richard L. *From the Rivers to the Sea: The U.S. Navy in Vietnam.* Annapolis: Naval Institute Press, 1992.

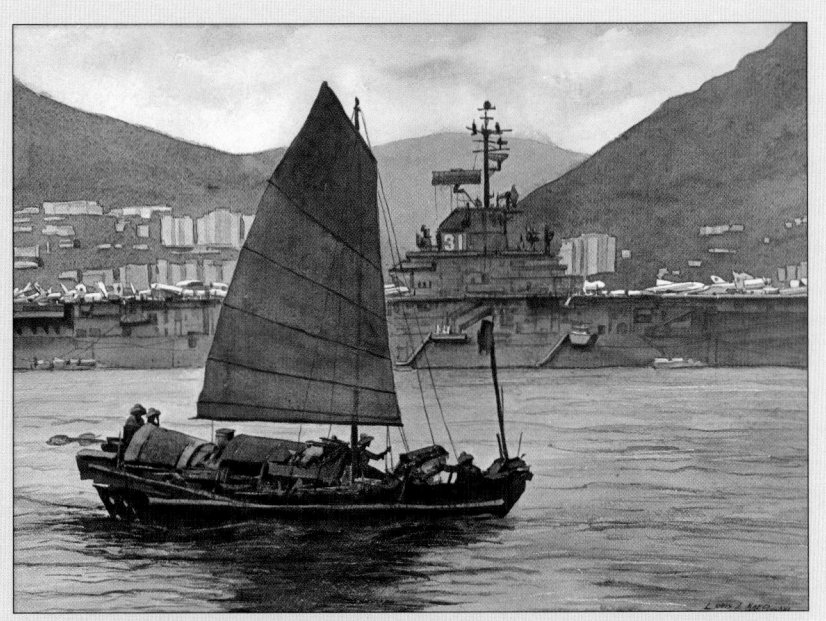

Bon Homme Richard in Hong Kong Harbor by Louis Kaep. Watercolor. Navy Art Collection.